Sex and Sexuality in Classical Athens

DEBATES AND DOCUMENTS IN ANCIENT HISTORY

GENERAL EDITORS

Emma Stafford, *University of Leeds* and
Shaun Tougher, *Cardiff University*

Focusing on important themes, events or periods throughout ancient history, each volume in this series is divided into roughly equal parts. The first introduces the reader to the main issues of interpretation. The second contains a selection of relevant evidence supporting different views.

PUBLISHED

Diocletian and the Tetrarchy
Roger Rees

Julian the Apostate
Shaun Tougher

Rome and its Empire, AD 193–284
Olivier Hekster with Nicholas Zair

Roman Imperialism
Andrew Erskine

King and Court in Ancient Persia 559 to 331 BCE
Lloyd Llewellyn-Jones

Sex and Sexuality in Classical Athens
James Robson

FORTHCOMING

The Family in the Roman World
Mary Harlow and Tim Parkin

Justinian and the Sixth Century
Fiona Haarer

The Emperor Nero
Steven Green

Sex and Sexuality in Classical Athens

James Robson

EDINBURGH
University Press

To Owain,
my *mochyn bach* and *muž-puž*

© James Robson, 2013

Edinburgh University Press Ltd
22 George Square, Edinburgh EH8 9LF

www.euppublishing.com

Typeset in 11/13 Minion by
Servis Filmsetting Ltd, Stockport, Cheshire,
and printed and bound in the United States of America

A CIP record for this book is available from the British Library

ISBN 978 0 7486 3413 2 (hardback)
ISBN 978 0 7486 3414 9 (paperback)

Published with the support of the Edinburgh University Scholarly Publishing
Initiatives Fund.

Contents

List of Illustrations

Series Editors' Preface

Debates and Documents in Ancient History is a series of short books
on central topics in Greek and Roman history. The works in the series
are written by expert academics and provide up-to-date and accessible
accounts of the historical issues and problems raised by each topic.
They also contain the important evidence on which the arguments are
based, including texts (in translation), archaeological data and visual
material. This allows readers to judge how convincing the arguments
are and to enter the debates themselves. The series is intended for all
those interested in the history and culture of the Greek and Roman
world.

Ancient Greek sexuality is a topic particularly suited to the *Debates
and Documents* series. Many of its constituent elements – women's
experience of sex inside and outside marriage, female and male prostitution, homosexuality – have been the subject of extensive scholarly
debate over the last forty or so years, informed by changing meth-
odological trends in the study of (ancient) cultural history and broader
discussions of gender and sexuality. Many of the issues concerned are
sensitive, in so far as they relate to universal human experience – study
of another culture's definitions, laws and customs concerning rape,
for example, can be uncomfortable as well as thought-provoking. At
the same time, the evidence available for the predominantly private
behaviours involved is scattered and often difficult to interpret. All the
more reason, then, for anyone taking up the subject to be aware from
the outset of the wide range of approaches which have been adopted,
and to engage directly with examples of the ancient source material.

This volume focuses on a single historical period and geographical
location – classical Athens. The limitation of time and space allows
the book to bring together a range of topics which are often treated
separately, but which are intimately related and mutually informing –
marriage, same-sex relationships, prostitution, sex and the law, ideas

about beauty, sexual attractiveness, fantasy and taboo. The result is a coherent account of what an individual man or woman might have experienced in the realm of sexuality, over the course of their life, in the particular time and place. The focus on classical Athens is also consistent with the wide range of evidence produced by the city's inhabitants during the period – in the media of vase-painting, drama (especially comedy), law-court speeches, philosophy and historiography – from which the majority of the sources presented here have been selected. The occasional inclusion of earlier and later evidence, and evidence from other parts of the Greek world, sets the particular case in the wider context of the history of ancient Greek sexuality.

Emma Stafford
Shaun Tougher

Preface

This book is about the sexual world of a very different culture from our own: a world in which same-sex desire was not only recognised, but regularly idealised; where prostitution was an accepted feature of daily life; and where adultery was subject to the harshest of penalties, but where sexual assault might sometimes go unpunished. This is also a culture where a relationship between an adult man and a teenage boy or girl was nothing out of the ordinary and where it was perfectly common for a man to marry his niece – or even half-sister. In terms of language, too, there is a world of difference: ancient Greek has no word for 'rape', for example, but it can boast a whole series of terms describing love, desire and affection – *agapē, erōs, himeros, pothos, philia* – none of which maps onto an English term or concept in a wholly straightforward way. In short, this is alien territory, and visitors must tread carefully.

There was a lot of sex about in ancient Greece. Hence my decision in this book to cover only one city-state – Athens – during one historical period, namely, the classical era (479–323 BC). Even this is a large topic and my specific approach has been to concentrate on sexual behaviour: that is to say, my interests as a social historian have always pointed me in the direction of examining what led one individual to have sex (or *want* to have sex, or *not* want to have sex) with another – which, in turn, has also entailed looking at the social and sexual assumptions, pressures and expectations in play in classical Athens. The five chapters in Part I (Debates), covering marriage, same-sex relationships, prostitution, adultery and rape, and, lastly, sex appeal, fantasy and taboo, very much flow from the same basic set of questions: who? With whom? How come? Adjacent concerns, such as the position of women in society and the views of philosophers or medical writers about sex and gender, are naturally of interest, but have not been my main concern here. As for the ancient material drawn on in this book,

while evidence from other parts of Greece and from outside the classical era has been included in this study, it is contemporary evidence in
the form of texts and images produced by those living in the city itself
during the fifth and fourth centuries BC that I have chosen to place
centre stage. Classical Athens, its art, literature and sexual actors, are
the stars of this particular show.

This book is conceived not only as an introduction to the topic,
geared towards those with little previous knowledge of the sex lives
of classical Athenians, but also as a book which speaks to research-
ers working in the field of Greek sex and sexuality. The format of this
series, which gives equal weight to debates and documents, enables
readers to gain an overview of the (often competing) claims that are
made about our evidence and the theoretical models that have been
proposed for understanding sex and sexuality, whilst at the same time
providing for scrutiny the original sources (both literary and visual)
upon which different scholarly interpretations rely. As the reader
will discover, juxtaposing subject matter which is so often treated
separately in scholarship (e.g. marriage and homosexual relationships;
prostitution and adultery) regularly serves to raise fresh questions
and suggest new perspectives. Part II (Documents), which contains
a rich mix of extracts from a wide range of literary genres – comic
drama, tragedy, legal speeches, philosophy, epic, lyric and iambic
poetry – as well as images from vase-painting, also contains some brief
biographical information on each author cited as further contextual
information. This not only allows readers new to the ancient evidence
to orientate themselves in regard to the sources but, importantly, also
serves to highlight changes taking place within the classical era in the
representation of, and attitudes towards, sexual practices (the nature
of which are very much a live topic of discussion amongst scholars).
Parts I (Debates) and II (Documents) are also fully cross-referenced,
allowing the reader to locate the original source relevant to a given
discussion and, conversely, the sections in the chapters in which a
given extract is used as evidence and/or discussed. References to Part
II sources are cited in Part I in bold type, thus: **Aeschines A**. This refers
to the extract under the heading 'Aeschines' entitled 'A Athenian laws
protecting boys from sexual exploitation' in Part II, the page number
for which can be found by consulting the contents list. Readers may
choose either to consult the texts and images which make up Part II as
they are encountered in Part I of the book or, alternatively, to review
them later.

My aim in this book has been to give different scholars' views as fair an airing as possible in order both to present an overview of the field as it currently stands and to move the debate forward. Naturally, I have also engaged with current controversies myself and develop some of my own ideas here, which I see as a strength of this study – adding nuance to debates and questioning various scholarly approaches in a way that I hope both students and scholars will find suggestive. The most important contribution to emerging debates perhaps comes in Chapter 5 in an area which is attracting increasing attention: the ancient body. This chapter brings together a diverse range of ancient sources and modern scholarship in an attempt to frame and answer new questions about what classical Athenians found sexually alluring and repelling, with my examination of the concept of sex appeal, in particular, revealing some fascinating correspondences between the ways in which male and female beauty are described and conceived. Certainly, I hope that students and scholars working in the fields covered by *Sex and Sexuality in Classical Athens* will find this book productive and thought-provoking: the central objective throughout has been to open up the field to further work and debate.

Thanks are due to colleagues, students and friends too numerous to mention whose support, advice, patience and interest I have benefited from hugely while writing this book. To single out those fellow classicists whose help I have particularly benefited from, I should like to extend my warm thanks to Sue Blundell, Helen King, Andrew Lear, Lloyd Llewellyn-Jones – and, of course, the series editor, Emma Stafford. Special thanks, too, go to Elsbeth Hymes for sharing her expertise on the body beautiful so generously with me. The staff at Edinburgh University Press, and Carol MacDonald in particular, also deserve thanks for their helpful and prompt input and their support for this project – not to mention their patience while waiting for me to complete the manuscript. The copy-editor, Fiona Sewell, also made a significant contribution to the finished product through her conscientious reading of my manuscript and many helpful suggestions for improvement. The translations in Part II were very much a joint effort, with credit due here to Dimitra Kokkini and, in particular, the wonderful Judith Owen, who prepared the lion's share for me (you little beaut!). I should also like to express my gratitude to my parents, Charles and Cynthia Robson, and niece, Charlotte Robson, who put me up – and put up with me – while I wrote and researched chunks of this book at their house in Lot-et-Garonne. As ever, my biggest debt of thanks goes to my partner, Owain Thomas, who is simply the most amazing and most supportive man I could ever have wished to meet

– and who also provided some characteristically thoughtful critiques of draft chapters. My parents also acted far beyond the call of duty in reading the whole manuscript for me prior to submission. I am a lucky man to have such wonderful family, friends and colleagues to fall back on.

Timeline

The following chronology provides dates (some more precise than others) for the major historical events and cultural trends relevant to this book, as well as the dates of key authors and their works, where known. Fuller chronological information on featured authors is also provided in Part II. All dates are BC.

750/700–480 BC Archaic era

?622/1	Draco establishes the first written legal code in Athens
?590s	Solon's legal reforms in Athens
530–525	The first red-figure vases are produced in Athens
514	Harmodius and Aristogeiton kill Hipparchus, the brother of Athens's tyrant, Hippias
510	End of tyranny in Athens with the death of Hippias
508	Reforms of Cleisthenes lay the foundations of democracy at Athens
500	Explicit sexual scenes and scenes of pederastic courtship begin to decline in popularity in Athenian vase-painting
490	Darius of Persia invades Greece; Battle of Marathon
480	Persian invasion of Greece, led by Xerxes; sack of Athens by Persian forces

479–323 BC Classical era

479	Greek victory in the Persian Wars
460–450	Birth of Aristophanes
451	Pericles' 'citizenship' law passed
450	'Adornment' scenes start to become popular in vase-painting; explicit sexual scenes and pederastic courtship scenes rarely occur in vase-painting after this date

431–404   Peloponnesian War between Athens and Sparta
429   Death of Pericles
?429   Birth of Plato
?428   Birth of Xenophon
416   Dramatic date of Plato's *Symposium*
415   Launch of the Sicilian Expedition (Athens' military campaign in Sicily)
413   Sicilian Expedition ends in disaster for Athens with the complete destruction of the expeditionary force
411   Aristophanes' *Lysistrata* and *Women at the Thesmophoria* first staged
411–410   Oligarchic coup in Athens leading to the rule of the 400 and the 5,000
406   Death of Euripides; Battle of Arginusae
404   Peloponnesian War ends with the defeat of Athens; rule of the Thirty Tyrants in Athens
403   Democracy restored in Athens; reinstatement of the Periclean 'citizenship' law
?400–395   Birth of Neaera
399   Trial and execution of Socrates
399–347   Composition of Plato's dialogues
?386   Death of Aristophanes
384   Birth of Aristotle in Chalcidice; birth of Demosthenes
?380   Death of the orator Lysias
354   Death of Xenophon
347   Death of Plato
346–345   Prosecution of Timarchus by his arch-rival Aeschines (Aeschines 1, *Against Timarchus*)
343–340   Prosecution of Neaera ([Demosthenes] 59, *Against Neaera*)
Before 340   Tightening of citizenship laws outlawing marriage between a citizen and non-citizen
336   Accession of Alexander the Great to the throne of Macedon
?324–320   Menander's first play staged in Athens

323–30 BC Hellenistic era

323   Death of Alexander the Great
322   Death of Aristotle; death of Demosthenes

Part I

Debates

CHAPTER 1

Sexual Unions: Marriage and Domestic Life

1.1 Introduction

Marriage was a hot topic in classical Athens. In 451 BC, Pericles famously proposed a law stipulating that, for a man to be an Athenian citizen, both his parents must be true-born Athenians – and not just his father, as had previously been the case (**Aristotle A** and **Plutarch C**). The reasons behind the introduction of this law are obscure (it receives little mention in contemporary sources), but one of its immediate effects must have been to elevate the status of Athenian women above that of the numerous women of foreign extraction living in Athens at that time. In order to produce children who could claim full rights in the city, a citizen had now to choose his wife from among a relatively small pool of women, and whereas a poor Athenian father might previously have struggled to find a husband for his daughter, his chances were now greatly increased (on this law, see Patterson 1981 and 2005; French 1994; Ogden 1996, 59–69). The rules of Pericles' citizenship law were occasionally relaxed, especially during the war-ravaged years of the late fifth century, in order to expand the depleted citizen body, and exceptions were occasionally made for individuals, too, most famously for Pericles himself, whose son by his foreign mistress, Aspasia, was granted citizenship (Plutarch, *Life of Pericles* 37). In 403 BC, however, once the Peloponnesian War was over, the citizenship law was reinstated. Moreover, at some point towards the middle of the fourth century Athens' laws were strengthened further, with the result that it became positively illegal for an Athenian citizen to marry a non-Athenian (**Demosthenes N** and **T**: on the dating of these legal reforms, see Sealey 1990, 17–19).

This brief summary of the changing nature of marriage laws reveals the keen interest which classical Athenians took in questions of citizenship, but barely hints at another contemporary obsession: inheritance.

The provision of legitimate – and preferably male – offspring was a major concern to citizen men and women alike and questions of inheritance would often inform the choice of marriage partners. In short, then, legal rules about citizenship and familial concerns with inheritance would routinely serve to dictate the person with whom you shared your marriage bed.

Citizenship and inheritance are two angles from which to approach the topic of Athenian marriage, but in order to build up a rounded picture of this institution, other, more homely considerations need to be taken into account, too. After all, marriage entails a whole array of practical arrangements: a betrothal, a wedding, the setting up of a marital home and – importantly in a Greek context – a dowry. All these details will be explored in the first sections of this chapter, along with questions such as how marriage partners were selected and the age at which men and women were wed. Further practicalities will be examined when we come to look at the mechanisms which existed for divorce, the consequences of the death of a partner, and remarriage. Importantly, too, the emotional and sexual side of the married couple's relationship will be considered, though here the nature of our sources (not least their male, upper-class bias) means that the realities of life for many sections of society are inevitably difficult to reconstruct – a further complication being that relations between husband and wife presumably varied not only from marriage to marriage but also from one stage of their lives to the next. We shall also look at those Athenian inheritance laws which had greatest impact on marriage and family life, especially the legislation surrounding the 'heiress' (*epiklēros*), i.e. a woman who found herself in the position of being first in line to inherit the family estate. Famously, Athenian law could require a woman's summary divorce from her husband and remarriage to a close member of kin in order to secure the line of succession.

Owing to the nature of our sources, this chapter is strongly skewed towards the experience of citizens in Athens. As a rule, ancient writers display little interest in the sex lives and marriage practices of other sections of society such as slaves and metics (i.e. resident foreigners and their descendants), except where these impinge on citizen lives. The discussion in the final sections of this chapter will nevertheless explore social categories such as the *pallakē* ('concubine') and the *nothos/nothē* ('bastard'), which lie at the fringes of the citizen life in Athens, and the marriage of non-citizens will also be considered. The term 'citizen' itself is not unproblematic either. Only an adult man could play a full role in the democratic institutions of classical Athens as a citizen (*astos/politēs*), of course. But in this chapter I shall follow the practice of ancient authors in referring to a woman who was the wife, daughter, mother or sister of an Athenian man as a 'citizen' (*astē*; sometimes *politis*), too, thus distinguishing this social group from other women in the city.

Central to any discussion of family life in ancient Athens are the concepts of *oikos* and *kyrios*. *Oikos* (pl. *oikoi*) is often translated 'household', but this word essentially has three overlapping meanings: namely a family's 'house', its 'property' and the 'family' itself (D. M. MacDowell 1989, 10; Cox 1998, 132). *Oikos* membership is not always clear-cut, however, and a married woman in particular often had allegiances to more than one *oikos*: both her marital *oikos* and the *oikos* of her birth. The *kyrios* (pl. *kyrioi*) is the name given to the head of a household. Always an adult male, the *kyrios* was the present owner and custodian of the family's estate and possessions (including slaves) and was the legal protector both of his children and of any women who belonged to his *oikos* (women and children were able neither to represent themselves at law nor to administer large sums of money or property: this required a *kyrios*). For a married woman, her *kyrios* was her husband, and outside marriage the role was traditionally played by a woman's father – unless he was dead, in which case these duties would have been assumed by her nearest male relative. In discussions of Athenian marriage practices, it is often assumed that a woman was given away in marriage by her father, but in his absence we find examples of this act being performed by a grandfather, brother, uncle and even a son.

1.2 Selecting the bride (and groom)

Kinship, geography and the circles in which your father moved seem to have been the major factors determining whom you married in classical Athens. One of the most common fates for a girl was to be married to her paternal uncle or cousin, with marriage to a half-brother also a possibility as long as the two siblings were born of different mothers (Themistocles' son and daughter from different wives married each other, for example: see Cox 1998, 216–19; see also **Demosthenes L**). One way to understand the prevalence in classical Athens of endogamy, i.e. marriage within the family group, is in terms of inheritance, since this ensured that property would remain within the confines of a fairly narrow bloodline (namely that of the father's family: marriage of a girl to her matrilineal relatives was far less common). Exogamy, on the other hand, i.e. marriage to members outside the family group, could potentially be used to shore up allegiances with individuals with whom the family had a close association or shared a common cause. And so another common scenario we find is for a girl to be married to a member of a neighbour's household or for a close friendship between two males to be cemented by the marriage of two men's kin (e.g. **Isaeus B**). As Cox demonstrates in her 1998 book, *Household Interests*, there is ample evidence of intermarriage between families whose estates had a common boundary, for example, or who had shared property interests in a particular locality (Cox 1998, xv–xvi, 27 and 38–67). Her study also shows that family groups often practised both endogamy and exogamy when marrying off their daughters, suggesting that they were careful to get the balance right between protecting their inheritance interests and building links with neighbours and associates (Cox 1998, 21–2 and 28–37).

This somewhat unromantic view of marital ties – as informed by familial concerns about inheritance on the one hand and social allegiances on the other – usefully serves to reveal some of the realities underpinning married life in classical Athens. In this light it is also worth noting that arranging the match was the job of the girl's *kyrios* (normally her father), who was evidently under no obligation to consult the girl herself. Nor was it only his daughters' marriages that a father would oversee: it seems to have been quite normal for a man's father, if he was still alive, to take an active interest in arranging a match for his son, too. Accounts of a father's actions in seeking a bride for his son (e.g. **Demosthenes F** and **Isaeus E**) often emphasize the role of consultation and persuasion, however – a quality we also find hinted at in descriptions of suitors asking for the hand of a girl from her guardians (e.g. **Isaeus B**). A further insight we find into the ideology which lay behind a father's choice of son-in-law comes from a speech of Demosthenes where the considerations mentioned are the worthiness of the match, convention and opinion (**Demosthenes A**): even if the bride-to-be was not consulted (unlike the prospective groom), a father is nevertheless likely to have considered himself to be acting in the girl's best interests. Interestingly, too, there are references in our sources to matchmakers, older women who were presumably employed when a father was unable to find a suitable candidate for his offspring to marry. The unlikely union of the rustic Strepsiades and his well-heeled urban wife in Aristophanes' *Clouds*, for example, is said to be the result of a matchmaker's work (**Aristophanes AI; cf. Xenophon E**).

It is tempting, then, to think of Athenian marriages as arranged by men in the interests of men, with the wishes of the girl neither sought nor taken into account. However, this may be to overlook the influence exerted by family members such as the girl's mother and, indeed, the girl herself (Dover 1974, 211). Given the narrow range of individuals an Athenian girl could generally be expected to marry – close family members, members of neighbours' households, family friends – there is every reason to suppose that the bride and groom would at least have seen each other, and perhaps even interacted with each other, at some stage in their lives prior to the betrothal and wedding. From previous contact with the prospective husband, many a father would be in a position to take an informed view as to the suitability of the match for his daughter, as would other members of his household – although the extent to which his own or others' opinions on such matters held sway is of course a matter of speculation. In the comedies of Menander (first staged in the late fourth century BC), we even find examples of romantic love leading to marriage, including one instance of a couple who, having grown up together, have come to expect that they will be wed (**Menander K**). Indeed, on the evidence of Menander's plays, Brown has surmised that 'there were chances for both boys and girls to form preferences (however inadequately based) about possible marriage partners, and perhaps also to communicate these preferences to their parents' (Brown 1993, 202). As Brown himself points out, however, in these same comedies, we also find instances of marriages being arranged with little or no consultation of the parties involved (Brown 1993, 199). Dover's view that 'in the middle and lower classes young men and girls . . . had a habit of getting their own way . . . despite the formal authority of their fathers' is one reading of our data (Dover 1974, 211). But it is also plausible that, by including in his plays marriages underpinned by romantic attachments, Menander was presenting his audience with something of an escapist fantasy (and a strange fantasy at that to modern tastes since, as we shall see in Chapter 4.7, these same plays regularly include instances of sexual assault).

Any debate about the extent to which the concept of romantic love existed in the classical era is further complicated by the fact that attitudes towards intimacy evidently shifted in Athens throughout the fifth and fourth century, although the exact nature of changes in social attitudes is hugely difficult to capture. Certainly it is a complex picture that emerges from our sources. To take the example of vase-painting, there is a distinct shift away from explicit erotic imagery after the sixth century, with fifth-century painters taking a greater interest in psychology and domestic life (sexual scenes become increasingly rare after 475 BC and all but disappear by 450 BC). This culminates towards the end of the fifth century in nuptial scenes which convey, as one scholar puts it, a 'romantic and idealized notion of heterosexual love' (Fantham et al. 1994, 101; on nuptial *erōs* see also Sutton 1997/8 and Stafford 2013). In popular drama, however, it is in this very same era, the late fifth century, that the use of obscenity and overt sexuality reaches its peak, as can be gleaned from study of the Old Comedy of Aristophanes (see e.g. **Aristophanes AZ** and **BK**). By the late fourth century, this earthy exuberance has given way to the largely genteel subject matter of Menander's New Comedy, with its more measured language and romantic love plots, and where spontaneous sexual acts routinely have their consequences (see e.g. **Menander L**). In short, our sources do not paint a wholly consistent picture and nor, perhaps, should we expect them to.

1.3 Betrothal (*engyē*)

In the normal course of events, before a marriage took place linking two citizen families, the bride's *kyrios* would promise the woman to her future husband in an act known as *engyē* or *engyēsis* – normally translated 'engagement' or 'betrothal'. This was no 'engagement' in the modern western sense of the word, however, rather a pledge made by the woman's current legal guardian to her future legal guardian, with the *engyē* requiring neither the woman's consent nor, indeed, her physical presence at the event. Evidently this pledge was not binding: we know of a number of examples of couples whose *engyē* did not ultimately lead to marriage (e.g. those of Demosthenes' mother and sister: **Demosthenes E**), but nowhere do we hear of any penalty for breaking the betrothal off. Nevertheless, the *engyē* constituted a key part of the process by which an Athenian man and a woman came to be seen as a legally married couple.

The importance of the *engyē* is perhaps most evident in fourth-century courtroom disputes about inheritance where the citizen status of certain individuals is in question (and thus the rights of them and their children to inherit). In legal speeches, evidence of the *engyē* was often provided – in the form of witnesses who had attended the ceremony – in order to underline that the marital union of which the individual was the offspring had been carried out according to established traditions (curiously, witnesses to the wedding itself are never produced in court to confirm the legality of a marriage, however: Ogden 1996, 84–5). There are, perhaps, two factors which serve to make the *engyē* so significant. First, an *engyē* could mark the difference between marriage and mere co-habitation: a man might happen to live with a woman (as a concubine, for example: see 1.15 below) but an *engyē* signalled that their relationship was on a more formal footing. The second consideration is the fact that, following the various reforms to Athenian marriage law in the fifth and fourth centuries, it was only citizen women who were eligible to be pledged to citizen men in an *engyē*; that is to say, for a woman to be a *gynē engyētē* ('betrothed woman'/'wife pledged in an *engyē*') she had not only to be acknowledged by her natal family as a true-born Athenian, but also accepted as such by the family into which she married. Crucially, the offspring of a marriage by *engyē* were 'legitimate' (*gnēsios*) true-born Athenians, who would grow up to enjoy citizen rights, whereas the offspring of other unions were generally destined to be *nothoi*, 'illegitimate'/'bastards' (Just 1989, 44–5; Ogden 1996, 62: on *nothoi* see 1.15 below).

The age at which a woman was pledged to her future husband could vary enormously, as the example of Demosthenes' family neatly illustrates. Just before he died, Demosthenes' father pledged his five-year-old daughter to one nephew of his (the girl's cousin) and at the same time pledged his wife to another nephew (**Demosthenes E**). The circumstances surrounding this double betrothal are unusual, however, and in the normal scheme of things the *engyē* probably took place just before the wedding (Just 1989, 49; Blundell 1995, 115) – and *not* when the bride was still a small child. The relationship of the man to the woman whom he was pledging could also differ. According to a law cited by Demosthenes, the expectation was for a woman to be betrothed by her father, paternal grandfather or a brother sired by the same father (**Demosthenes J**), but clearly other close male relatives could assume this duty, too, if they were the woman's legal *kyrios*. We have already met the example of Demosthenes' father pledging his wife (as well as his daughter) on his deathbed, and we find instances of a betrothal being overseen by a stepfather (albeit with the consent of the girl's young brother: Isaeus 9.29), as well as jointly by a woman's brothers (**Isaeus B**; here as elsewhere, the word *ekdosis* is used to describe the act of marrying a woman off – literally 'giving away' a woman in marriage – from the verb *ekdidōmi*: see Just 1989, 71–2).

There are two sources which give us the words spoken by a girl's *kyrios* when performing the *engyē*. One of these is Herodotus' *Histories*, where we find our earliest specific reference to an Athenian marriage: the wedding of Megacles and Agariste, the daughter of Cleisthenes, the tyrant of Sicyon, which took place in the mid-sixth century BC. The words of Cleisthenes' pledge to Megacles are quoted by the historian (**Herodotus B**), but these are perhaps neither typical nor illustrative of Athenian practice, not least because the pledge is made by a non-Athenian. A more reliable source for the words spoken at the *engyē* is probably Menander's New Comedy, where we find the same formula repeated in more than one play (albeit with slight variations); namely, the woman's father saying to the future bridegroom, 'I give (her) to you for the cultivation (lit. 'ploughing') of legitimate children' (e.g. **Menander C**; see Gomme and Sandbach 1973, 531). For some scholars the wording of the pledge is significant as it casts the woman in the role of a possession (a piece of land) and a passive object, in contrast to the man who is her owner and takes on the active role of ploughing (e.g. Patterson 1991, 52). No doubt, the ideas of fertility and reproduction evoked in these words are also suggestive, however (Blundell 1995, 122). Not all scholars are convinced that a standard form of words existed for the *engyē*: A. R. W. Harrison suggests that all that was required from the two parties was 'some expressions of intention' (A. R. W. Harrison 1968–71, 18).

1.4 The bride's dowry

The *engyē* was usually the point at which the bride's father handed over the dowry (*proix*) to the woman's future *kyrios*, her husband-to-be (Blundell 1995, 115). The dowry was essentially a sum of money (sometimes property, too: Cox 1998, 76) which was set aside by a father for his daughter's upkeep and represented a woman's share of her paternal inheritance (although a lesser share than would be received by a son: Golden 1990, 174). Whilst there was no legal requirement to provide a dowry, it was nevertheless customary for a substantial sum of money to follow the bride to her new home: this was entrusted to her new guardian to provide for her material needs for the duration of the marriage. There is debate as to the extent to which the legal prohibitions on women owning and administering large sums of money in Athens were occasionally flouted (Sealey 1990, 37–40 and 42–9), but certainly the general expectation was that a citizen woman in Athens did not undertake major financial transactions (**Isaeus M**): this was the job of her *kyrios*. The dowry, then, was essentially available for the husband to draw on and invest as he saw fit, and in many ways to treat as part of his own estate, but with one important proviso: if he and his wife divorced or she died childless, the dowry had to be returned to her natal family. If he failed to do so, he was required to pay interest on the dowry at the rate of 9 obols a month per 100 drachmas (i.e. 18 per cent per annum) until his debt was cleared (**Demosthenes T** and Demosthenes 27.17; A. R. W. Harrison 1968–71, 55–9).

For an Athenian father, the provision of a generous dowry was an opportunity to make a show of his wealth to the broader community (Lacey 1968, 109; Schaps 1979, 74–5). Whilst the dowries of society's poorest girls could no doubt be modest, the average size of a dowry amongst elite families in the classical era was around 30 to 40 minas (i.e. 3,000–4,000 drachmas: Cox 1998, 75; cf. **Demosthenes E, Isaeus B** and **L** and **Menander C**). Some dowries could be a good deal more. Alcibiades, for instance, is said to have received the famously large sum of 10 talents when he married Hipparete (i.e. 60,000 drachmas: **Andocides B** and **Plutarch A**). Estimates vary, but the sum handed over in respect of a daughter's marriage might perhaps represent between 5 per cent and 20 per cent of the father's wealth (Schaps 1979, 78; Leduc 1992, 279–80), the size of the dowry presumably determined in part by the number of children between whom a father's estate had to be divided. The attraction of wealth to potential suitors evidently led to an element of competition in the provision of dowries; or in other words, to attach a large sum of money to a girl made her a more attractive proposition and could help to secure an advantageous match. In turn, a sizeable dowry no doubt provided the woman with a certain degree of security and influence within her new marriage and made the prospect of divorce that much less appealing for her husband (**Euripides B**; cf. **Andocides B** and **Plutarch A**). What is more, a generous dowry might also encourage what Cox calls 'marital intimacy' (Cox 1998, 70). Since it was her offspring who inherited the money on their mother's death, the only way for the husband to ensure that the dowry would remain the property of his *oikos* was for the couple to have children.

It was not just first-time brides who were provided with dowries in classical Athens: they would also be provided to men who married widows and divorcees (see **Demosthenes E** and **Isaeus L**; Hunter 1989, 295). While the inability to furnish a woman with a sizeable dowry could evidently be a source of embarrassment and regret for a family (see e.g. **Isaeus L**), for a man to marry a girl whose dowry was small or non-existent could conversely be presented as a noble act worthy of praise (e.g. Lysias 19.14–18). We find examples, too, of friends and extended family contributing to the dowry of a girl of poor parents as well as the city of Athens providing a dowry for the daughters of men who had served the state (Plutarch, *Life of Aristides* 27; Aeschines 3.258). Indeed, there appear to have been specific laws in place in

Athens which ensured that orphaned girls and daughters of the poor could obtain a dowry (**Isaeus A** and **Demosthenes W**).

1.5 The wedding rituals

As various scholars have suggested, the rituals which marked the marriage of the bride and groom in ancient Athens would not have held the legal significance of a modern wedding ceremony (e.g. Maffi 2005, 254). Since weddings were neither presided over by a representative of the state nor officially registered, a marriage was essentially judged to be legitimate by virtue of the couple having gone through various stages in their relationship, including the betrothal, 'living together' (*synoikein*) and, ideally, the production of offspring (*paidopoiein*). So, as Cynthia Patterson puts it, marriage is perhaps best regarded as a 'social process rather than a legal moment' (Patterson 1998, 109) – albeit a process in which the wedding ceremony had an important role to play, not least in terms of the ritual and emotional lives of the married couple, their friends, families and the community at large. Significantly for the bride, her wedding also marked the point at which she left her natal home to be incorporated into a new *oikos* – that of her marital family – and gained a new *kyrios* in the form of her husband. For most women marriage would also have entailed their sexual initiation (unlike the older groom, who is likely to have gained sexual experience prior to his wedding). For a first-time bride, then, her wedding was a rite of passage from girlhood to adulthood in more ways than one.

The wedding rituals were divided into three distinct phases: the *proaulia* (preparations), the *gamos* or 'wedding' itself (including the feast and procession), and *epaulia* (celebrations after the wedding night). In its canonical form, a wedding seems to have lasted three days – one day for each of these phases (Cantarella 2005a, 246) – though we find examples of celebrations taking place over a longer period as well as weddings being completed in a day and a night (Oakley and Sinos 1993, 10). The information we have about marriage celebrations in ancient Greece is vast, since the wedding (*gamos*) surfaces as a motif in numerous sources, most notably in lyric poetry, drama and Athenian vase-painting. In the absence of a single authoritative account from the classical era, however, there is inevitably a certain amount of uncertainty as to the precise order of events and the exact nature of the rituals practised by fifth- and fourth-century Athenians – which may, in any case, have varied from wedding to wedding. The following account of Athenian marriage rituals is based largely on the study of *The Wedding in Ancient Athens* by Oakley and Sinos (1993), who synthesize a large number of disparate sources.

Essential elements of every marriage ceremony included appeasing the gods, the ritual preparation and adornment of the bride and groom, feasting, the ceremonial transfer of the bride to her marital home, and the couple's first night together in the marriage chamber. The initial sacrifices to the gods of marriage – Zeus Teleios, Hera Teleia, Artemis, Aphrodite and Peitho (Persuasion) – were evidently a cause for celebration and an occasion for music, dancing and the singing of marriage songs (**Euripides I**). This was followed by the ritual bathing and adornment of each partner, which in the case of the bride constituted a particular focus of interest for vase-painters in the fifth century. One common scene shows the solemn procession undertaken by the companions of the bride to fetch water for the bath, and surviving examples of the type of jug used for this purpose, the loutrophoros, are typically painted with wedding imagery. A more popular subject still on red-figure vases is the adornment of the bride by her companions, who are often shown carrying boxes containing perfume and jewellery, one key moment of the bride's preparation being the binding of the woman's hair (**Fig. 1**; see also **Fig. 2**). Such 'adornment' scenes are particularly popular in the second half of the fifth century (Blundell and Rabinowitz 2008, 136; but see also Lewis 2002, 135, who questions whether all adornment scenes are necessarily wedding-related). For the wedding, the bride would be dressed in a crown and a veil and would wear special shoes called *nymphides* (one detail we lack is the colour of the dress, however – no literary source directly informs us of this and vase-painters fail to portray the dress in a distinctive colour; Llewellyn-Jones argues that the veil was most likely of a reddish hue: Llewellyn-Jones 2003, 223–7; cf. Oakley and Sinos 1993, 16). A common feature in bridal scenes on vases is the presence of an Eros figure, often taken as suggestive of the seductive powers of which the bride is possessed (Sutton 1992, 27; Oakley and Sinos 1993, 19–20 and 47; Lewis 2002, 144; see also Stafford 2013 for discussion). To add to their allure, both partners would have been anointed with perfume, and whilst the groom's bath and adornment are rarely depicted, we nevertheless know that he wore a special cloak which was 'bright' and intricately woven (Aristophanes, *Peace* 859; *Wealth* 530).

No vase-painting depicts the wedding feast, but it could clearly be a rowdy affair (**Plutarch F**), and towards the end of the fourth century it even became the subject of specific legislation restricting the number of diners to thirty (Oakley and Sinos 1993, 22: this was perhaps aimed at curbing ostentatious displays of wealth). The location of the meal varied but evidence from New Comedy indicates that families often collaborated to lay on the feast, which featured meat from the prenuptial sacrifices. Unusually, men and women dined together on this occasion, albeit on different sides of the table, and at nightfall the bride's father would unite the couple for the first time. This was perhaps the occasion for the unveiling of the bride, too, the *anakalypteria*, though the conflicting accounts we find in our sources means that the timing of this event is uncertain (Oakley and Sinos 1993, 25–6; see Llewellyn-Jones 2003, 227–47, on ancient accounts and modern views as to when the *anakalypteria* took place, his own suggestion being that there were multiple unveilings at different points in the ceremonies). Significantly, the groom gave the bride a gift at her public unveiling which she formally accepted – a detail which, it has been suggested, is symbolic of the bride giving her consent to the union (Patterson 1991, 55).

A further major event was the torchlight procession conveying the bride and groom to the marital *oikos*. An early description of this event occurs in Homer (**Homer A**, where the role of song and dance is neatly highlighted), and the procession was also a popular subject in vase-painting (on black-figure vases, in particular, e.g. **Figs 3** and **4**). The marital procession could either be accomplished on foot (the so-called *chamaipous*) or in a cart (in vase-paintings depicting the latter we occasionally find the bride accompanied not just by the groom but also by what is perhaps a best-man figure, the two men protecting the bride by sandwiching her between them as they ride along). Vase-paintings sometimes contain another female figure, too, in addition to the bride, generally taken to be a *nympheutria*, or 'bridesmaid'. Processions could again prove rowdy events and served the important purpose of informing the wider community that the wedding had taken place.

From this point in the celebrations the groom's family home became the focus of activity. The moment at which the bride entered the house was a further signature moment and forms the subject of a number of vase-paintings, where the bride's uncertainty is often apparent as she is led inside by her new husband (e.g. **Figs 5** and **6**; cf. **Sophocles E**). Following her arrival, the bride was incorporated into her new *oikos* by a ritual known as the *katachysmata* (a ceremony also used in respect of new slaves) during which she had dates, nuts, dried fruit and figs poured over her head. Finally, the newly-weds would retire to the previously adorned marital chamber, which would be guarded for the night by a friend of the groom acting as a door-keeper. Friends of the bride would also keep a vigil outside the door, providing a comforting sound for the bride, perhaps, as they sang songs (Oakley and Sinos 1993, 37). According to post-classical sources their singing also muffled the sounds of the bride as she was violated by her husband (scholiast on Theocritus 18) – the presence of the door-keeper serving to 'prevent the women from helping the screaming bride' (Pollux 3.42). These post-classical notions of the violated, 'screaming' bride are arguably at odds with the romanticized image of the bride we find in Athenian vase-painting, however, where she is often accompanied by the goddess Peitho ('Persuasion'), the emphasis here being on her seductive charms, perhaps – or, alternatively, the seduction which is practised upon her by the groom (see Oakley and Sinos 1993, 46–7, and Stafford 2000, 135–8). The day following the wedding and this sexual initiation was an occasion for further feasting, songs and dances and was also the time for giving the gifts, the *epaulia*, which gave their name to the whole day.

At some point subsequent to the wedding, the groom would traditionally hold another feast called the *gamēlia* for his phratry (i.e. one of the kinship groups to which most – if not all – male Athenian citizens belonged). This put down a further marker that a legitimate wedding had taken place and paved the way for any sons born to him from the union to be enrolled in the phratry at a later date. Now the married couple could be said to be 'living together' – *synoikein* – a word which, in the absence of any more precise term (**Aristotle H**), effectively denoted 'being married' in classical Athens (**Demosthenes X**; see Just 1989, 62–4 and Ogden 1996, 79–80). If a citizen man was living with a woman who was not his legitimate wife – e.g. if she had not been pledged in an *engyē* or, after Pericles' citizenship law of 451 BC, if the woman was non-Athenian by birth or descent – the relationship might instead be described as 'being together' or 'co-habiting', *syneinai*. In the eyes of the law, children born from such a union would normally be classed as 'illegitimate' (*nothoi*), and enjoy only limited civil and inheritance rights (see 1.15 below).

1.6 Men and women's age upon marriage

From the depictions of wedding processions and other marital scenes we find on Greek vases, it would be easy to conclude that the age gap between husband and wife was relatively small, since both are customarily depicted in the bloom of youth (**Figs 5** and **6**). From our literary sources we know that the reality was somewhat different, however, and in the case of first marriages at least, the couple would typically be made up of a teenage bride and an adult husband perhaps twice her age or more.

Most modern scholars concur that the age of an Athenian girl at the time of her wedding was usually fourteen, although some would allow slightly more leeway: Lacey, for instance, suggests that girls were married 'not later than 16' with a tendency 'to be earlier than this rather than later' (Lacey 1968, 117), whereas Blundell suggests that 'girls were probably married for the first time between fourteen and eighteen' (Blundell 1995, 119). Certainly fourteen was the age upon marriage of the bride in Xenophon's *Oeconomicus* whom her husband, Ischomachus, must instruct in the management of the home (**Xenophon I**). Fourteen has also been suggested as the average age in Athens of menarche (i.e. the onset of periods: Amundsen and Diers 1969; Sourvinou-Inwood 1988, 25–8), and given the emphasis on female virginity before marriage and the threat that a sexually mature girl could potentially pose to her family's honour (the pubescent girl's wild nature is often emphasized in our sources: e.g. **Anacreon C**), a father's desire to marry off his daughter while she was still a young teenager is perhaps understandable. This is not to say that all Athenians considered marriage advisable at such a young age. Plato suggests that women should marry between the ages of sixteen and twenty (**Plato E**), for example, whereas Aristotle, who advocates marriage for girls at about eighteen, warns that younger women are more likely to have stunted and female offspring and are at greater risk of dying in childbirth (**Aristotle J**). These suggestions by Plato and Aristotle are probably best understood as attempts to correct contemporary practice rather than to reflect it, however, and so do little to call into question the hypothesis that Athenian brides were routinely young teenagers.

For a man, the time for marriage seems to have been when he was in his late twenties to mid-thirties. Ischomachus in Xenophon's *Oeconomicus* is a man of roughly thirty years when he marries his bride, and in his poetry the sixth-century statesman Solon advises men to marry and have children between the ages of twenty-eight and thirty-five (Solon, fr. 27.9–10 W = 23 G-P; Hesiod's advice, too, is for men to marry at around thirty: **Hesiod B**). Plato's advice is in a similar vein, namely for a man to marry between the ages of thirty and thirty-five (**Plato E**). The highest age we find recommended is in Aristotle, who advises men to marry at around thirty-seven (**Aristotle J**; cf. **Demosthenes F** where we find an example of a peculiarly young eighteen-year-old groom, albeit one whose father has special reason for wanting him to marry quickly).

The age difference between husband and wife has been accounted for in various ways by scholars. For Keuls, what she calls the 'premature marriage' of girls, i.e. before they had reached full physical maturity, was a 'technique for keeping women physically under control' (Keuls 1985, 103). Pomeroy, on the other hand, suggests that the requirements of military service meant that it was preferable for men to marry late, and points out that a young widow could potentially serve as a wife in multiple marriages and therefore provide heirs for more than one household. In this way, she argues, the early age of marriage for girls helped to make up for the low numbers of females in the population (caused, she claims, by female infanticide – a suggestion that has proven controversial – as well as a higher mortality rate among girls than boys: Pomeroy 1975, 64; cf. Oldenziel 1987, 98–100). One theme to emerge from ancient sources is that young girls are most easily educated in the ways of the new household (**Hesiod B**; Xenophon's *Oeconomicus*). For Strauss it is significant that an ageing man would generally look to hand over the running of his house to his son before he died (Strauss 1993, 67–70; cf. **Aristotle J**), since a gap of roughly thirty years between generations would mean that a man in his early sixties would hand over control to a son when he was around thirty years of age. The point at which the son took over the management of the household might thus seem an appropriate time of life for him to take a wife and seek an heir of his own – one advantage of this arrangement being that a young wife could play a role in looking after her husband's ageing father. This is roughly the scenario we find in a legal speech by Isaeus, for example, where the ageing Menecles adopts a son who had recently married. Menecles proceeds to leave his new son in charge of the *oikos*, while his new daughter-in-law helps to care for him (**Isaeus E**). Whether many fathers lived long enough to 'retire' in this way is another matter, however: Strauss estimates that only a third of twenty-five-year-old men, and a fifth of thirty-year-olds, would have had fathers who were still alive (Strauss 1993, 68). Perhaps significant, too, is that it was at thirty that Athenian men gained their full quota of citizen rights: before this age, a man was ineligible for civic roles such as generalships and magistracies, as well as serving on juries and Athens' Council (*Boulē*).

Also hugely relevant to the question of when men and girls married, no doubt, is the role of social expectation: unlike Plato and Aristotle, who have their own suggestions to make, presumably few Athenians thought to question the marriage practices of their city. Rather, for most citizens, the assumption would be that they and their family members would simply follow the established traditions of their society. This said, there are at least some indications in comic drama that the model of the twenty-eight- to thirty-five-year-old man marrying a young teenage girl was not always adhered to. On the one hand, we find a character in Menander scolding an older man for seeking a young bride's hand in marriage rather than letting her marry someone her own age (**Menander K**). On the other hand, we find an indication in Aristophanes that old men marrying young brides was not at all unknown (**Aristophanes BF**). Indeed, there is every reason to suppose that age in itself was not a bar to men finding wives, whereas for girls, the age range during which it was open for them to marry for the first time may have been relatively narrow (**Aristophanes AW**).

1.7 Divorce

Whilst, in the words of one scholar, 'divorce was easy' in classical Athens (Lacey 1968, 108), it seems to have been a far from routine occurrence. The most common mechanism by which divorce occurred was 'repudiation' – *apopempis* or *ekpempsis* – literally a 'sending away' or 'sending out' of the bride by her husband. Divorce in this manner could evidently be undertaken at will by the husband without justification (Cantarella 2005a, 246), but apparently the decision to separate could also be arrived at by common consent (**Isaeus C**; **Plutarch B**). Another form of divorce was that initiated by the woman. This required the wife to leave the conjugal house in an act known as *apoleipsis* or 'abandonment' and for her and her new *kyrios* (e.g. her father) to present themselves in front of the archon (one of Athens' ruling magistrates). Only two examples of *apoleipsis* are attested in the classical era (Cohn-Haft 1995, 4), including what is perhaps the most dramatic of all Athenian divorce sagas, the attempted 'abandonment' of Alcibiades by his first wife, Hipparete. Rather than allow her to see the divorce through, Alcibiades apparently provoked a cause célèbre by having her dragged home by force through the marketplace before she could reach the archon (**Andocides B** and **Plutarch A**). There is also evidence to suggest that a third form of divorce was possible, paternal *aphairēsis*, that is the 'taking back' of the bride by her father (see Katz 1992, 693–4 and Cohn-Haft 1995, 5–6; but cf. Rosivach 1984, who questions whether this procedure was ever used). Most scholars think that this form of divorce was only possible if the woman was still childless (e.g. A. R. W. Harrison 1968–71, 309–11, and Cantarella 2005a,

247). The existence of this procedure raises interesting questions about the legal rights that the natal family still had over the bride and the extent to which – prior to motherhood, at least – she was truly integrated into her marital *oikos* (see also 1.12 below on the laws pertaining to the *epiklēros* or 'heiress').

The reasons we find cited for divorce are something of a mish-mash (Cohn-Haft 1995, 9–14). For Alcibiades' wife it was her husband's habit of bringing *hetairai* (i.e. prostitutes/mistresses) back to the family home that sent her over the edge (on *hetairai*, see Chapter 3.3). In a legal speech by Isaeus, we find a man called Menecles who is so concerned that he and his wife are unable to have children that he delicately approaches his brothers-in-law suggesting that she be found another husband so that she, at least, might not die childless (**Isaeus C**; childlessness was perhaps among the more common reasons for divorce: Blundell 1995, 127). A slightly less touching story is that of one Protomachus, who, when the opportunity arises for him to marry an heiress, decides to seek a divorce, persuading a friend to marry his wife in his place (**Demosthenes M**). Regardless of the circumstances under which a divorce occurred, the husband was bound to return his wife's dowry: this explains Alcibiades' reluctance to let his wife leave him, for instance (**Plutarch A**; cf. **Euripides B**). In the case of Menecles, he simply passed the dowry he had received for his wife onto her new husband (**Isaeus C**).

The question remains as to how Athenians regarded divorce. In Euripides' *Medea* we are told that women are held in bad repute if they divorce their husbands (**Euripides J**), though perhaps here it is *apoleipsis* in particular which is being alluded to (i.e. the wife's 'abandonment' of the marital home). While Cox suggests that 'a woman's divorce could lead to gossip about her behaviour and thereby bring shame on her' (Cox 1998, 71; cf. Scafuro 1994, 163), there is in fact little evidence to indicate that divorce initiated by a husband (which could often be undertaken by mutual consent) was frowned upon. An obvious exception to this rule is when a man was obliged to seek a divorce, e.g. if his wife was guilty of adultery (**Demosthenes V**); or if his wife had been pledged to him under false pretences, e.g. if his wife proved to be a non-citizen ([Demosthenes] 59.81–3; cf. **Demosthenes T**). As Cox reminds us, however, we hear of relatively few separations in the legal speeches of the era, the implication being that the divorce rate in Athens was low. The general view – albeit 'idealized', she suggests – 'is that husband and wife try to make the marriage work' (Cox 1998, 72; cf. Coln-Haft 1995, 14, who counts just nine recorded instances of divorce in classical Athens).

1.8 Widow(er)hood

A far more common ending to a marriage than divorce was the death of one of the partners. By one estimate, the median life expectancy (i.e. the age which only 50 per cent of people reached) was 44.5 for men and 33.6 for women (Angel 1972, 94; cf. Garland 1990, 245), with disease, warfare and death in childbirth regularly bringing marriages to an early end. In the case of the death of a wife, there were perhaps few practical consequences: if she died childless, the dowry would simply be returned to her natal *oikos* and the husband would be free to remarry; if there were children, these would generally remain in their paternal home (see e.g. **Isaeus L**), and the woman's son(s) would inherit her dowry (it is not known what happened to the dowry if a woman died leaving only female offspring: Sealey 1990, 27; cf. Leduc 1992, 280). If the husband died when the couple were still childless, the wife would normally return to her original home taking her dowry and other possessions with her. As stated above, if the dowry could not be repaid immediately, the debtor (i.e. the husband, if alive; his next of kin, if not) was liable to pay the wife's family interest of 18 per cent a year of the capital sum.

There was evidently more flexibility when a man died leaving a widow and (non-adult) children. In these circumstances a range of solutions seems to have been possible to the problem of where the widow and her offspring lived. We certainly find cases of women remarrying and leaving their children behind to be reared by the dead husband's family (e.g. Lysias 32.8). However, alternative scenarios were also possible whereby the mother would take her children with her to the *oikos* of a member of her natal family (usually a brother, who would then act as her *kyrios*: e.g. Lysias 3.6 and 19.33), or where a widow who had remarried would live with her children in her new husband's household (e.g. Isaeus 7.7 and 9.27). In the event of widowhood, women could generally rely on the protection of their male relatives (and failing that, the archon, who had special duties in respect of a widow left without a *kyrios*, e.g. the responsibility to prosecute offenders on her behalf: Demosthenes 43.75; [Aristotle], *Constitution of Athens* 56.7). Minor children would routinely have guardians appointed to act on their behalf and administer their dead father's estate until they came of age.

1.9 Remarriage

Remarriage was evidently customary for divorcees, widows and widowers alike. Cox suggests that 'remarriage of a widow still in her childbearing years was often a very hasty transaction' (Cox 1998, 182), an assessment that chimes with Pomeroy's view, outlined above, that the relative shortage of suitable women of childbearing age made them valuable commodities for households requiring an heir (Pomeroy 1975, 64). It is also plausible that an older woman would have a certain amount of say as to whom she married: Demosthenes' mother failed to marry the man to whom her dying husband had betrothed her, for example (**Demosthenes E**), and in a legal speech of Hyperides we find an example of a widow who had supposedly promised herself to one man, Lycophron, but subsequently married another, Charippus (one of the juicier allegations in this legal speech being that Lycophron had tried to persuade the woman on her wedding day to save herself for him and not to sleep with her new husband: Hyperides 1.3 and 1.7).

It is interesting, too, to consider the effects that the intermarriage of kin, death and remarriage could have on the make-up of a household. To take one example, in a legal speech by Lysias we find a certain Diogeiton living in the same house as his fraternal nephews – who are also, we note, his grandsons – along with his second wife and the couple's children (Lysias 32). Remarriage could evidently lead to tense domestic situations on occasions, too, as can be judged from legal disputes between stepchildren (e.g. Demosthenes 39 and 40), or between children of a previous marriage and a new wife (Antiphon 1 contains a particularly compelling portrait of an allegedly wicked stepmother). Of a wholly different order are the domestic arrangements of Callias, which we learn about in a speech by Andocides. In the late fifth century he is alleged to have made his wife's mother his mistress while all three were living under the same roof. The wife supposedly attempted suicide out of shame before fleeing, and later Callias threw her mother out of the house, too – but not, it seems, before making the latter pregnant (**Andocides A**; see also 1.13 below on the so-called 'bigamy concession').

1.10 Married life

The variables affecting the relationship between man and wife in classical Athens make it impossible to talk of a 'typical' marriage. For a woman, factors such as social class, whether she had been married before and whether in her new household she was surrounded by relatives (in the case of a marriage to a member of her kin) or lived close to natal family (if, for example, she had married a neighbour), would no doubt have had a significant impact on her life. The anxieties of the new bride are arguably captured on the faces of women being led towards their marital homes on red-figure pottery (e.g. **Figs 5** and **6**) and in tragedy we similarly find some telling examples of women articulating the uncertainties and stresses that marriage brings them (e.g. **Euripides B** and **J** and **Sophocles E**).

Reconstructing the nature of the lives lived by women in classical Athens has been a popular pursuit in modern scholarship. One point of consensus is that the picture we sometimes find in our texts of citizen wives and daughters confined to the home, rarely coming into contact with men, is essentially an idealisation of how women might and should behave (e.g. **Lysias H**). For most women, especially the non-elite, the realities of everyday life would have been somewhat different. In his ground-breaking study, *Law, Sexuality, and Society*, David Cohen dispels the myth of female 'seclusion' by examining the wide range of activities in which we regularly find women engaged in our sources: not only did women of the lower classes often work outside the home, but females of all social strata participated in public religious activities, visited neighbours, fetched water, assisted in childbirth, and so on (D. Cohen 1991, 150–4). Cohen concludes that 'what statements to the effect that the women never leave the house in fact mean is that they never leave the house without a purpose, a purpose that will be regarded as legitimate in the eyes of the watchful community' (D. Cohen 1991, 163). In short, a citizen woman's life was typically centred on, but not wholly restricted to, the house, and largely, if not exclusively, spent in the company of other women (thus Cohen prefers to talk of the 'separation' of women from men rather than their 'seclusion': D. Cohen 1991, 149). While men enjoyed far greater freedom of movement, their time would chiefly be spent with other males, too, their contact with women mainly limited to female family members – as well as prostitutes (see Chapter 3).

For a typical newly wed couple, the gap in age and education between husband and wife might plausibly have led to the kind of paternalistic relationship we find described in Xenophon's *Oeconomicus*. In this dialogue, Ischomachus seeks advice from no less a figure than Socrates on how to train his young bride in household management, and while a partnership is evidently envisaged between husband and wife, the marriage is hardly seen as a pairing of equals: rather, the man is clearly the one in charge (see also Aristotle's much-quoted assessment of men's intellectual superiority to women: **Aristotle I**). It is in some of the smaller details that Xenophon's work is particularly revealing, however: we learn not only that husband and wife rarely converse with one another, for example (**Xenophon H**; but cf. **Aristophanes AD**), but also – in common with other married couples in our sources – that they do not share a bed (*Oeconomicus* 9.6; cf. **Lysias C**). Such pen portraits have led many scholars to conclude that Athenian marriages were generally devoid of affection and sexual passion. Pomeroy, for instance, talks of marriage in Athens as 'characterized by a lack of friendship in the modern sense of the word' (Pomeroy 1975, 74); Cantarella suggests that marriage 'can hardly be considered the most appropriate venue for Eros' (Cantarella 2005a, 247); and Keuls ventures that a man slept with his wife only 'reluctantly, for the sake of offspring' (Keuls 1985, 215; see also Lewis 2002, 176). To be sure, marriage is regularly portrayed in a negative light in our sources (e.g. **Aristophon A**; **Euripides J**), but ancient authors do sing its praises, too. For example, marriage can also be presented as a mutually beneficial and mutually pleasurable union (at least if the right women is secured: **Semonides A**); as giving rise between husband and wife to a bond of *philia*, 'affection' or 'friendship' (**Aristotle F** and **Xenophon A**); and, even when things go wrong, as something worth patching up for the sake of the children (**Demosthenes G**). Interestingly, too, we find real-life accounts of married couples displaying affection for each other (e.g. **Isaeus C**) and caring for each other when unwell (Demosthenes 30.34, 50.61, 59.56). Numerous epitaphs also express the sorrow of the husband at the death of a wife (albeit in conventional wording, e.g. **Inscription A**) and images on Greek vases, specifically white-ground lekythoi which were created as offerings for the dead, often show poignant scenes of mourning for women (the white-ground technique involved covering the clay with a white slip, which thus provided the vase-painter with a light background on which to paint images). While such evidence may allow us to discuss how relationships between husband and wife were presented in art and literature, however, we must be careful to bear in mind the extent to which our sources are artistic creations and, crucially, composed almost exclusively by men and for a largely male audience (on the representation of marriage in our sources, see esp. Just 1989, 126–52). As a result we have precious little access to the thoughts and emotions of women. Equally important to consider is just how different ancient conceptions of 'love' and 'affection' may have been from our own (Konstan 2000, 122) and the extent to which the expectations of ancient brides and grooms would have differed from those of their modern, western counterparts.

There may be evidence of affection, co-operation and mutual regard in some Athenian marriages, but is there any reason to doubt the validity of Pomeroy's assertion that 'the sexual experience of the majority of Athenian citizen women was not satisfying' (Pomeroy 1975, 87)? We find occasional references to husbands feeling *erōs*, 'desire', for their future or current wives (e.g. **Menander B**), but less indication that this feeling was reciprocated; even in Old Comedy, where younger women are routinely portrayed as sex mad, there are few references to citizen women enjoying sex with their husbands (instead it is women's alleged extra-marital dalliances that take centre stage, e.g. **Aristophanes BE** and **BG**; cf. **Plato K** and **L** for a mythical example of a devoted wife). Similarly, the fact that most citizen couples routinely lived, ate and slept apart does little to suggest that emotional and sexual intimacy was a standard feature of married life. What is more, since citizen men had a variety of more or less socially approved outlets for their emotional and sexual needs in the form of same-sex relationships (see Chapter 2) and prostitutes (see Chapter 3), there was arguably less reason for them to seek intimacy at home. Indeed, in Xenophon's *Memorabilia*, Socrates explicitly states that sex for pleasure with prostitutes is something different from marital sex, the purpose of which is instead reproduction (**Xenophon D**; Carson 1990, 149, detects a contrast in Greek thought between reproductive sex which is considered 'work' and non-reproductive sex which is considered 'play'). Athenian wives did not enjoy the same sexual freedoms as their husbands, of course, and if a woman had sex with a man to whom she was not married she risked severe punishments (see Chapter 4.4). Instructively, too, in a legal speech by Isaeus, the fact that one Pyrrhus serenaded, argued and feasted with a woman is presented as evidence that she cannot have been his wife, but rather a prostitute (**Isaeus F**). The suggestion here is that intimacy and a heightened emotional connection between husband and wife are far from normal.

1.11 Children

The production of children was the primary object of marriage for classical Athenians (**Menander C**; cf. **Demosthenes X**). As can be gleaned from the account of reproduction provided by Xenophon in his *Memorabilia*, for example, the desire to have children was seen as a fundamental and natural part of the human condition (**Xenophon**

D) and, as one modern scholar comments, for women, marriage and motherhood were considered 'the fulfilment of the female role' (Just 1989, 40). Children played a key role not just in inheritance (see 1.12 below) but also in the continuation of the religious traditions of the household, since they were the means by which family cults would be maintained in future generations (**Isaeus K**). In addition, parents could expect their children to care for them in old age – indeed, they were legally bound to do so (Plutarch, *Life of Solon* 23.1 and 4; Strauss 1993, 65) – which provided further motivation for a couple to reproduce (Lacey 1968, 117; **Isaeus D**).

Life expectancy in Athens was low by modern western standards, with death in childbirth a particularly common cause of female mortality (Blundell 1998, 49, estimates that up to one in five births may have resulted in the death of the mother; see also **Aristotle J**). Infant mortality was also high: Golden reckons that between 30 per cent and 40 per cent of children failed to survive their first year (Golden 1990, 83), making it likely that most Athenian mothers would have buried at least one child in their lifetime (Blundell 1995, 141; cf. French 1994, 73, and Ingalls 2002, 246–7, whose figures suggest that only 50 per cent of newborn babies would have reached adulthood). The question as to whether the exposure of healthy newborn infants was practised by married couples in classical Athens has been the subject of intense debate, but there is little doubt among scholars that this is a fate that regularly befell illegitimate, unhealthy or handicapped children (e.g. Blundell 1995, 130, who notes, however, that no real-life instances of exposure are recorded; see also Patterson 1985 and Oldenziel 1987 on scholarly debates about infanticide). Certainly boys were more prized than girls – but while in Old Comedy we find listed among the scandalous misdemeanours of women the introduction of a supposititious male child into a household (presumably as a substitute for a stillborn or female baby), we have no way of knowing the extent to which such ruses were ever employed in real life (**Aristophanes BE**). Interestingly, the children of those families mentioned in legal speeches do not show any strong gender bias (Lacey 1968, 166; Ingalls 2002, 249), which perhaps suggests that the exposure and substitution of female children were in fact rare. Legal speeches, too, provide us with useful data about the number of surviving children typically found in an Athenian family: anything up to five seems normal (Lacey 1968, 163; see e.g. **Demosthenes H** and **Isaeus B**), with stepchildren often living alongside children from the new marriage (e.g. **Isaeus L**). Childlessness is seen as highly problematic, but while medical remedies for infertility were characteristically aimed at women (Blundell 1998, 44), it was evidently not always the wife who was thought to be at fault (**Isaeus C** and **Plutarch D**; cf. Byl 1990, 309).

1.12 Inheritance, adoption and the law of the 'heiress' (*epiklēros*)

A situation which every citizen householder in Athens would have been eager to avoid is the demise of his *oikos*. The ideal way to ensure its continuation was to have sons who in turn married and produced sons, thus providing a clear line of succession. This ambition was not always realized, of course: Patterson, for example, estimates that around 20 per cent of *kyrioi* would have died childless, with a similar number having only daughters (Patterson 1998, 93). The standard way in which a *kyrios* would have made up for the absence of a male heir was by the adoption of an adult male into his household (**Isaeus D** and **K**). Adoption could take place either while the *kyrios* was still alive or by will after his death; but either way, the adoptee was obliged to marry the *kyrios*' daughter if there was one. The adoptee – who was most often a close kinsman of the *kyrios* (e.g. his brother or nephew: Humpreys 2002, 342; but cf. Rubenstein 1993, 22–6) – would forfeit any inheritance rights he had in his natal family, his key task in the adoptive household being to sire a male heir through which the family estate might be transmitted in the future. Once he had provided this heir he was, it seems, at liberty to return to his natal *oikos* if he so chose, although this entailed giving up his rights in his adoptive family. These complex rules were evidently aimed at preventing two *oikoi* merging into one, designed as they were to ensure that the same man did not inherit twice. (A further stipulation was that the adoptee did not properly 'inherit' the *kyrios*' estate; like a dowry, the estate remained under his administration to use as his own, but had to be passed on to his offspring intact: Isaeus 8.31; Sissa 1996, 220–1.)

When a *kyrios* died, Athenian law dictated that his son – whether natural or adopted – came into possession of his estate; if the deceased had more than one son, the estate was divided equally between them (which in turn could lead to the creation of new *oikoi*: **Demosthenes H**). In the absence of a living son (or his descendants), the next in line was the dead man's daughter(s) (or her descendants), and then the deceased's brother (or his descendants), his sister (or her descendants), then paternal uncle(s), paternal aunt(s) and so on, with the members of an individual's extended family able to inherit – the so-called *anchisteia* – limited by law to the children of the deceased's first cousins

(Isaeus 11.2; see also Just 1989, 85–8). Importantly, then, Athenian law allowed for the estate to be settled on a female, most often the daughter (or daughters) of the deceased. A woman who found herself in this position was known as an *epiklēros*, usually translated as 'heiress' (the word literally means 'on the estate' or 'with the property'). As a female, however, she was unable to administer the inheritance herself. For this, she needed a *kyrios* in the form of a husband – and to protect the bloodline of inheritance, this man should ideally be a close male relative.

Once a woman became an *epiklēros*, she automatically became the subject of a judicial procedure called an *epidikasia*, the precise purpose of which has been the subject of debate. Most scholars think the *epidikasia* served to determine the member of her family to whom the heiress would henceforth be married, bypassing the usual convention of the 'betrothal' (*engyē*). However, it has been suggested that this procedure merely established which man was to become her *kyrios* – with this man then gaining the right either to wed her himself or to give her away in marriage to another member of family (Cudjoe 2005). Either way, the job of the archon, who oversaw this procedure, was clearly to make an official adjudication about the *epiklēros'* future and, if more than one relative sought to claim her, to decide which one should prevail (with preference given to the man most closely related to her: see Katz 1992, 695).

In line with the standard order of inheritance in Athens, the deceased man's brother or nephew was the obvious candidate to claim the hand of the *epiklēros*, but it was evidently not obligatory for him to do so (**Isaeus I**). If no family member came forward to claim the *epiklēros* (a real possibility if she was a poor man's daughter), the extended family had a social and legal duty to provide her with a dowry and to find her a husband (**Isaeus A**; Demosthenes 43.54). Here, then, we find another example of Athenian laws which are designed to avert the extinction of an *oikos*. Once married, the *epiklēros'* husband enjoyed a status similar to that of an adoptive son: he forfeited his inheritance rights in his natal family and, while the estate was his to administer, it remained the property of his wife, the heiress (Isaeus 10.12; who might as a result turn into something of a demanding wife: **Menander J**). The key task of the husband, then, just like the adoptive son, was to sire a male heir to inherit the *oikos*.

Complications arose when either the *epiklēros* or her prospective husband were married at the time when the *kyrios* died. In the case of a married woman, the legal process of the *epidikasia*, which saw

her allotment to a member of her natal family, evidently entailed her
divorce from her existing husband (**Isaeus H**). The law may have
provided some flexibility, however: in a legal speech by Isaeus we find
an example of a woman who remained with her existing husband after
becoming an heiress (**Isaeus N**), though in this case it is clearly her
natal family rather than she and her husband who took possession of
the estate. Some scholars believe that the woman was not obliged to
divorce her husband if she had children (Maffi 2005, 257); others if
she had a son (for discussion, see A. R. W. Harrison 1968–71, 309–11).
And if she already had sons there was always another possibility:
namely for one of these to be adopted into her natal family (Cox 1998,
95, who also notes examples of grandsons inheriting without being
adopted; see also **Isaeus P**). In his *Life of Solon*, Plutarch also details
some of the finer points of the law concerning the *epiklēros* that Solon
supposedly framed in the sixth century BC (**Plutarch D**). These include
the requirement of the new husband to sleep with his wife at least three
times a month – a rule presumably aimed at encouraging the production of an heir and deterring a relative (especially one in extreme old
age) from claiming the woman's hand purely for financial gain. Solon's
law as cited by Plutarch also suggests that the heiress could remarry
within the family group in the event that husband was unable to
provide her with offspring (or perhaps even, tantalisingly, that she was
allowed to have extra-marital sex with kin members for the purpose of
securing an heir, depending on how the Greek word *syneinai* is to be
understood: **Plutarch D**).

In the case of men who were already married when they claimed
an heiress, we find evidence that that they, too, divorced their existing wives. In **Demosthenes M**, for example, Protomachus, is said to
have done just this, arranging for his wife's remarriage to a friend of
his when he became eligible to claim the hand of an heiress. However,
the wording of this passage might well suggest that the divorce did not
happen straight away and that he was still married to his original wife
at the point when he was allotted the *epiklēros*. (This is only problematic, of course, if the *epidikasia* is thought to result in the marriage of
the *epiklēros* and the kin member; not if the *epidikasia* merely gives the
kin member the status of *kyrios* and the right to marry the woman in
the future.) On this and other evidence, Lacey goes as far as suggesting that a man might sometimes have taken a wife awarded to him as
epiklēros in addition to his existing wife (Lacey 1968, 143–4). Nor is
this the only circumstance in which it has been suggested that a man in
classical Athens could legally be husband to more than one wife.

1.13 Athens in crisis: the 'bigamy concession'

The shortage of men towards the end of the Peloponnesian War – especially acute following the Sicilian disaster of 413 BC – called for some desperate measures on the part of the Athenians. Strikingly, citizenship was extended not just to those metics and foreigners but also the slaves who had fought on behalf of the city at the Battle of Arginusae in 406 BC, thus allowing them to intermarry with Athenians and produce citizen offspring (citizenship had previously been extended to other select groups of foreigners, too). Diognenes Laertius, writing in the third century AD, also informs us that, at a stage in the late fifth century usually guessed to be some point after 413 BC, Athenian men were allowed to 'marry one citizen woman but also have children by another' (**Diogenes Laertius A**; cf. Aulus Gellius 15.20). The precise meaning of this passage has been much discussed by scholars, one key point of disagreement being whether the second woman with whom a man was permitted to sire citizen offspring was regarded as a legitimate 'wife' (for discussion, see Ogden 1996, 72–5). The existence of a 'bigamy concession' would certainly help to make sense of later traditions that figures such as Socrates had two wives, however (Pomeroy 1975, 66–7), and may even be the reality behind the tangled domestic situation in which Callias found himself at the end of the fifth century (**Andocides A**: see 1.9 above). If this 'bigamy concession' did exist, it was doubtless abandoned in 403 BC, shortly after the war ended, when the city passed legislation reinstating the requirement for would-be citizens to demonstrate that both their parents were Athenian. This 403 BC legislation also required those who were already citizens 'to be let be without examination' (scholiast on Aeschines 1.39), thus forbidding the mixed bag of people who could now legitimately lay claim to Athenian citizenship from being questioned about their parentage and origins.

1.14 Non-marriage

Clearly not everyone in Athens got married. In the case of citizen women, for whom 'marriage and motherhood were considered the primary goals' in life (Pomeroy 1975, 62), spinsterhood must have been a particularly cruel fate (see **Aristophanes AW**; cf. Lysias 12.21). Such was the emphasis on marriage for females that, in the event of a girl dying unwed, she was often envisaged as a bride of death, and her grave marked by a loutrophoros, the vessel in which the water for the bridal bath was traditionally carried (Oakley and Sinos 1993, 6). In tragedy, too, it is her failure to marry and have children that the virgin Antigone bewails before she dies, for example (**Sophocles A** and **B**; see also Seaford 1987, esp. 106–7, and Rehm 1994 on female death before marriage). Some citizen men evidently could not afford to marry or preferred not to (in a speech by Demosthenes, for example, we find one Archiades who chose to live alone: **Demosthenes I**) – not that failure to marry would necessarily spell the end of an *oikos*, since it was still open for unmarried men to adopt an heir. For Plato, at least, remaining unmarried amounted to a dereliction of one's civic duty. In the *Laws*, he proposes that any man who reached the age of thirty-five unwed should be fined (*Laws* 774a–c).

1.15 Alternatives to marriage: the Athenian *pallakē* (concubine)

As we have seen, various resolutions passed in the classical era served either to discourage or expressly to forbid marriage between a citizen and non-citizen in Athens. However, there was nothing to prevent a citizen man from having a long-term relationship with a non-citizen woman or even setting up home with her – as long as he did not try to pass her off as his 'wife' (**Demosthenes N**). A woman who found herself in this position was known as a *pallakē* or 'concubine'.

Significant differences between 'marriage' (*synoikein*) and mere 'co-habitation'(*syneinai*) included the fact that concubinage occurred without an *engyē* and that a *pallakē* would routinely come with no dowry. The arrangement was therefore far more casual than marriage and could presumably be terminated by either party at will (a *pallakē* is summarily dismissed by her citizen boyfriend in **Menander M**, for example). Typically, a concubine might be a former prostitute with whom a man chose to settle down in widowerhood (see Chapter 3.6) or a woman set up in accommodation separate from the family home by a wealthy, married man as his mistress. The orator Lysias kept a young prostitute at the house of a friend, for instance ([Demosthenes] 59.22), whereas in Isaeus 6 we learn that Euctemon installed his lover, Alce, in the Kerameikos before eventually abandoning his wife and children to move in with her (**Isaeus J**). The extent to which married Athenian men like Lysias and Euctemon kept *pallakai* as mistresses in addition to their wives is essentially impossible to know, but as Blundell asserts, '[a]mong the upper classes, the practice of keeping a concubine appears to have been relatively common' (Blundell 1995, 124). Certainly it was not the done thing for a man to lodge his *pallakē* under the same roof as his citizen wife: indeed, even bringing mistresses and prostitutes home could be grounds for divorce, as we saw earlier (**Andocides B**). Nor is it likely that a wife and mistress would have placidly accepted each other's existence. As Humphreys notes, the fact that a number of fifth-century tragedies depict a wife locked in conflict with a concubine (e.g. Sophocles' *Trachiniae* and Euripides' *Andromache*) suggests that this theme had contemporary resonance in Athens (Humphreys 1983, 63).

Pallakai were, then, a luxury that a man generally indulged in either after or at the same time as a citizen marriage – an added extra rather than an alternative to a conventional union and the production of legitimate offspring. If a citizen man did have children with a foreign or metic *pallakē* rather than a legitimate wife, these were regarded as *nothoi* or 'bastards' in the eyes of the law (on citizen–metic unions, see sp. Bakewell 2008/9). As *nothoi* (sing. *nothos*) these children would have enjoyed few of the rights and responsibilities of citizen children: despite having a citizen father, their status in the city would essentially have been that of metics and they were also released from the obligation of supporting their father in old age and carrying on the ancestral rites of their paternal family. Crucially, too, in the classical era *nothoi* were entitled to inherit a maximum of 500 or 1,000 drachmas, the so-called *notheia* or 'bastard's share' (our sources differ as to the amount: see Ogden 1996, 38–9). This important difference between the inheritance rights of a citizen man's offspring by a legitimate wife and his offspring by a concubine accounts for the number of allegations we find in legal speeches that children by concubines have been passed off as citizens (e.g. Dinarchus 1.71; Isaeus 6.21). The *pallakē* is also capable of being cast as a hate figure by the man's marital family: in Isaeus 6, for example, Euctemon's mistress, Alce, is portrayed as a woman of few scruples who schemes to get her eldest son passed off as an Athenian citizen (**Isaeus J**). In fifth-century comedy, too, a key element of the mockery to which Pericles' foreign lover, Aspasia, was subjected seems to have hinged on her being openly referred to as a concubine (**Plutarch B**): in Aspasia's case at least, *pallakē* was evidently used as a term of abuse.

An interesting question to consider is the extent to which citizen women might have become *pallakai* in classical Athens. Clearly the category of *pallakē* existed in the city long before Pericles' citizenship law differentiated between citizen and non-citizen women, since 'concubines' are mentioned in Solon's early sixth-century law on justifiable homicide (**Demosthenes D**; cf. **Lysias G**), and there is every reason to suppose that, in this earlier stage of Athens' history, some 'Athenian' girls did become concubines. But whether the tradition of 'citizen' *pallakai* continued to any great degree into the late fifth and fourth centuries is impossible to estimate from our scanty evidence (see Ogden 1996, 158–63). Possibly concubinage was an option for citizen girls from poorer families whose meagre dowries would have made them an unattractive match, or for widows, divorcees or women whose families had, for whatever reason, failed to marry them off young. As various scholars have pointed out, however, the difference in status enjoyed by a wife and a *pallakē* was marked and so presumably this was a fate which most families would sooner avoid for their womenfolk (see e.g. Patterson 1991, 284, and 2005, 58). The lack of a dowry meant that the concubine had no protection from being discarded, for example (Wiles 1989, 44), and her children enjoyed relatively low social status and only a meagre claim on their father's estate. Evidence from legal speeches also confirms that the legal status of *pallakai* was lower than that of wives (e.g. **Lysias G**; cf. **Demosthenes X**).

Such evidence that there is for citizen *pallakai* is often confusing and disputed. In a legal speech by Isaeus, we even find a puzzling reference to concubines receiving what are arguably dowries – but, as has been pointed out, it is probably unwise simply to assume that the speaker is talking about contemporary Athenian practice here (**Isaeus G**; Ogden 1996, 159). There is also the vexed question as to whether, following Pericles' law, the offspring of two citizens linked not by marriage but by concubinage were considered 'legitimate' (*gnēsioi*) or 'bastards' (*nothoi*) – or in other words, could a citizen *pallakē* bear citizen children? Given the importance so often given in legal speeches to establishing that a woman was a *gynē engyetē* (i.e. 'wife pledged in an *engyē*'), the answer is most probably 'no', though scholarly opinions differ (for discussion and an overview of scholarly debate, see Ogden 1996, 151–65).

1.16 Non-citizens: metics and slaves

Metics formed a large and varied class in classical Athens, perhaps accounting for a third or more of the free residents of the city. We are relatively well informed about the scandalous details of the love lives of certain metic women, namely those who were romantically involved with high-profile citizens, or who were named as mistresses in legal speeches, or who worked as high-class prostitutes (see Chapter 3.7), but our sources tell us little about the relationships which metics formed between themselves. As has been noted, 'metics must have had a marital and legitimacy system of some kind' (Ogden 1996, 133), since we find not only examples of married metic couples in our sources, but also tantalising references to legal cases involving metic heiresses and questions of inheritance ([Aristotle], *Constitution of Athens* 58.3). It seems plausible, then, that the processes of betrothal and wedding ceremonies – and, indeed, divorce and inheritance – were experienced in a similar way by metics and by citizens in Athens, the key difference being the lack of citizen privileges to which these resident aliens and their offspring could lay claim.

Whilst slaves had no mechanism by which they could enter into a legal marriage, some do seem to have been allowed to form lasting unions with each other (and if the evidence of Roman Comedy is to be trusted, then domestic Athenian slaves may occasionally have performed unofficial 'wedding' ceremonies: see MacCary and Willcock 1976, 107–8, on Plautus, *Casina* 68 and 71–2). Since a proportion of Athenian slaves were home bred, sexual relations cannot have been uncommon among slaves, though these are likely to have taken place primarily at their master's discretion. In Xenophon's *Oeconomicus*, Ischomachus explains how he keeps the door between the men's and women's quarters bolted and allows only what he considers to be the 'good' slaves to breed (**Xenophon J**).

Not every slave's sex life would have involved a long-term relationship with a kindred spirit. Vast numbers of slaves would have worked in Athens' brothels, for example (and similarly many metics – both male and female – would have eked out a living as jobbing street-walkers in Athens' red-light districts: see Chapter 3.4). In a domestic setting, too, it seems likely that slaves and their owners occasionally had sexual liaisons. Old Comedy offers an array of models here, generally presented from the man's point of view as stolen pleasures, ranging from kissing a slave-girl while the wife is in the bath (*Peace* 1138–9) to the full-blown rape of a neighbour's slave-girl who has been caught stealing (**Aristophanes AA**; cf. **Aristophanes BG**, where sex with slaves is listed as a supposed *female* misdemeanour). Other sources hint at sex between masters and slaves, too. The banter in which Euphiletus and his wife engage in Lysias 1 is suggestive of the contexts in which a master might make advances on a slave (**Lysias D**), whereas in *Oeconomicus* we find Ischomachus talking openly about the choice to be made between his wife and a female slave, his preference being for consensual sex with his wife (**Xenophon L**). Scholarly opinion differs as to the extent to which citizen men would have attempted sexual activity with their female (or indeed male) slaves, although Blundell is probably right when she says that such liaisons 'were not accepted as a matter of course' (Blundell 1995, 146; see E. Cohen 2000a, 122–3, for discussion). Any offspring that a slave bore a citizen would presumably be exposed or raised as a slave.

1.17 Conclusion

By exploring the nature of marriage and other long-term relationships in this chapter, we have seen how social structures, cultural expectations and legal statutes served to shape the domestic arrangements – and thus the sex lives – of classical Athenians. Clear themes emerge here, such as the Athenian obsession with legitimacy and inheritance, the close connection that women maintained with their natal family even after marriage, and the relative lack of control that women in particular had over their choice of marriage partner. What is also clear is the importance of citizen marriage not just to the *oikos*, but to the *polis* or 'city-state' as a whole. After all, the production of legitimate offspring by a married couple was the chief mechanism by which the household and its traditions were continued and by which Athens was able to replenish its stock of citizens.

While marriage seems to have been a topic of continued interest for Athenians during the classical era, it is also instructive to trace the way in which ideology surrounding this institution shifted over time. What Blundell describes as a 'growing cultural emphasis on marriage during the fifth century' (Blundell and Rabinowitz 2008, 137) is particularly evident in the war-ravaged years of the late fifth century, for example, when the subtly changing role played by women in the city is an issue we find explored in numerous contemporary sources (e.g. Thucydides 2.44 and 46; Aristophanes' *Lysistrata* and *Women at the Thesmophoria*). As Blundell notes, the interest in marriage during this period is particularly evident in vase-painting, where there is a marked trend for artists to depict women in domestic settings being adorned for weddings (Blundell and Rabinowitz 2008, 137). In this period of uncertainty, then, we arguably have evidence of a contemporary response to the perceived crisis in Athens: namely, to promote marriage and domesticity as an ideal for women. In a city where citizen numbers are dwindling due to a prolonged war, marriage is also an appropriate focus for male erotic energies, of course, since this is the one socially sanctioned context in which reproductive sex could take place.

Another detail to emerge from the discussion in this chapter is the difference in the sexual freedoms typically enjoyed by men and women in Athens. Respectable women were expected to be virgins when they married and extra-marital sex was punished severely by law (see Chapter 4.4). For citizen men, things looked very different, since they lived in a world where it was socially acceptable to keep a mistress, where prostitutes were plentiful and where same-sex relationships between males were a common – if not universally praised – feature of life. Importantly, the existence of an array of sexual choices for men meant that marital sex could be contrasted with other forms of sexual activity. And, as we have seen, when such comparisons are made in our sources, wives are routinely associated with the *oikos* and legitimate offspring, whereas sexual pleasure is seen as deriving from elsewhere (e.g. **Demosthenes X**).

The next two chapters explore two of these alternative sexual outlets: same-sex relationships and prostitution.

CHAPTER 2

Same-Sex Relationships

2.1 Introduction

The subject of 'Greek Love' has caused students of classical Athens all manner of difficulties. Historically, social attitudes towards same-sex relationships have at best made the topic an awkward one to address, and at worst made it strictly taboo. Indeed, it was not until 1978, with the publication of Dover's *Greek Homosexuality*, that the subject could claim its first English-language 'classic'. But taboos are not the only problem. Studying ancient sexuality also forces scholars to confront some difficult issues – difficult not least because they have a bearing on the sexual politics of the contemporary world and how we view our own sexual identities. After all, interpreting ancient evidence requires us to confront highly challenging questions about human sexual behaviour, such as whether categories like 'homosexual' and 'heterosexual' (so meaningful to us in modern industrialised societies) are in fact universal, innate traits or, alternatively, culturally specific constructs: neither word has an equivalent in Classical Greek, after all, and many men in ancient Greece seemed to have enjoyed sexual relationships with both males and females. And with a topic as potentially emotive and as politically resonant as (homo)sexuality, how objective can scholars really be when assessing ancient evidence? When Devereux suggests that Greek homosexuality is a result of 'inadequate fathering', for example (Devereux 1968, 70), or when Halperin equates penetration with power (Halperin 1990, 29–39, developing the ideas of Dover 1978, 100–9), to what extent are not only these judgements themselves, but also our own reactions to them, influenced by the beliefs and prejudices that we bring with us – our cultural baggage?

But it is not just the social and political climate of the modern world that has posed problems for students of Greek homosexuality: it is also the ancients themselves. Dover may have been able to talk of Greek culture's 'sympathetic response to the open expression of homosexual desire' (1978, 1), but when it came to acting on this desire, same-sex relationships in classical Athens (as well as individual sexual acts) seem to have been governed by a whole raft of protocols, as we shall see. Nor do the words that classical Greeks use when discussing sexual relationships make scholars' lives any easier. For one thing, many important Greek terms have their own complex associations and nuanced meanings and consequently resist straightforward translation into English: the word *erōs*, for example – the root of our word 'erotic' – seems to overlap with a range of concepts in English ('love', 'desire', 'sexual desire'). But in addition, we regularly find that when a source seems about to yield an important piece of information about sexual behaviour we run smack in to a brick wall. Perhaps the worst offenders in this regard are the speakers in legal cases, who generally prefer to allude to the fact that an adversary's sexual behaviour is scandalous without saying what they are actually supposed to have done (e.g. **Aeschines E**). For the sake of *aidōs* ('decency', 'shame', 'modesty'), either real or feigned, the juicier details of homoerotic liaisons are often glossed over.

The purpose of this chapter is to outline the characteristics of same-sex relationships in classical Athens – not only the written and unwritten rules that seem to have governed homoerotic activity but also behaviour that appears to run contrary to these 'rules'. This will entail surveying a wide range of evidence. In terms of visual sources, vase-paintings play a particularly important role – and it should be noted that the bulk of the relevant images come from the sixth and early fifth centuries and so slightly predate the classical era (which modern historians conventionally date as running from 479 to 323 BC). Whilst there are important literary sources from the sixth century (e.g. lyric poetry) and the fifth century (e.g. Old Comedy), much of our key written evidence comes from later in the classical era: notably legal speeches, such as Aeschines' *Against Timarchus*, and philosophical texts, such as Plato's *Symposium* and *Phaedrus*, dating from the fourth century. Marrying up the visual and literary sources – the words and pictures – can often be a challenging affair, made all the more complex by the fact that attitudes towards homosexuality evidently underwent something of a shift in the classical era, although scholars dispute the precise nature of these changes and the reasons behind them (see Lear, forthcoming, for discussion).

In this chapter, then, we shall explore the nature of homosexual relationships from the sixth to the fourth century BC through the lens of different kinds of primary evidence (especially vase-painting, legal

speeches and philosophy) whilst also looking at some of the major theoretical approaches taken to the much-debated topic of Greek homosexuality. In the discussions which follow, the words 'homosexual'
and 'homoerotic' are used to refer to (sexual) relationships between
two males, with 'lesbian' and 'lesbianism' used to describe (sexual)
relationships between two females. Of course, the use of these words
should not be taken as implying any fundamental continuity between
ancient same-sex relations and those experienced in the modern world:
as many scholars have been at pains to point out, ancient and modern
conceptions of sex and sexual orientation differ in a number of crucial
respects. Nevertheless, 'homosexual', 'homoerotic', 'lesbian' and 'lesbianism' remain the most convenient umbrella terms under which
to discuss a diverse range of phenomena pertaining to same-gender
relationships and sexual activity.

2.2 Greek pederasty: men, youths and boys

For any student of ancient Greek homosexuality, an essential concept
to get to grips with is pederasty. The Greek word *paiderastia* com-
bines the root *paid-*, meaning 'child' or 'boy', and *erōs*, which is often
translated as '(sexual) desire' or 'love'. 'Boy-love', then, might be a
convenient short-hand for this phenomenon. When scholars discuss
homosexuality in classical Athens, it is only rarely that the topic under
consideration is a relationship between two adult males: rather, we can
generally assume that the focus of erotic attention is a boy or youth.

The essential feature of a conventional pederastic relationship is that
there is an older partner – the *erastēs*, usually translated 'lover' – and
a younger partner: the *erōmenos* or 'beloved' (also referred to in our
sources as *ta paidika*). At the centre of such homoerotic relationships,
then, is routinely a differential in age (and thus status): older *plus*
younger; more senior *plus* more junior. This inequality in ages is also
mirrored by a lopsidedness in the roles each partner plays. On the one
hand, the *erastēs* is the one who is inflamed by *erōs* ('love'/'desire') and
who pursues the boy. The *erōmenos*, on the other hand, whilst not incapable of returning an *erastēs*' affection, is first and foremost the object
of *erōs* (see e.g. **Plato I**). Confusingly, a boy may have several *erastai*,
since *erastēs* can signify not only the 'lover' who has successfully wooed
the object of his affection, but also, more generically, a boy's 'admirer'.

Our evidence suggests that the *erastēs/erōmenos* divide had emerged
not long before the classical era and certainly appears to post-date
Homeric epic (which was probably composed towards the end of the

eighth century BC). Indeed, the relationship between Achilles and Patroclus as depicted in Homer's *Iliad* (which, it must be said, is not *explicitly* sexual in the poem: **Aeschines M**) evidently confused classical Athenians for whom it was simply not clear who was the 'lover' of whom. In a lost tragedy by Aeschylus, *Myrmidons*, Achilles was evidently portrayed as the *erastēs* of Patroclus (**Aeschylus B**). One of the speakers in Plato's *Symposium*, Phaedrus, says that Aeschylus got it wrong, however, and that it must have been Achilles, as the younger and more beautiful of the two, who was the *erōmenos* (**Plato L**). These are revealing examples of how classical Athenians seem instinctively to conceptualise homosexual relationships in terms of the *erastēs/erōmenos* divide. But what these extracts also reveal are the criteria which a classical Athenian might use to determine which man played which role in a relationship. For Phaedrus in *Symposium*, beauty and youth are characteristics of the *erōmenos*, while Aeschylus presumably casts Achilles in the role of *erastēs* owing to his greater status in the Greek army. After all, unlike Patroclus he is both a demi-god and the Greeks' greatest warrior.

Much has been made of the power differential between the two partners, with the *erastēs* seen as the dominant partner owing to his greater age (and therefore public standing: e.g. Dover 1978, 100–9; Halperin 1990, 29–39). However, our sources often hint – maybe rhetorically, maybe not – that it is the *erōmenos* who exercises the real control. In lyric poetry, for example, lovers regularly give voice to their helplessness in the face of their desire for a boy (e.g. **Anacreon A, Ibycus A** and **Pindar A**). The *erōmenos*, on the other hand, since he is not maddened by love, is in a position to make a cool-headed decision as to whether or not to respond to an admirer's attentions. Importantly, too, since youths were thought to be in their prime for a relatively short time (see Chapter 5.5), demand would have inevitably outstripped supply, leading to intense competition between *anterastai* or 'rival admirers' for a boy's affections (see Yates 2005). Tellingly, *erōmenoi* are often entreated not to be too scornful towards their admirers (c.g. **Demosthenes Y.3** and **Theognis B**) and are chastised for abandoning their lovers (**Theognis A**). It is also up to the *erōmenos* to decide the extent to which he will 'grant favours' (*charizesthai/charisasthai*) to his *erastēs* – a term which is generally understood to have sexual overtones but which, depending on context, may also have referred to more innocent 'favours' (the granting of 'favours' is also associated with prostitutes: Chapter 3.7; see also Davidson 2008, 46–50, for discussion of the possible meanings of *charizesthai*).

One recurring debate in the study of Greek homosexuality concerns the ages of *erastai* and *erōmenoi*: just how old would the pair have been in practice? One difficulty we are presented with here is that ancient Athenians did not celebrate birthdays, and in all likelihood most Greeks would have had only a vague idea themselves of their precise age (at Plato, *Lysis* 207b, for example, we find two boys in disagreement about which of them is the elder). Evidence from vase-painting certainly suggests that there routinely remained an all-important gap in physical maturity between each partner, but when it comes to pinning down the ages of the participants, we are presented with something of a puzzle, since the average age of those depicted as involved in homoerotic relationships undergoes a shift in the period that concerns us here. Scenes on vases dating from the mid-sixth century depict homoerotic courtship scenes where bearded men court youths, but in the fifth century the older partner comes to be depicted more and more often as a youth, the younger as a barely pubescent boy (Shapiro 1981, 135; Lear and Cantarella 2008, 67). The question here is whether this shift represents a change in practice or in artistic convention. Stewart suggests it was the latter, arguing that the change in the age of the partners can largely be accounted for on aesthetic grounds: by lowering the age of the participants, a painter could depict two sexually appealing figures – a youth and boy – and do away with the need to paint a less desirable adult man (Stewart 1997, 80). Other factors cannot be ruled out, however: perhaps pederasty really did begin to be practised more by younger males and/or perhaps relationships between younger partners had always occurred but became an increasing source of interest in Athenian society (see also Lear and Cantarella 2008, 67, who suggest that the shift marks a decreased emphasis on the pedagogical nature of pederastic relationships). Literary evidence from later in the classical era – our richest vein coming from the fourth century – is generally at odds with the evidence of fifth-century vase-painting, however, since here the older partner in a homosexual relationship is characteristically conceived of as an adult. In other words, whilst fifth-century vase-painters came to favour the representation of youthful *erastai* and even younger *erōmenoi*, the combination of bearded man *plus* youth seems to have remained the standard – if not exclusive – model of a homosexual pairing throughout the classical era (see also Lear and Canterella 2008, 2–6, on the ages of the partners).

It has been suggested by Davidson that an understanding of the (notoriously confusing) Athenian system of age-classes can shed some light on the age of those who engaged in homoerotic activity

(Davidson 2008, 71–82; cf. Davidson 2006, 38–51). We know that boys in Athens were registered as citizens when they were deemed to have reached the age of eighteen and that part of this process involved a physical examination to determine whether or not the candidate was sufficiently physically mature to pass from being a 'boy' (*pais*) to a 'youth' or 'young man' (*meirakion* or sometimes *neaniskos*: [Aristotle], *Constitution of Athens* 42.1–2). Davidson, who believes that on average puberty took place several years later in ancient Greece than in the modern world, suggests that height and stature as well as whether or not the boy had begun to grow body hair and facial hair would have played important roles in determining whether he was deemed to have come of age (Davidson 2008, 72 and 78). After two years of being a 'youth' or 'young man', these age-mates would each then graduate to being a 'man', *anēr* (i.e. at roughly twenty years old), and would finally become a 'senior', *presbytēs*, ten years after that (i.e. at roughly thirty, the time at which a man finally came to enjoy the full quota of citizen rights: see Chapter 1.6). If we take the further step of relating these age-classes to the different kinds of figures we find in homoerotic vase-paintings, then we might surmise that the pubescent 'boys' we find are perhaps thirteen and over and that the 'youths' (who tend to be markedly taller and who often sport sideburns or patches of facial hair: see e.g. **Fig. 7**) are between eighteen and twenty. As for the age of the bearded men we find on homoerotic vases, there can be less certainty, since it is generally difficult to tell which would qualify as 'men' and which as 'seniors'. The assumption is often made that homosexual activity was largely confined to unmarried men (e.g. Henderson 1991, 206–7, and Hubbard 2003, 5). Indeed, some scholars have even explored the idea that Athenian males underwent a sort of sexual progression from *erōmenos* to *erastēs* to husband as they grew older (e.g. Devereux 1968, 72; Kilmer 1993, 14–15). However, such theories should be treated with caution, not least because there are plenty of examples in classical literature of men who are past marriageable age continuing to be attracted to boys and youths (e.g. **Aristophanes AG**, **AK** and **BJ** – where the speakers are all older men – and **Aeschines L**; cf. **Lysias H**). In a similar vein, Golden has proposed that homosexuality 'was in part an institution of transition from the subordinate . . . status of boyhood to the status of adult free citizen': Golden's thesis is that a youth negotiated his journey into adulthood by learning to exercise and respond to social and sexual power in same-sex relationships, first as an *erōmenos* and then as an *erastēs* (Golden 1984, 309; 318–19).

2.3 The archaic era, and the evidence of vase-painting

Whilst courtship scenes on vases are not, of course, snapshots of daily life in ancient Athens, they nevertheless comprise important evidence for how homoerotic relationships were perceived and portrayed. Black-figure vases such as **Figs 8** and **9**, both dating from the mid-sixth century, provide useful indications of the age difference between the partners. Interestingly, too, these black-figure courtship scenes can take different forms: sometimes we find an isolated pair; sometimes a pair is surrounded by other figures; sometimes there is a series of couples at different stages of courtship, and so on. Vase-paintings like these, when looked at alongside literary evidence from and relating to the period (e.g. **Solon A**; Thucydides 6.53–9), serve to indicate a strong tradition of pederasty in archaic Athens – among the upper classes, at least, at whose drinking parties the painted cups would have found use (on the development of pederasty in the archaic and classical eras, see esp. Bremmer 1990).

It is fruitful to analyse these sixth-century images of homoerotic courtship further. As was first identified in an article by John Beazley as long ago as 1947, whilst there are variations in the precise details of the activities depicted, three specific scene-types are particularly common (cf. Kilmer 1997a). One scenario is for an *erastēs* to reach for the *erōmenos'* chin and genitals in what Beazley called the 'up and down position' (the hand reaching towards the chin being generally read either as an affectionate gesture or as an act of supplication: Beazley 1947, 219; cf. Golden 1984, 315, and Lear and Cantarella 2008, 115). In such scenes the boy may respond with differing degrees of enthusiasm – for example by clutching the *erastēs'* wrist, which is often seen as a sign of resistance (see **Fig. 8**), but which could, alternatively, be read as an indication of the boy's flirtatious accept-ance of the older man's advances (DeVries 1997, 14–24). Another scenario is for the *erōmenos* to be offered gifts – commonly an animal such as a cock, hare, dog or deer (and since these gifts are connected to 'manly' pursuits such as cock-fighting and hunting they may be thought to fit neatly into the picture that emerges from other parts of Greece, namely that pederasty originated as a form of initiation rite, whereby an older man gave instruction to a youth). Other gifts presented by *erastai* to their beloveds include flowers, plant fronds, slabs of meat and small bags, which some scholars suggest contain money, others knuckle bones (used for a child's game: see Lear and Cantarella 2008, 78– 86, for discussion). The third recurring scene-type is for the couple to be involved (or about to engage) in copulation.

It is worth considering these scenes of copulation in greater detail since scholars have reached radically different conclusions about how they should be interpreted. What is perhaps most striking is the extent to which the sex depicted is discreet. Often the couple is wrapped in a cloak, for instance, and when they are not, the younger partner is only very exceptionally depicted as sexually aroused (although DeVries identifies a number of vases where the younger partner, while unaroused, nevertheless conveys his sexual responsiveness by such means as loving gestures, e.g. eye-contact or clutching his lover: DeVries 1997). The position adopted in all but a handful of these scenes is 'intercrural' sex: that is to say, the couple stands facing each other while the older partner inserts his penis between the *erōmenos'* thighs (see **Fig. 9** and the couple on the left-hand side of **Fig. 10**). Characteristically, the *erastēs* stoops in order to achieve this position and the *erōmenos* looks away, generally looking over the *erastēs'* head and sometimes with his gaze fixed on the gift that his lover has brought him (a motif which also occurs on red-figure vases: e.g. **Fig. 11**). What do such poses signify? Is the *erastēs* gratifying his own desires whilst the unaroused and impassive boy merely tolerates his attentions? This certainly chimes with the account of pederastic sex found in Xenophon's *Symposium*, for example (**Xenophon N**), and echoed in different forms by various scholars (Halperin 1990, 93, for instance, states that if a youth submitted to sex, he did so 'out of a feeling of mingled esteem, gratitude, and affection'). Or are the boys who stare at their gifts to be thought of as motivated primarily by these rewards – or even, as Schnapp has suggested, to be thought analogous to the hunted hares that occasionally feature on vases of this type (Schnapp 1989, 79–81, and 1997, 255; cf. Lear and Cantarella 2008, 86–7, and Lear, forthcoming; see **Figs 10** and **11**)? An alternative view is that the *erōmenos'* impassivity indicates that *he* is being depicted as the one in control, unlike his aroused lover who has clearly succumbed to his passions (Golden 1984, 313–16; Hubbard 2003, 10). In this light, the *erōmenos'* small, flaccid penis and his upright posture can be read as symbols of his modesty and self-control (*sōphrosynē*), whereas the *erastēs'* awkward posture and absorption in the sexual act could be said to indicate a certain enslavement to his desires.

Of course, one of the reasons why scholars debate how these vase-paintings should be 'read' is that there are no explicit statements from the artists themselves telling us how to understand the imagery. So it is the task of scholars to interpret the evidence, on the one hand trying to build up an understanding of artistic conventions by looking closely at the images themselves, and on the other by integrating visual and literary sources. Studies of imagery reveal the importance of eye-contact, for example (probably best understood as exciting arousal in an *erastēs* even in cases where an object of desire appears unresponsive: Hubbard 2003, 19; cf. Cairns 2002a). The act of undressing is also important (i.e. one way a boy has of signalling his willingness to be seduced seems to be by letting his cloak fall away and revealing flesh: Hubbard 2003, 19). Hubbard also sees it as significant that (on some vases at least) the *erastēs* is more successful in his pursuit the younger he is and/ or the more expensive his gifts are (Hubbard 2003, 19). It should be said, too, that it is not at all clear how extensively 'intercrural' sex was practised in Athens (the term originates with Dover 1978, 98; it simply means 'between the thighs'). Unhelpfully, accounts of homosexual sex we find in literary sources are often couched in euphemistic language, but while boys' thighs do feature prominently in homoerotic poetry (e.g. **Anacreon B** and **Solon A**), it seems likely that anal sex – and not intercrural – was the norm among real-life couples (Dover 1978, 99). Indeed, Lear suggests that intercrural sex was 'a kind of visual euphemism' used by vase-painters: that is, 'a portrayal of sex, but at the same time, a way of avoiding the portrayal of other kinds of sex considered less admirable' (Lear and Cantarella 2008, 106; cf. 190).

Attention to the conventions of vase-painting also allows us to see when the 'rules' dictating the ways in which pederastic courtship is generally depicted are being broken. For instance, there are a small number of scenes where, instead of intercrural sex, oral or anal sex is depicted (these are the 'other kind of . . . less admirable' sex referred to by Lear). Nor is there always an obvious age difference between the participants in a sexual encounter: a small number of vases depict youths of a similar age (e.g. the scene on the red-figure vase shown in **Figs 12** and **13**). Indeed, **Fig. 10** demonstrates well the principle that it is youths in the company of other youths who are often depicted as the most sexually experimental: while a bearded man performs 'conventional' intercrural sex with an upright youth on the left-hand side of the picture, two youths to the right of the scene engage in the rarely depicted act of anal intercourse. And some vases confound all expectations, such as a much-discussed scene on a so-called Tyrrhenian amphora which shows a youth penetrating an older bearded man from behind (Orvieto 2664, ABV 102.100: Lear and Canterella 2008, fig. 3.14). Such vases have naturally provoked a good deal of discussion.

Some scholars postulate the existence of a 'boys will be boys' attitude when it comes to youths and their sexuality, for instance, leading vase-painters to relax the protocols that generally prevent them from depicting adults engaging in orgiastic and anal sex with other males (e.g. Shapiro 2000, 18–19; Lear and Cantarella 2008, 117–20). As for the rule-breaking Tyrrhenian amphora showing a youth penetrating a bearded man, this might reasonably be said to belong to an artistic tradition all of its own. Tyrrhenian amphorae were probably produced for export to Etruria and so the images which adorn them, with their distinct iconographic conventions, were plausibly designed to appeal to non-Athenian sensibilities (Kilmer 1997a, 44–5; Skinner 2005, 90; Lear and Cantarella 2008, 123–7). Importantly, too, scenes which portray homosexual orgies, and our 'rule-breaking' Tyrrhenian amphora which portrays young-on-old anal sex, tend to display few of the iconographic conventions associated with pederasty (Lear and Cantarella 2008, 118). Such paintings may show homoerotic sexual activity, but they have little or nothing in common with vases whose painters depict *erastai* and *erōmenoi* adhering to the normal conventions of pederastic courtship, such as gift-giving and sexual discretion.

2.4 From black-figure to red-figure: the late sixth and early fifth centuries

Somewhere around 530 or 525 BC, 'red-figure' vases were produced in Athens for the first time (i.e. vases where black is used to fill in the background of the image, leaving the figures to stand out in the rich red colour of the Attic clay). This new technique had great advantages for the portrayal of the human form, allowing details of anatomy to be picked out with fluid painted lines. This innovation was keenly exploited by Athens' vase-painters and by 500 BC there were few painters of note still employing the older 'black-figure' technique (i.e. where black figures were painted on a red clay background: the contrast in styles can be seen clearly by comparing **Figs 7** and **8**). The differences between black-figure and red-figure images are apparent not only in the basic technique, however. The evolution in vase-painters' style means that red-figure vases tend to be less stylised and more psychologically involving. In terms of pederastic courtship scenes, the action in red-figure tends to centre on the gymnasium and *palaistra* (wrestling ground: Kilmer 1993, 12, 16–17), and it is in the period immediately following the switch to red-figure that the age of the participants in pederastic courtship scenes begins to undergo the change noted earlier, whereby the older partner typically comes to be depicted as a beardless youth, the younger partner a smaller, pubescent boy. But the trend is also for the popularity of male–male courtship scenes to diminish: pederastic imagery suffers a sharp decline after 500 BC and scenes of foreplay and explicit sex are rare on pots after about 475 BC (Stewart 1997, 157; Lear and Cantarella 2008, 175). Certainly by the beginning of the classical era (479 BC) the scenes that Athenian vase-painters are producing are, taken as a whole, less obviously erotic than was true of images painted in their grandfathers' day. This is true not only of homoerotic scenes: the fashion across the board in the classical era is for subject matter to become more domestic and less risqué in nature as the fifth century progresses.

There are large questions surrounding the interpretation of homo-erotic vase-paintings. To what extent do the scenes depicted reflect reality and to what extent are they stylised or merely fantasy? Who bought these homoerotic vases? While they were produced in Athens, the vast majority of surviving vases were unearthed in Etruria (western/central Italy), and so it seems likely that the imagery of some of the vases was geared, at least in part, towards an export market (esp. the 'Tyrrhenian amphorae', discussed above at 2.3). Also, are we in danger of overrating the importance of these homoerotic vase-paintings? After all, out of the tens of thousands of vases that survive only around a thousand images are erotically themed, of which only a hundred and fifty or so depict figures engaged in sexual activity (on erotic vase-painting, see also Chapter 5.6).

One group of vases requires special mention at this point: namely those which carry *kalos*-inscriptions. These are vases where the painter has included the words *ho pais kalos*, 'the boy is beautiful', or simply *kalos*, '(he is) beautiful' (e.g. **Fig. 14**, where a bearded man offers a cock-erel to a boy). In about a thousand cases, a specific boy is named; e.g. *Leagros kalos*, 'Leagros is beautiful' (and, indeed, Leagrus is named as *kalos* on perhaps as many as eighty vases: Shapiro 2000, 27; cf. Kilmer 1993, 181 n.22). Interestingly, there is not always an obvious con-nection between the inscription and the iconography: sometimes the scene is homoerotic, sometimes not – and in the vast majority of cases no explicit sexual act is depicted. Indeed, it is not always the case that there is a young male figure in the scene to whom the *kalos*-inscription might reasonably be thought to refer (Dover 1978, 118, discusses one vase, for example, where the words 'the boy is beautiful' are painted in a scene depicting a balding, older man copulating with a female prostitute). These inscriptions, which mirror graffiti on walls and trees from the ancient Greek world where boys are similarly praised (Lear and Cantarella 2008, 164), begin to appear on vases from around the mid-sixth century and continue to feature right up to the 420s BC.

Kalos-inscriptions raise a whole host of difficulties. First is that the word *kalos* has a range of meanings in Greek: it can indicate not only physical beauty but also moral worth and nobility (these three qualities being linked in Greek thought). Are these qualities separable and, if so, which of them is being praised, exactly? What are we to make of the fact that we find scenes where no viable candidate is depicted who might plausibly be described as a beautiful boy? One intriguing suggestion as to how these inscriptions might best be understood is made by Lear and Cantarella, who remind us that Greeks did not read silently, but rather would have tended to read aloud the words they found written on pots. On this basis they propose that these inscriptions might have been intended to be spoken as impromptu toasts at the drinking parties where so many of these painted vessels would have found use (Lear and Cantarella 2008, 171). Whether or not this is the case, it is worth bearing in mind that the fate of the vast majority of Athenian painted vases was to be exported to Italy: that is to say, for most buyers, the inscriptions would presumably have been indecipherable.

2.5 Homerotic contexts: the gymnasium and symposium

Two physical settings for homoerotic activity which emerge again and again in both visual and literary sources are the gymnasium and the symposium. The gymnasium in particular often forms the backdrop to courtship scenes on red-figure vases (in **Fig. 7**, for example, the bags on the walls are athletes' kit bags). As for the symposium, it is guests at these all-male drinking parties who would have been the chief users of the cups, drinking bowls, and so on, on which (homo)erotic imagery is characteristically found. A glimpse of the symposium can be seen on a homoerotic vase such as **Fig. 15** where the reclining figures – a bearded man and two youths – are symposium guests.

The gymnasium and *palaistra* (i.e. wrestling school, sometimes attached to a public gymnasium) are in one sense an obvious focus of homoerotic attention: these were exclusively male preserves, where boys and youths would have trained and competed in the nude and developed their bodies physically. Gymnasia were centres for more than physical education, however: in the classical era they became venues for public talks by sophists and philosophers as well as more informal intellectual and moral instruction (Plato's Academy takes its

name from the gymnasium in Athens where his philosophical school
was founded). The homoerotic associations of gymnasia did not escape
the attention of Athens' legislators, either: a law cited by the orator
Aeschines in the fourth century (but probably in place long before
that) seems to have laid down rules about the supervision of youths in
these places (**Aeschines A.9–12**) – and also to have forbidden slaves
from exercising there. But even if the reality was that the law served
to protect free-born youths from being seduced as they exercised their
minds and bodies, gymnasia nevertheless remained a fertile source of
homoerotic fantasy, as evidenced not only in vase-painting but also in
literature throughout the classical era (**Aristophanes AG**, **AK** and **AL**
and **Plato I**; see also Chapter 5.5).

The symposium, or all-male drinking party, was a very different environment altogether. Symposia were essentially an adult affair limited to
a small number of participants and traditionally took place in private
houses in a special dining-cum-drinking room called the *andrōn*, or
'men's room' (presumably while other family members were at home,
though these would have been excluded from the party). Symposia
could be highly charged sexual environments, where songs and banter
would regularly be erotically themed and where guests would be enter-
tained by female musicians-cum-prostitutes (see Chapter 3.5). In the
two fourth-century works we possess called *Symposium* – one by Plato,
the other by Xenophon; both set at such drinking parties – we find
examples of same-sex couples (an *erastēs* and an *erōmenos*) drinking in
the company of their friends, and playful flirtation amongst the guests.
Not that this is the only form of homoerotic flirting that took place,
it seems: according to an ancient anecdote, the tragic poet Sophocles
took the opportunity at a symposium craftily to steal a kiss from the
boy pouring his wine (presumably a slave) – much to the delight and
amusement of his fellow guests (**Athenaeus B**).

The links between homoeroticism and the symposium go deeper
still, as can be judged from the abundant homoerotically themed sympotic poetry we possess, dating largely from the sixth century. These
poems would have formed the text of songs sung by guests at drinking
parties, and many of their lyrics were no doubt capable of taking on a
new significance depending on the performance context. It is interesting to imagine how poems like **Anacreon B**, **Ibycus A**, **Pindar A** or
Theognis C, for example, might be sung to the kind of youthful par-
tygoers or serving boy depicted in **Fig. 15**; or how **Theognis A** might
have been sung teasingly or sympathetically to a recently rejected
fellow guest.

As for connections between these two key homoerotic contexts – the gymnasium and the symposium – one theme that clearly links them is that of education. Just as gymnasia were venues of education and philosophical instruction, the symposium was equally no stranger to discussion and debate: in the (admittedly atypical) drinking party we find in Plato's *Symposium*, for example, the topic under consideration is the nature of *erōs* itself. Of great significance, too, is the fact that the gymnasium and the symposium – and for that matter, the composition of poetry (be it sympotic or otherwise) – were primarily the domain of the leisured, monied classes. That is to say, pederasty was largely (perhaps even exclusively) an elite pursuit and a distinctive feature of the aristocratic lifestyle.

2.6 Classical Athens:
poikilos pederasty and the fourth-century 'crisis'

Pederasty and Athenian democracy are intricately bound together thanks to the actions of a same-sex couple: Harmodius (the *erōmenos* of the pair) and Aristogeiton (his *erastēs*). The facts are these: in 514 BC Harmodius and Aristogeiton killed Hipparchus, the brother of Athens' tyrant Hippias, and thereby contributed to a chain of events that led to the end of the tyranny and the birth of the democracy in 508 BC. But these 'facts' were not allowed to get in the way of a good story: as the historian Thucydides tells us (*History of the Peloponnesian War* 1.20), most later Athenians believed that Harmodius and Aristogeiton had performed no less a deed than killing the tyrant himself. In consequence, the couple were celebrated in classical Athenian oratory, philosophy and even popular drinking songs as tyrant slayers and founders of the democracy (**Aeschines L.140, Plato M.182c** and **Drinking Songs A** and **B**). Statues of the pair took pride of place in the Athenian agora (perhaps the first in Greece to be dedicated to non-mythical figures: Lear and Cantarella 2008, 15) and were considered important enough to be replaced after the originals were removed by the Persians when they sacked Athens in 480 BC.

Despite the importance of pederasty to the democracy's foundation myth, the relationship that classical Athens enjoyed with homosexuality was nothing if not complex. Later in the classical era in particular, the institution of pederasty seems to have come under a great deal of scrutiny. In fourth-century philosophy and oratory, for example, we find appeals to an ideal of *sōphrōn*, i.e. 'modest' or 'chaste', pederastic love, whereas *im*modest *erōs* is demonised (e.g. **Aeschines L,**

Demosthenes Y and **Plato M**; see also Xenophon, *Symposium* 8.9–27, and Lear, forthcoming). The impression given is perhaps that pederasty had fallen into disrepute (in some quarters at least), leading its supporters to articulate the virtues of the 'right' kind of relationship. Various discussions of pederasty from the fourth century highlight the potential of public opinion to be harmful as well as beneficial to a boy (e.g. **Plato H, I** and **M**). Indeed, whilst it is an enviable thing to be a boy who is *kalos*, 'beautiful' (in mind, body and comportment), and pleasing to attract admirers (*erastai*), it seems that youthful beauty is also capable of attracting scandal, and simply by spending time alone with a man to whom he is not related a boy can become the subject of gossip and even blackmail (Hubbard 2003, 12; D. Cohen 1991, 196). In a word, the situation in Athens regarding pederasty is *poikilos*, 'many-hued', 'intricate', 'subtle': the term used by Pausanias during his speech in Plato's *Symposium*, where he emphasises the complexity of the unwritten rules governing same-sex relationships in Athens, especially in comparison with many other Greek states (**Plato M.182b**).

The question often asked by scholars is what the nature of the 'crisis' is to which writers in the fourth century are responding. How had society and/or the institution of pederasty changed between the sixth and fourth centuries? Was it simply that the aspects of pederasty which were potentially morally problematic were coming under the spotlight: the euphemisms used to speak about sex ('granting favours', etc.), boys' acceptance of gifts in return for their attentions, and so on? Perhaps. But other solutions have been proffered too. According to Hubbard, for example, the key point is that pederasty, as an aristocratic pursuit, was regarded by the masses with suspicion and antipathy (Hubbard 1998). On this reading, what we are seeing in these fourth-century accounts of pederasty, then, is a response by members of Athens' aristocracy to a fundamental hostility towards the institution – a hostility born partly of the fact that pederastic relationships generated close ties between aristocratic males and were therefore perceived as helping to perpetuate an exclusive elite clique (Hubbard 1998, 69). Hubbard detects hostility towards pederasty in sources throughout the classical era, some of the more striking examples of which come from late fifth-century comedy. In Aristophanes' plays, we find real-life individuals from the city of Athens mocked as effeminates (most notably the tragic playwright Agathon and the politician Cleisthenes: **Aristophanes AJ, BB, BC** and **BH**); politicians accused of prostituting themselves (e.g. Cleon, i.e. the 'Paphlagon' figure in *Knights*); and boys' motives for involvement in pederastic relationships similarly impugned (**Aristophanes**

BM; and note that in Hubbard's view, the poets of Old Comedy were hostile to all those alleged to have engaged in pederasty, regardless of whether they were 'active' *erastai* or 'passive' *erōmenoi*: Hubbard 1998, 55–9). In addition, public antipathy is also evident, Hubbard suggests, in the apologetic statements made by certain speakers in fourth-century oratory when relating in court incidents involving homoerotic behaviour (e.g. **Lysias H**). Hubbard might be said to overstate his case here (it is less easy to detect hostility towards homoerotic behaviour in comic passages such as **Aristophanes AG** and **BJ**, for example, and there are other explanations as to why speakers in law courts might choose to express themselves apologetically: see below). However, the overarching thesis nevertheless has the potential to be illuminating: namely, that pederasty was an activity associated with the elite and so (like many aspects of the lifestyle and values of the city's nobility) came under increasing scrutiny in democratic Athens, with its lofty ideals held up by some for ridicule.

Davidson takes a different stance towards the fourth-century 'crisis'. What *he* detects in the rhetoric of the era are anxieties about 'whorish-ness' (Davidson 2008, 64–7 and esp. 446–65). On this view, the public relations disaster that pederasty had encountered was a perception that there were boys in Athens who gave in too easily to the sexual demands of lovers, who submitted for the wrong reasons (e.g. financial reward), or who were simply prostitutes – and so what we find in our sources are writers trying to shore up pederasty's tarnished reputation. According to this theory, those who defend pederasty as an institution are thus seeking to define its noble ideals – and set out to show how these are distinct from the wanton behaviour of a minority lest all those involved in same-sex relationships be tarred with the same brush (see 2.7 below). Davidson also floats the idea that, in vase-paintings, boys who do not submit so readily to their lovers' advances are being put forward as an ideal. For him, it is not just physical beauty, nobility and intellectual worth that are being praised as *kalos* in *kalos*-inscriptions but also, quite specifically, sexual modesty (Davidson 2008, 426–39; the boy named as *kalos* in **Fig. 14**, who remains tightly wrapped in his cloak despite his lover's offer of a gift, potentially provides a good example of a praiseworthy, reluctant *erōmenos*).

A further key point to take into account when trying to understand fourth-century accounts of pederasty is the change in the intellectual climate that took place in Athens during the classical period. The appe-tite for discussing ethical and social issues grew hugely towards the end of the fifth century with the presence in the city of various sophists and thinkers such as Socrates – and this continued into the next century and beyond. In one sense, then, fourth-century discussions of pederasty represent an inevitable development in an intellectual and philosophical tradition in which the discussion of contemporary social mores loomed large. Furthermore, the potential of pederastic relationships to play a role in the educational and moral development of the young must also have made them an obvious topic for discussion in philosophical circles. And so it is perhaps unsurprising that it is this educative side to same-sex relationships which comes to form a central part of the pederastic ideal while the physical dimension is seen as increasingly problematic.

2.7 Platonic love: philosophical views of pederasty

Among fourth-century discussions of homosexual behaviour two Platonic dialogues stand out as particularly informative on the subject of Greek Love. Plato's *Symposium* contains a series of speeches on the subject of *erōs*, which, tellingly, is conceived by the speakers as either exclusively or predominantly homosexual in nature. Whilst some of the speeches are highly rhetorical (e.g. Agathon's) or largely fantastic (Aristophanes': **Plato N**), taken as a whole they provide a series of fascinating insights into contemporary views of (homo)sexual relationships. The contrast between modest and immodest desire that we find in other fourth-century texts looms large in Pausanias' encomium of *erōs* in *Symposium*, for example, where morally superior, non-physical desire is said to derive from Heavenly Aphrodite, whereas base, physical desire is the province of Common Aphrodite (**Plato M**: the speech is also highly instructive as to the pitfalls that pederastic relationships can create for a boy). Previous speakers have already praised the loyalty that can exist between same-sex couples as well as the other virtues that pederastic relationships promote (**Plato K and L**). Later in *Symposium*, too, Socrates' speech emphasises the desirability of learning to value intellectual beauty above physical beauty (the 'ladder of love': *Symposium* 210a–212a). In another of Plato's works, *Phaedrus*, we again learn a good deal about the moral and social tensions inherent in pederasty, since Plato once more articulates the difference between man's worthy and immodest instincts. Using the famous allegory of the soul as comprising a charioteer and a good and a bad horse, Socrates explains to his interlocutor how the good horse is governed by a sense of *aidōs*, 'decency', 'shame' or 'modesty', whereas the bad horse is heedless of his master's whip and desirous of physical love (*Phaedrus*

253c–254e). In both of these texts, then, intellect and self-control are what receive a positive press and, whilst the power of physical desire is certainly recognised, it is far from prized.

Some of the most striking comments on pederasty in the fourth century emerge in the philosophical dialogues of Xenophon, who (like Plato) often features Socrates as a central character in his work. They are remarkable because they cast the pursuit of boys by an *erastēs* in a very dim light. In *Memorabilia*, for instance, Xenophon has Socrates liken a lover's desire to 'rub up against' his beloved to a piglet wanting to rub itself against stones (1.2.31) – hardly a flattering image – and he later has the philosopher advise his followers to avoid sex (*ta aphrodisia*) with boys altogether, claiming that a single kiss from a boy can destroy a man's ability to exercise self-control (*sōphronein*: 1.3.8–13). One difficulty these passages cause us is that we do not know to what extent they reflect Socrates' own views or whether Xenophon has essentially put words into Socrates' mouth (certainly they do not fully chime with the stance taken by Plato's Socrates towards pederasty – nor, indeed, is pederasty always presented in a negative way in Xenophon's work). Whatever their origin, it is interesting to consider how Xenophon's negative remarks about pederasty bear a number of interpretations. They might, for example, reasonably be seen as indicating the importance of *sōphrosynē*, 'self-control', 'modesty', and the value of intellect as compared to physical desire (and as such might even be seen as part of a fourth-century backlash against 'whorish' behaviour). They might (also) serve to characterise Socrates as a man of the people who had little truck with 'elite' pederasty (thus Hubbard 1998, 49 and 69). A further complication is that Xenophon (like Plato), as a follower of Socrates, was evidently keen to paint a positive picture of the philosopher following his trial and execution in Athens in 399 BC (where one of the charges was that Socrates had corrupted the city's youth). Could this, too, have a bearing on the views Xenophon has him express?

So much for philosophical discussions of pederasty. Let us now move on to look at what Athenian law and speeches delivered in Athens' courts can tell us about homosexuality in the classical era.

2.8 Athens' law courts: legal sanctions and public attitudes

The *cause célèbre* of the Athenian law courts in 346–345 BC was undoubtedly the prosecution of the politician Timarchus by his arch-rival Aeschines. The charges laid against Timarchus were that he had formerly prostituted himself with men – not that such a profession was illegal in itself, but what *did* contravene Athens' laws was for a former prostitute to take an active role in the life of the city, such as by holding public office or addressing the Assembly (**Aeschines C; Demosthenes C**). Whilst accusations of prostitution are common enough in fourth-century political debate (see e.g. E. Cohen 2005, 205–6), this is the only certain use of the law to mount a prosecution in court (although insinuations of prostitution were also made in court against the tax collector Androtion in 356 BC: Demosthenes 22.21–32). And what made the case of Timarchus so special was the fact that the protagonists were such high-profile politicians. Aeschines' suit was successful and Timarchus suffered the ignominy of *atimia*, the loss of his citizen rights.

Aeschines' speech, *Against Timarchus*, provides a unique insight into social attitudes towards homoerotic relationships and male prostitution in the late classical era. To make it effective as a piece of rhetoric, Aeschines has to choose not only which stories to tell about Timarchus and what emphasis to give them, but also what insinuations to make (a task made all the more vital given that Aeschines seems to have precious little evidence to back up any of his claims: see e.g. Lape 2006, 141). The bulk of the speech is taken up with charting Timarchus' supposed progress as a whore, residing with men with whom he had no family connection, consorting with Athenians and foreigners alike, and giving himself up to all manner of wanton acts (the nature of which is often hinted at rather than spelt out: **Aeschines D.41, E** and **F**). Of particular interest is that Timarchus is characterised as a shameless slave to his desires – which include a passion for fine foods, gambling and also *female* prostitutes and free wives (**Aeschines D.42** and **I**). Presumably Aeschines is keen to convey to the jury the sheer range of Timarchus' wanton tastes and his utter lack of restraint (Davidson 1997, 256, suggests that the impression his opponent is aiming for is that Timarchus pays for one vice by indulging in another). But does Aeschines also mention these female prostitutes in order to imply that Timarchus is, in the words of one scholar, 'gay for pay' (Davidson 2008, 455)? Aeschines relates as well an incident where Timarchus is denounced in public as another man's 'woman': Hegesandrus' 'woman', in fact (and, the speaker adds, Hegesandrus also used to be a 'woman' himself: **Aeschines J**). Is the emphasis here simply that Timarchus is playing a subordinate role to a man with whom he is in a relationship? Or is there an added implication that Timarchus was taking the passive (and thus 'womanly') role in sex and that this is a cause for shame?

One striking feature of this speech is that Timarchus' prosecutor tackles the subject of pederasty head on in an extended excursus, the content of which is not at all untypical of fourth-century discussions of homosexuality (**Aeschines L**). Here, Aeschines says that he is himself a 'lover' (or 'admirer': *erastēs*), and admits to having quarrelled over boys and to having written homoerotic poetry. However, he suggests that there is a difference between *erōs* ('love'/'desire') that is *sōphrōn*, 'modest' or 'chaste', and that which is *hybristos*, 'outrageous', such as hiring a (citizen) prostitute. He then goes on to offer an interpretation of Athens' laws governing homoerotic behaviour in a passage where we learn, for instance, that slaves in Athens were forbidden from following free-born boys around and even 'falling in love' (*eran*) with them (presumably what was in practice forbidden was for a slave *actively* to display his 'love' for a boy). Aeschines claims that by forbidding slaves to do these things, however, the law-giver was tacitly endorsing the same actions when carried out by citizen men, the benefit being, he states, that boys are thus watched over by modest (*sōphrōn*) adult admirers who in turn safeguard the boy's modesty (*sōphrosynē*).

Aeschines' account of pederastic behaviour in this passage has the potential to be highly valuable as an historical source. Juries in Athens consisted of hundreds of citizen members, a significant number of whom were drawn from the lower classes, and so Aeschines' words here (always assuming the published version we possess reflects what was said in court) represent a rare public airing of the ideals of pederasty aimed at a largely non-elite audience. To be sure, part of Aeschines' purpose here may well be to counter any slurs that the defence mean to make about his own sexual behaviour (there are hints in the speech that Aeschines' homoerotic poetry was not as 'chaste' as it might have been and so Aeschines may be taking the opportunity here to suggest that his own behaviour – unlike Timarchus' – has been wholly honourable). But this aside, what are we to make of the sentiments expressed? Can the emphasis on 'whorishness', not just here but in the speech as a whole, be taken as supporting Davidson's hypothesis that sexual voracity had become something of a public obsession? And/or can we also detect in this passage a defensive stance to 'elite' pederasty in line with Hubbard's approach to the fourth-century 'crisis'?

One reason why legal speeches like this are so vital to scholars, of course, is that they represent important sources of information for piecing together the law governing sexual behaviour in the classical era (see also Chapter 4). Indeed, no single speech is richer in detail than *Against Timarchus* where the laws covering homosexuality are concerned. In the course of his prosecution, Aeschines cites not only laws about the protection of boys at schools (**Aeschines A.9–12**); sanctions against those who act as pimps for free-born boys (**Aeschines A.13**); and the measures that can be taken against citizen prostitutes (**Aeschines C** and **N**; which we also learn about from other speeches: **Demosthenes C**); but also the penalties for those who commit acts of *hybris*, 'outrage', against boys (**Aeschines B**) – a category which quite feasibly covered sexual as well as physical assault (see D. Cohen 1991, 177–90, for discussion). What emerges, then, is certainly not that Athenian law forbade homoerotic liaisons per se, but that it did specifically seek to protect boys from sexual exploitation, from the attentions of slaves and (in all likelihood) from sexual assault. What is more, Aeschines' account of Athens' legal code in **Aeschines A.9–12** suggests that the laws governing conduct in schools and gymnasia (not to mention the chaperoning of boys by slave-attendants, *paidagogoi*) sought to restrict contact between boys and potentially immodest (i.e. non-*sōphrōn*) adult men. In particular, regulations seem designed to limit the possibilities for sexual liaisons when a boy was outside the care of an immediate family member, such as when he was under the tutelage of teachers or physical instructors (on Athenians laws concerning homosexuality, see esp. D. M. MacDowell 2000 and Fisher 2001, 36–53).

Since Athenian law was so concerned to protect boys from sexual exploitation, how did it regard pederastic relationships – and in particular sex between an adult citizen and a free boy? Our knowledge of the legal code suggests that it was only when force was applied or when money changed hands that action was possible, though David Cohen goes as far as to suggest that *any* act of sexual intercourse between a man and a boy was potentially actionable under the law of *hybris* (D. Cohen 1991, 177), his logic being that a boy's family might launch a lawsuit on the basis of damage to the boy's honour, even if the boy had consented. Cohen's reasoning may be sound: perhaps an action could, theoretically, be brought against a gratified *erastēs*. However, as Cohen himself admits, we have no evidence of the law ever having been used in this way (D. Cohen 1991, 180). Importantly, too, there appears to have been no age of consent in classical Athens (and therefore there was no concept of statutory rape: see Chapter 4.8).

What legal speeches also provide are glimpses into the real-life disputes of Athenians and the ways in which speakers present and justify their actions to a jury – not that their words are always easy to interpret. The speaker of Lysias' *Against Simon*, for example, expresses embarrassment at having to address the court about his attachment to the Plataean youth Theodotus (the possession of whom is the subject of his long-running dispute with Simon: **Lysias H**). Is the liaison a source of embarrassment itself, or is it merely, as he says, that others may think he is too old to be carrying on in this way? Similarly, when a certain Xenaenetus is accused in court of 'buggering away' his inheritance, does the slur rely on disdain for squandering money on boys in particular, or sexual liaisons and/or relations with prostitutes in general (**Isaeus O**; see Chapter 3.7)? Importantly, in a number of legal speeches, *Against Timarchus* included, we also gain an indication of how same-sex relationships were conducted by ordinary citizens: oratory can therefore help us look beyond the pederastic attachments between elite males, centred on the gymnasium and symposium, which are most often represented in literature and art (see also Chapter 3.8 on male prostitution). Also revealing are some of the incidental details we glean from legal speeches. For example, we learn of the sums of money which were exchanged to obtain a boy's attentions: in *Against Simon*, the Plataean boy, Theodotus, is said to have been given a sum of 300 drachmas by the defendant in what appears to be a contractual agreement to secure his services (**Lysias I**). We are also told that Timarchus lodges with a certain Euthydicus in the Peiraeus ostensibly to learn a profession (in this case medicine: **Aeschines D**), but with a pederastic attachment between the two also in evidence. So did engaging an apprentice routinely mean mixing business with pleasure? Interestingly, too, in another speech we learn of a boy's lover being designated as his legal guardian in his father's will (Lysias, *Against Teisis*, fr. 17.21–2). This seems to indicate a pederastic relationship which was conducted openly and with the full approval of the boy's family. Here, then, is one *erastēs* at least who had little reason to fear prosecution under the Athenian law of *hybris*.

2.9 The *kinaidos,* the *katapygōn* and anal sex

For a man in classical Athens, being called a 'woman' was far from a compliment. As we have seen, Timarchus is insulted as 'Hegesandrus' woman' in the course of his trial (**Aeschines J**), and in Old Comedy men such as Agathon and Cleisthenes are also mocked as effeminate (**Aristophanes AJ**, **BB**, **BD** and **BH**: the latter perhaps simply because he was incapable of growing a beard, however, and thus resembled men who trimmed their beards to attract either boys or admirers by appearing more youthful). Effeminacy is something of a catch-all insult in Athens: men who allegedly lead a luxurious lifestyle, who go in for soft living, who are cowardly – and even those who supposedly commit adultery with other men's wives – can all be charged with being 'womanish' (see Chapter 4.5). However, in the case of those men mentioned above, their characterisation as 'women' plausibly hints at a specific accusation: namely that, although past the age of boyhood, they willingly play the passive role in sexual acts with other men.

This allegation makes sense when we consider the fourth-century scare-figure of the *kinaidos*, the most extreme form of sexual deviant, as discussed, for example, in Plato's *Gorgias* (**Plato D**). Most scholars take the view that the word *kinaidos* indicates a man who willingly and habitually chose the passive role in homosexual sex, or in Winkler's formulation, 'a man socially deviant on his entire being', whose behaviour 'flagrantly violated or contravened the dominant social definition of masculinity' (Winkler 1990b, 177). As such, the *kinaidos* is to be equated with the man described by Plato in *Laws* who 'imitates the woman' in bed (**Plato F**) and the 'contrary to nature' (*para physin*) man whose predilections are discussed at length in the pseudo-Aristotelian *Problems* (where the desire to be anally penetrated is put down to abnormal physiognomy: *Problems* 4.26 = 879a37–880a6). Davidson, however, has suggested that the essential feature of the *kinaidos* is his sexual insatiability rather than his passivity per se (Davidson 1997, 173–80, and 2008, 55–60, who also stresses the importance of effeminacy to the characterisation of these figures, however). And although this notion of insatiability might not fully square with the evident repulsion expressed by Socrates' interlocutor in *Gorgias* at the mention of this category of men (**Plato D**), the inability to find sexual satisfaction is plausibly part of what makes the *kinaidos* so repugnant a figure: his sexual voracity is (at least in part) what renders him so shameless.

Kinaidos is essentially a fourth-century term and starts to appear in our sources at roughly the same time as the word *katapygōn* falls out of use in Athens, one word seemingly replacing the other in common parlance (Davidson 1997, 167 and 173). *Katapygōn*, a term which implies sexual orientation towards the *pygē*, 'buttocks', is a word mainly to be found in Old Comedy: a number of men – often public figures such as politicians and/or those who are also characterised as effeminate – are insulted as *katapygones* in Aristophanes' plays or alternatively as 'widearsed', *euryprōktos*, and 'buggers' (*kinoumenoi*: literally 'men who get screwed'; **Aristophanes AN** and **BD**), and so on. The frequency with which words seemingly relating to passive homosexuality are used as insults in comedy is often taken as evidence that popular opinion in

Athens took a dim view of a man who took the passive role in anal sex (see e.g. Henderson 1991, 209–13; but cf. Davidson 2008, 55–64 and esp. 113, who equates 'wide-arsedness' with 'farty . . . windbag speech', and Hubbard 2003, 7, who suggests that *kinaidos* could be used to denote not just sexual passivity but 'anyone who is perceived as sexually excessive or deviant'). Certainly, the *kinaidos*-cum-*katapygōn* has proven to be an important figure in modern scholarship, since the negative views that classical Athenians supposedly held about male sexual passivity play a key role in a much-vaunted modern theory of Greek sexuality which places penetration at its heart.

2.10 Theorising homosexuality: essentialism, constructionism and penetration

When it comes to theorising ancient sexuality, two schools of thought which have proven particularly influential are 'essentialism' and 'constructionism'. The nature of essentialist approaches varies, but at their core is the belief that our sexual instincts are biologically determined. To be sure, the prevailing norms of the society in which we live may serve to influence the precise way in which our sexual urges are expressed, but importantly, categories such as 'heterosexual' and 'homosexual' are hard-wired into our genes. Evidence from different civilisations and different eras is used to suggest that – in spite of some striking variations – there are nevertheless substantial underlying transcultural and transhistorical similarities in patterns of human sexual behaviour (Skinner 2005, 8; see esp. Boswell 1990 and, for further references, Halperin 1990, 159–60 n. 21).

This is all well and good, but of course, an essentialist model of sexuality proves problematic when applied to a society like classical Athens where many male Athenian citizens' sexual experiences would have ranged from being an *erōmenos* and an *erastēs* in same-sex relationships, to frequenting prostitutes (see Chapter 3), to being married to a woman (who at the time of marriage might be little more than a pubescent girl: see Chapter 1.6). This suggests a culture which recognises a wholly different set of sexual norms from those of modern western societies and one whose members cannot be usefully categorised as (exclusively) hetero- or homosexual. Perhaps it is no surprise, then, that many scholars choose to take a 'constructionist' approach to the question of ancient sexuality, an approach foreshadowed by Dover and subsequently developed by Foucault in the second volume of *The History of Sexuality: The Use of Pleasure* (Foucault 1985).

Underpinning constructionism (also called 'social constructionism')
is the notion that human sexual behaviour is shaped not primarily by
biology, but rather by the prevailing cultural norms of the society into
which we are born. Scholars differ in the precise theoretical approach
they take, but one key notion is that the classical Greeks lived, as the
title of the 1990 collection of essays edited by Halperin, Winkler and
Zeitlin suggests, in a time *Before Sexuality*: that is to say, human sexual
identity in ancient Greece was simply not categorised as hetero-, bi- and
homosexual (cf. Foucault 1985, 3–6 and 187–93). As evidence for this
Halperin, for example, lights on the fact that Ancient Greek possessed
no terms equivalent to 'heterosexual' and 'homosexual' – indeed, as he
points out (Halperin 1990, 15), the word 'homosexual' only entered
the English language in the late nineteenth century: hence the title of
his 1990 book, *One Hundred Years of Homosexuality*. Winkler makes
the same point in *The Constraints of Desire* when he remarks on the
impossibility of writing a history of homosexuality, 'since neither it
[i.e. homosexuality] nor heterosexuality nor even sexuality are time-
less facets of human nature' (Winkler 1990a, 4). However 'natural' it
might seem to us in modern industrialised societies, then, according
to the constructionist view our sexual orientation is a cultural con-
struct rather than a 'given'. And so the categories of 'heterosexual'
and 'homosexual' were unavailable to classical Greeks, who instead
conceptualised sexual behaviour according to different principles. (For
a particularly thoughtful contribution to the debate, see Parker 2001,
who examines the systems used by a variety of non-western cultures
for categorising gender and sexuality.)

According to scholars of the constructionist school, such as Dover,
Foucault, Halperin and Winkler, sexual acts in the world of classical
Greece were defined primarily with reference to penetration – or rather
who was penetrating whom (e.g. Dover 1978, 100–9; Halperin 1990,
29–39). Thus a sexual act is made up of an active and passive partner,
one person being the penetra*tor*, the other the penetra*ted*. Importantly,
too, this is not a value-neutral exercise: sex is a zero-sum competition
in which the active partner is the winner, the passive partner the loser
(see e.g. Foucault 1985, 215–25; Halperin 1990, 32; Winkler 1990a, 11).
In terms of heterosexual acts, then, penetration is uncontroversial in
an ancient Greek context since it simply serves to confirm the man's
natural superior status to the woman. Homosexual sex might also be
unproblematic if a citizen were to penetrate a slave or foreigner, since
the act of penetration would simply serve to reinforce the difference
in status between the two partners. However, sex between two free

males is another matter, since here one of the partners is by necessity placed in an 'unnatural', inferior (and feminising) role. This explains why Timarchus is insulted as a 'woman' and why the *kinaidos* figure is a source of such horror: sexual passivity is feminising and degrading, and since a *kinaidos* chooses to be penetrated, he is therefore 'a man who desires to lose' the zero-sum competition of sex (Winkler 1990a, 54 = Winkler 1990b, 186). The constructionists' model of sex also helps to explain the nature of pederastic relationships: the age-inequality between the partners mirrors the inequality inherent in the active and passive sexual roles, and the 'intercrural' position adopted by same-sex pairs in vase-paintings can be read as less shaming for the *erōmenos* than anal sex would be (Dover 1978, 101–3). The anxieties surrounding homosexual courtship, not to mention the scandal that a boy is capable of attracting simply by being alone with a man, are also products of this obsession with penetration. Since sex is degrading for the passive partner, if it became known, or even alleged, that a boy had granted his *erastēs* sexual favours – let alone been penetrated anally – then he could be charged with being 'womanish'. In consequence, the utmost discretion in the conduct of courtship and sexual acts was necessary.

Constructionism has not been without its critics. Thornton, for instance, finds Halperin's and Winkler's work theoretically flawed, and criticises their narrow understanding of 'power' and the monolithic application of what he calls their 'rigid' theory to a society as 'self-consciously complex' as that of ancient Athens (Thornton 1991, 185; for a similarly stinging critique of construction, see also Davidson 1997, 167–82 and 250–60, and 2008, 101–66; see also Fisher 2001, 44–53, for a balanced response to both Davidson and the constructionist school). Furthermore, as various scholars have pointed out, there is at least some evidence of individuals being characterised in ancient Greece in terms of their preferences for boys or women (**Archilochus A, Athenaeus B** and **Theognis D**; see esp. Hubbard 2003, 2–3), in addition to which Aristophanes' speech in Plato's *Symposium* (fantastic and comic as it undeniably is) purports to explain the origin of three distinct modes of sexual attraction: male–male; male–female and female–female (**Plato N**; on which see esp. Thorp 1992). So was modern categorisation of people according to their 'sexual orientation' – i.e. hetero- and homo-sexual – such a foreign concept to the ancient Greeks after all?

As for the supposed centrality of penetration to the classical Greek view of sex, there have also been objections raised. For a culture alleg-edly so obsessed with penetration, it is certainly noteworthy that the focus of erotic attention in homosexual vase-paintings tends to be on the *erōmenos'* penis (which is not infrequently stared at or fondled) rather than the anus (thus Hubbard 2003, 10, who suggests that the interest in the boy is as an 'active agent with sexual capabilities' rather than a 'passive receptacle'). Furthermore, where anal sex *is* depicted, the partners tend to be similar in age: that is to say, the emphasis does not seem to be on the inequality of the participants' social status (Hubbard 2003, 11; see **Fig. 10**; cf. **Figs 12** and **13**). And not only is anal sex depicted only rarely on vases, it also features relatively infrequently in our literary sources (outside Old Comedy at least): the constructionist view that anal (or for that matter oral) penetration occupied such an important position in the Greek psyche is, then, essentially based on inference rather than direct, unequivocal testimony. And if sex *was* a zero-sum competition that men were keen on winning, why do we never find examples of boastful *erastai* talking of their conquests? Importantly, too, it is English rather than Greek which tends to use sexual metaphors to express power ('Fuck you!', 'You're really screwed!'). Is the idea that penetration is synonymous with power in fact a concept that scholars have imported from the modern world into an ancient setting (Davidson 2008, 119–20)?

All this said, a constructionist position clearly has its value, not least because – in its questioning of the 'essential' nature of the categories 'homo-' and 'heterosexual' – it tackles head on the problem of accounting for the differences between modern and ancient attitudes towards sex and sexual practices (and here it should be noted that it is in theory possible to be a constructionist without adhering to the 'penetration' model of sex – and equally possible to be an essentialist who believes in the importance of penetration to the ancients). What is more, even if penetration plays a less central role in Greek consciousness than some constructionists would have us believe, it seems undeniable that the homosexual anal sex was a taboo topic for classical Athenians: why else did the painters of pederastic scenes assiduously avoid depicting it on vases, opting for intercrural sex instead? Was this – in part at least – because it rendered the passive partner 'womanish', or for other reasons? Oral and anal sex are certainly those acts most likely to be implied by the speakers of various legal speeches when they talk of unmentionable, shameful deeds (**Aeschines D.41** and **E**: see also Chapter 5.6).

Any coherent explanation of classical Greek homosexuality has to account for a wide variety of data from a culture whose attitudes were certainly *poikilos* ('many hued'). And within the rich mix of data we have from classical Athens, there are also examples of opinions and behaviour that seem to go against many of the trends and 'rules' we have discussed so far, such as adult *erōmenoi*, as well as areas of homosexual behaviour about which we are woefully underinformed, such as lesbianism. These form the subject matter of the following section.

2.11 Marginal figures: adult *erōmenoi* and non-citizens

The drinking party of Plato's *Symposium* is hosted by Agathon, a suave and well-groomed tragic playwright who, in 416 BC when the symposium was supposedly held, would have been in his late twenties. In *Symposium* he is at times gently teased by his guests, and at one point Alcibiades and Socrates enter into an extended joke where they pretend to be two *erastai* ('admirers') vying for his affections as an *erōmenos* (Plato, *Symposium* 222c–223a). The reason why the joke has bite, however (and why, presumably, Agathon was later mocked as an effeminate, sexually passive *katapygōn* by Aristophanes: **Aristophanes BD** and **BH**), is that he was involved in a relationship with one of the guests: despite his age he was *erōmenos* to the older Pausanias' *erastēs*. In another of Plato's dialogues we learn that the couple had been together since Agathon's early adolescence (*Protagoras* 315d–e); and some years later, when Agathon left Athens for the court of King Archelaus of Macedon, Pausanias went with him (Aelian, *Historical Miscellany* 2.21). Here, then, we have an example of a long-term homosexual couple – and one which, by definition, involves the unusual spectacle of an adult *erōmenos*.

But just how unusual was it to find relationships involving two adult citizens? In his *Nicomachean Ethics* Aristotle explicitly talks about the difference between pederastic attachments which fade and those where the couple 'come to love each other's character' and which survive into adulthood (**Aristotle G**; see also **Plato M.183e**). The word Aristotle uses to describe such adult relationships is *philia*, often translated as 'friendship' or 'affection', and it would obviously be interesting to know what such relationships might have involved in practice. Whether or not *philia* could involve being more than just 'friends', however, couples like Agathon and Pausanias clearly lay outside the norm. These two lovers belong to a select group of high-profile couples in the Greek world, the strength of whose continuing, intense attachment to each other was evidently seen as worthy of note (although cf. Davidson 2008, esp. 131–2, 381–8 and 508–16, who suggests that committed adult same-sex couples were not uncommon).

Another way in which the norms of pederasty are occasionally breached is with regard to the relative ages of the *erastēs* and *erōmenos*. In particular, as noted earlier, youths of similar ages are sometimes to be found in vase-paintings involved in experimental sexual acts (e.g. **Fig. 13**) and, less salaciously, in literary sources there is also evidence of young homosexual couples who are age-mates (Timarchus was clearly of a similar age to his *erastēs*, Misgolas, for example: Aeschines 1.49). Educational establishments are plausibly one place where young homosexual love between peers might have flourished: we learn in Xenophon's *Symposium*, for instance, that Critobulus' infatuation with his near age-mate Cleinias began when he started to attend the same school (Xenophon, *Symposium* 4.23; cf. **Theopompus A**: see also Stafford 2013 on the association of Eros with the gymnasium, including the cult of Eros at the Academy). As for other 'unexpected' behaviour, as noted above, some vase-paintings seem deliberately to break the rules (e.g. where a youth penetrates a bearded man anally: see 2.3 above; or where an *erōmenos* initiates intimacy, **Fig. 16**). In addition, one fragment of comic drama suggests the existence of 'cruising' spots in classical Athens, where men are said to behave 'in an unseemly fashion' amongst the ruins of old buildings (**Cratinus A**). If homosexual relationships in Athens were indeed bound by a notional set of rules, it appears that it was perfectly possible to break them.

The concentration on pederasty in this chapter largely reflects the nature of our sources, which tend only to be interested in the sexual behaviour of citizen men and free youths/boys. For this reason, we are poorly informed about the homoerotic sex lives of large swathes of Athens' population, such as slaves and foreigners – and also poorer citizens. Indeed, foreigners and slaves tend only to be mentioned when their sexual conduct comes to bear on the lives of free males (e.g. when the Plataean boy, Theodotus, is the object of dispute between rival *erastai*, or when slaves are forbidden from harassing Athenian boys: **Aeschines A.9–12** and **Lysias H**; cf. **Aeschines P**). To be sure, we know something of the role played by foreigners and slaves in prostitution (see Chapter 3.3–3.8), but as for sexual relations between, say, masters and their male slaves (consensual or otherwise), we are very much in the dark. Where our knowledge is also poor is in relation to lesbianism. From elsewhere in Greece, we have erotically themed poems by the sixth-century poetess Sappho of Lesbos (e.g. **Sappho A** and **B**), and Plutarch (writing in the first and second centuries AD) tells us that there was female pederasty in Sparta in the classical era (*Lycurgus* 18.4). As for classical Athens, however, the most compelling literary evidence we have for lesbianism is Aristophanes' speech in Plato's

Symposium (**Plato N**), where women who 'turn to women' are called *hetairistriai* (a word of uncertain meaning, but linked etymologically to the word *hetaira*, meaning 'companion' but also 'prostitute': see Chapter 3.3). In addition to this, there exist a number of images on Athenian vases representing female intimacy, some more obviously erotically charged than others (the most frequently discussed image of female intimacy is without doubt **Fig. 17**). It should be said, however, that these were produced by male artists and presumably sold to male buyers: we have no way of knowing whether these paintings represent reality in any meaningful way (on female homoeroticism as displayed on vases, see Rabinowitz 2002, esp. 126, 131–2 and 148–50). Lastly, it is worth bearing in mind that for classical Athenians, the word *lesbiazein* meant 'to suck dick': despite the spell cast on the modern world by Sappho of Lesbos, it was not a fondness for same-sex relationships for which residents of that island were famous, but rather a different activity entirely.

2.12 Conclusion

In this chapter we have seen how the sources pertaining to male homosexuality in classical Athens can be challenging to understand, not least because attitudes towards same-sex relationships and sexual acts shift over time and vary depending on the author, genre and audience. Faced with the array of scholarly interpretations of this evidence, it is all too easy, however, to lose sight of the fact that the kind of survey provided by this chapter comprises neither a comprehensive nor a rounded picture of homosexual activity in the city of Athens. Above all, it is important to bear in mind that ancient sources and their modern interpreters over-emphasise certain aspects of homoerotic behaviour and tend to ignore others. The institution of pederasty is a case in point: the reputation of pederasty as an institution and the 'rules' of pederastic courtship are of great interest to elite, ancient male authors, but perhaps only a fraction of those living in Athens (chiefly elite males) would ever have been involved in the kind of relationship we find described, alluded to and discussed in lyric poetry, philosophy and oratory. As far as the homoerotic lives of the bulk of Athens' inhabitants are concerned – its poor, immigrants, slaves and, of course, women – there remain large gaps in our knowledge. And since, as we have seen, one key point of contention amongst scholars is the extent to which non-elite Athenians were suspicious of and hostile towards homosexuality, it may well prove useful here to separate out

same-sex attraction in general from pederasty in particular. The pederastic pursuit of boys required leisure time for its realisation, money for
the purchase of gifts and, no doubt, status if a man was to win a noble
erōmenos round. And like any exclusive activity, this may have been
one in which some non-aristocrats sought to participate and which
they saw as conferring status, but which others were increasingly wont
to question and even deride as the democracy matured. But if a scholar
such as Hubbard is right that the non-elite were hostile towards pederasty (or if certain Athenians were at least suspicious of it), this is not the
same as saying that the masses were ill-disposed towards all forms of
homosexuality. Indeed, the occasional homoerotic fantasy in a popular
genre such as Old Comedy (e.g. **Aristophanes AG**) – not to mention
homoerotic themes in poetry, the existence of homoerotic graffiti, and
so on – suggests a widespread recognition and acceptance in classical
Athens of same-sex attraction as a fact of life.

A further point to make is that homosexual acts are distinct from
homosexual relationships. In most discussions of classical homosexuality (this chapter included), sex acts and intimate relationships are
discussed alongside each other, not as separate categories. But sex is
only one aspect of sexuality, of course, and same-sex relationships in
classical Athens could evidently involve affection and respect as well as
quarrels and jealousies – that is to say, they operated on an emotional
and not just a physical level. In other words, Greek homosexuality was
not simply characterised by the sex acts on which the constructionist-
cum-penetration model of Greek sexuality tends to focus our minds.

In the next chapter we go on to examine another strand of sexual
behaviour in classical Athens which, perhaps surprisingly, involves not
just sexual acts but also long-term attachments, both heterosexual and
homosexual: namely, prostitution.

CHAPTER 3

Prostitution

3.1 Introduction

Athens in the classical era was home to a huge range of sex workers (**Xenophon D**), ranging from the lowliest slave working in one of Athens' many brothels to famous courtesans (*hetairai*) such as Phryne and Gnathaena whose looks and wit became the stuff of legend. The conditions for prostitution were ripe at Athens. Like Corinth (the most famous centre for commercial sex in the Greek-speaking world), it was a prosperous, bustling city with a large passing trade in the shape of sailors, merchants and other visitors. A further key factor in the development of the sex industry is the attitude taken by Athenians towards prostitution. Views were extremely liberal by modern standards inasmuch as there seems to have been little or no opprobrium attached to using prostitutes per se: prostitutes were openly frequented by figures such as Alcibiades and the orator Lysias, and major statesmen in the classical era, such as Themistocles and Pericles, are also said to have co-habited with (former) sex workers (although see e.g. Henderson 2000, 140, for the possibility that these stories originate in comic slanders). Prostitutes may even have accompanied some military expeditions (Xenophon mentions *hetairai* in a military camp at *Anabasis* 4.3.19, for example: see Loman 2004, 49–50). Importantly, too, prostitution was entirely legal and controls exercised over the industry by the state were fairly minor. Prostitutes were registered and taxed (**Aeschines K**; and therefore provided what was no doubt an important revenue stream for the public purse) and the maximum fees that some sex workers could charge also appear to have been subject to legislation (**Aristotle B**). For the slaves and metics (i.e. 'resident immigrants') who made up the bulk of sex workers in the city, state interference in their lives ended here, and it was only for those few citizens who prostituted themselves that additional legislation applied:

for citizen women, the law placed certain limits on the religious role they could play in the city (e.g. [Demosthenes] 59.75), whilst for boys it restricted the civic functions they could fulfil in adult life (**Aeschines C**). These laws can only have served to discourage citizens from becoming sex workers, and encouraged the perception that prostitution was largely a low-grade occupation. But if prostitution was essentially practised by non-Athenians and poverty-stricken citizens, it was certainly not a profession that attracted universal scorn. There are, after all, examples of ordinary, respectable Athenian men who set up home with former prostitutes in later life – as well as a select handful of glamorous courtesans who achieved nothing short of celebrity status.

In this chapter, we shall look at the range of prostitutes working in classical Athens, from brothel-workers and street-walkers to entertainers at symposia (drinking parties), sex-slaves, live-in lovers and expensive courtesans. Not that the distinction between various categories of prostitute in classical Athens is always easy to draw: sex workers, it seems, resist easy compartmentalisation (indeed, as more than one legal dispute shows, it seems that even the line between prostitute and wife was not always wholly clear). Of particular interest are the terms *pornē* ('whore', 'prostitute') and *hetaira* ('companion') which classical Athenians regularly used to describe sex workers, the precise difference between which modern scholars have sought to define in various ways, as we shall see. In the course of this survey, we shall also look at male prostitution and expenditure on sex as well as the ways in which modern scholars have attempted to define the ideological basis of prostitution in classical Athens.

3.2 Neaera: the whore of Corinth

One figure that crops up again and in again in discussions of Greek prostitution is Neaera, a Corinthian prostitute born some time around the beginning of the fourth century. Her importance to modern scholars stems from the fact that she is the subject of a legal speech delivered in the late 340s BC, *Against Neaera* ([Demosthenes] 59), in which the alleged details of her professional and personal life are spelt out in gory detail. Her prosecutor, Apollodorus, seeks to establish that, although a foreigner, Neaera had been living with an Athenian citizen as if she were a wife (an important consequence being that children of the union would not be Athenian citizens: see Chapter 1.1 and 1.15).

As various scholars have pointed out, we should no doubt be

sceptical about many of the details contained in *Against Neaera* (Glazebrook 2005; Gilhuly 2009, 29–57), but the speech is nevertheless an invaluable source for students of ancient prostitution, and from it we can gain a vivid (if perhaps not wholly truthful) impression of how varied and tumultuous a prostitute's life could be. According to the speaker, Neaera is bought as a young girl by Nicarete, who sets her up along with her other 'daughters' in a high-class brothel in Corinth and puts her to work as a prostitute when Neaera is still very young, probably pre-pubescent ([Demosthenes] 59.22; cf. **Metagenes A**). She is later sold to two regular clients of the brothel but eventually buys her freedom. She manages to raise the capital for this thanks to donations from former clients, but above all the Athenian Phrynion, to whom she evidently remains much beholden. Phrynion takes her to Athens, where he treats her outrageously (**Demosthenes Q**), and so she runs away, taking clothing, jewellery and two maidservants with her. She meets Stephanus in Megara, and returns with him to Athens, where Phrynion features in her life once more when he tries to take her from Stephanus' house by force. Phrynion's attempt fails, but Neaera subsequently has to submit to the conditions of an out-of-court settlement between these two men, whereby she has to return to Phrynion what she stole and live with him and Stephanus on alternate days ([Demosthenenes] 59.40 and 45–7). Later in the speech, Phrynion fades from view and the prosecution case focuses instead on the children Neaera supposedly has with Stephanus and an assortment of outrages that the two have supposedly committed ([Demosthenes] 59.50–87).

These are the bare bones of the account we have of Neaera's life. To be sure, the course of her career as described in this speech was probably far from typical both in its upheavals and in the fact that she achieved a modicum of fame in Corinth and beyond: Neaera's name even features in fourth-century Athenian comedy (Philetaerus' *Huntress*, fr. 9 KA, and Timocles' *Neaera*, a play apparently named after her: Athenaeus 13.567d–e). What the picture of Neaera presented in this speech neatly demonstrates, however, is how a prostitute might fulfil multiple roles in the course of a career (brothel-worker, sex-slave, live-in lover) – and also how much the life of a slave-prostitute was under the control of her owners (and in Neaera's case, of the man who had helped to buy her freedom, too: a purchase which evidently came at a high price for her).

3.3 *Pornai* and *hetairai*

In Classical Greek there is a whole range of ways to denote female prostitutes – including a number of words which provide interesting insights into how and where women might ply their trade: 'ground-beater', 'bridge-woman' and 'alley-treader', for example (Davidson 1997, 78). As mentioned in the introduction to this chapter, perhaps the two most commonly used terms in our sources are *porně* and *hetaira*. *Porně* derives from the verb *pernanai*, 'to sell', and is often translated 'whore' or 'prostitute', whereas *hetaira* is a more euphemistic term meaning 'companion' and – if it is translated at all – is most often rendered as 'courtesan' or 'mistress' (the male equivalents of these terms are *pornos* and *hetairos*). Modern scholars of ancient prostitution have often sought to characterise the difference between *pornai* and *hetairai* (see E. Cohen 2006, 97–9, and Glazebrook and Henry 2011b for concise surveys). Some see promiscuity as the key difference: the *porně* sells herself to all-comers; the *hetaira* enjoys a series of longer-term relationships (e.g. Cantarella 1987, 50). For Dover, 'emotional attitude' is crucial, with the *hetaira* 'nearer to a "mistress" than to a "prostitute"' (Dover 1978, 20–1). For Kurke, who examines the origins of these terms in archaic Greece, the *hetaira* is linked with elite ideology and gift-exchange, whereas the *porně* comes to represent democratic commodification (Kurke 1997). Indeed, most scholars see the distinction between the two figures as one of status, with the high-class *hetaira* thus standing in contrast to the common *porně*. Edward Cohen adds a further nuance to the picture by suggesting that an important aspect of the *hetaira*'s greater status is that she works unsupervised – unlike the slavish *porně* who works under another's jurisdiction (E. Cohen 2003, 214–18, and 2006, 99; see also Nowak 2010 for an attempt to arrive at a quasi-legal definition of prostitution in Athens).

One thing that emerges from scholarly discussions of the difference between *pornai* and *hetairai* is that the label which a speaker or writer chooses to assign to a given sex worker can, on occasion, be highly significant. The contrasting associations of the two terms can be used to great rhetorical effect in the characterisation of a woman, as is the case when Neaera is deliberately characterised as both a luxury-loving *hetaira* and a common *porně* in the prosecution speech made against her (Miner 2003). At other times the terms are used relatively casually, however – even interchangeably – with the distinction between them not always sharp.

In reality, of course, we find not two different and easily separable

types of prostitute in Athens, but a multitude of sex workers falling
into a whole host of different categories – some slaves, some free; some
foreign, some Athenian, and so on – with a wide spectrum of working
practices, living conditions and prices demanded for their services.
Attempts by some feminist scholars to collapse the distinction between
different types of sex worker may serve as a useful reminder of the
exploitation that (in modern eyes at least) the profession entails, but
these are less successful in communicating the gradations between different kinds of prostitutes – and these will often have held great importance for the women concerned (Keuls, for example, sees the 'refined
hetaira' as 'a fabrication of the male mind' and maintains that in reality
Athenian men simply divided women into two categories: 'mothers'
and 'whores': Keuls 1985, 199 and 205). This said, in the following
survey of the Athenian sex industry, one key point which will emerge
again and again is the permeability of the categories of prostitute: the
same woman might work in a variety of different environments in the
course of a career (just as Neaera supposedly did), and different kinds
of sex workers continually rub shoulders with one another in brothels,
on street corners, at parties and in private homes – and therefore often
defy straightforward categorisation as a *pornē* or *hetaira*.

3.4 Street-walkers and brothel-workers

The sex workers most likely to have been referred to as *pornai* in classical Athens were the women who paced Athens' streets and worked
in Athens' brothels – women whose lives have left little trace in the
archaeological or literary record. Most street-walkers would probably
have belonged to the class of Athens' residents known as 'metics': that
is, immigrants from other Greek states and their descendants, although
presumably some women from Athens' citizen class were also driven
to prostitution through poverty (a fictional citizen prostitute features
in **Antiphanes A**, for example: instructive here is that she has no
kinsmen to support her financially). The majority of street-walkers
would no doubt have plied their trade in the city's red-light districts,
the most notorious of which were the Peiraeus, Athens' busy port
(**Aristophanes AY**; cf. **Metagenes A** where 'merchants' are mentioned), and the Kerameikos, or potters' district, which incorporated
the famous Dipylon gate northwest of the acropolis (**Alexis B** and
Aristophanes AR; although Glazebrook argues that the Kerameikos
was not a 'disreputable part of town' in itself, merely one in which
sex workers were concentrated: Glazebrook 2011, 48). The area of the

Kerameikos beyond the city-walls was the site of an ancient cemetery where the tombstones may well have provided a setting for a variety of outdoor sex acts. Just inside the city-walls in the Kerameikos was a structure known as 'Building Z' which was rebuilt several times during the classical period and at one point contained at least twenty small rooms. In its remains archaeologists have unearthed symposium-ware along with various female accoutrements such as a mirror and jewellery. Whilst some scholars take the presence of drinking vessels to indicate its use as an inn, others believe that Building Z was an ancient brothel, with the small rooms well suited for use by the brothel's inhabitants and their clients (Davidson 1997, 85–6; E. Cohen 2006, 105 and 120; Glazebrook 2011, 39–41).

Unlike street-walkers, women working in a brothel (*porneion*) were all slaves, owned by a *pornoboskos* (lit. 'whore-herder'). Many slaves in Athens were foreign-born, from areas such as Thrace and Caria, and so men who frequented brothels would have grown used to encountering women whose Greek was poor or heavily accented, perhaps working alongside Athenian-bred slaves as well as slave-women from other parts of the Greek-speaking world (it was often a woman's fate to be enslaved when her city was captured in war, for example). Evidence for how life was lived inside a brothel is fairly scant, but scholars often presume that living and working conditions there were poor and that the lives of brothel-based *pornai* were difficult and unpleasant (e.g. Keuls 1985, 156). Certainly in comedy, *pornoboskoi* (i.e. brothel-keepers) are typically presented as 'mean, manipulative [and] money-grubbing' men (Davidson 1997, 94; **Alexis A**) and for at least one slave-woman, the thought of being placed in a brothel made her adopt extreme measures. In a speech by Antiphon, *Prosecution of the Stepmother for Poisoning* (Antiphon 1), we learn of the poisoning of Philoneus (and a dinner guest) by a slave-concubine whom he was about to place in a brothel. The woman's defence was that she thought the poison was a love potion, but whether or not this was true, she was subsequently tortured and executed. But if some brothels were squalid, as many assume, others seem to have been less so: Building Z may have boasted a courtyard garden, for example, and the drinking vessels and dining equipment found on site may well indicate that the surroundings were found comfortable enough by customers to extend their stay (see Davidson 1997, 94, and esp. Glazebrook 2011, 42–5). Brothel-workers are likely to have resided in the buildings in which they worked (E. Cohen 2006, 102, who points out that business premises were generally co-extensive with private residences in classical

Athens). This would no doubt have provided ample opportunity for the inhabitants to swap tips on how to deal with some of the occupational hazards of the job, such as unwanted pregnancies (on contraceptives and abortifacients, see Riddle 1992, 17–18, 23–4 and 74–82).

Some brothels seem to have been very well appointed indeed. The brothel in which Neaera worked (albeit in Corinth rather than Athens) evidently catered for an exclusive clientele, and so the indications are that this was a far from down-at-heel establishment. What is more, Nicarete, the brothel's madam, evidently invested a good deal of time training her 'daughters' from a young age to be desirable companions for clients ([Demosthenes] 59.18), an education which must have encompassed far more than simply instruction in sex. Consequently, the girls' clients could be called on to pay extremely high fees: when Timanoridas and Eucrates (Neaera's eventual purchasers) were staying at the brothel, for instance, they were required to pay 'all the daily expenses of Nicarete's household' (**Demosthenes P**). It is also worthy of note that in Nicarete we have a female brothel-keeper. We hear of other women, too, typically former prostitutes themselves, who fulfilled the role of *pornoboskos* or pimp (see Keuls 1985, 196–8; E. Cohen 2005, 207–8; Glazebrook 2011, 50–2). Examples include the former courtesan Antigone who procures the perfume-seller's son in Hyperides 3 (**Hyperides A**), and perhaps Pericles' lover, Aspasia (**Aristophanes AB**; instructively, the gender of the brothel-keeper imagined in **Alexis A** is also female).

Inevitably, the glimpses we gain of the Athenian brothel in art and literature represent a male perspective on the institution, with the focus in our sources tending to be on the availability of the women and the act of choosing. A number of vase-paintings depicting men inspecting naked or partially clad women are thought to represent brothel scenes (e.g. **Fig. 18**), not least because they closely correspond to descriptions we find of brothel-prostitutes being paraded naked or bare-breasted as the clients make their choice (a parade of women in front of the client is characteristic of many modern brothels, too). In a fragment of the fourth-century comic playwright Xenarchus, we learn of good-looking girls in whore-houses, drawn up in columns with their breasts exposed, from amongst whom the client can select whichever girl is most to his taste in terms of age and body-type (**Xenarchus A**; cf. **Eubulus A**). In another comic fragment, this time by Philemon, naked prostitutes are also mentioned, and the emphasis here is on the ease of the transaction: not only is the sex cheap, but 'it's straight off to the woman you want, however you want it' (**Philemon A**). Xenarchus also mentions the way in which some prostitutes lure clients into the brothels by dragging them in and calling them pet names ('little father', 'kid brother'), the implication being that at least some of the girls would have worked outside the brothel, perhaps mingling with street-walkers. Tricks of the trade used by prostitutes and their owners to make them more attractive to customers also feature in comedy: good features are emphasised, bad ones disguised (**Alexis A**). An ancient sandal provides a clue as to another tactic that prostitutes might have used to attract clients back to the brothel: nails in the sole of the sandal are arranged in such a way as to spell out 'follow me' (*akolouthēi*) when trodden in the dust (see Halperin 1990, 109 and n. 147).

Inevitably, a brothel would have been busier at certain times of day than others and it is unlikely that the slave-workers were allowed to sit idle. Indeed, there is evidence to suggest that when demand for sexual services was slack during the day, many brothels were turned into a very different kind of sweatshop: a textile factory with slave-prostitutes working and weaving wool. On the site of Building Z, for example, over a hundred loom weights have been found, and there are various vase-paintings depicting what have become known as 'spinning *hetairai*': these show seated women, spinning or winding wool, while young men approach or wait nearby with gifts or bags (presumably containing money). What seems to secure the identification of these women as *pornai* is the fact that on one vase two of these wool-workers are labelled with names appropriate to prostitutes: Aphrodisia, 'Sexy', and Obole, 'Cut-Price' (lit. 'One Obol': see Davidson 1997, 86–90, and E. Cohen 2006, 104–5). A further intriguing source which may provide evidence of the double life of the brothel comes in the form of the *phialai exeleutherikai*: tablets dating from around 320 BC, which record the occupations of a number of former slaves. Over half of the freed-women whose occupations are listed on these tablets are *talasiourgoi*, or 'wool-workers', an occupation which, Edward Cohen suggests, they most likely learnt and practised as prostitutes (E. Cohen 2003, 222–7, and 2006, 105–8). Cohen's logic here is that a slave working as a poorly paid wool-worker would have little chance of accumulating enough money to buy her freedom, whereas a wool-worker-cum-prostitute stood a far greater chance of amassing the necessary funds. This is not to say that all wool-workers were prostitutes, however, or that all brothel-prostitutes worked wool, but rather that there appears to have been a significant overlap between the two occupations. If Cohen's suggestion is right, then for some slave-women at least, life in a brothel was not without its financial benefits, and buying one's way out of slavery was a realistic objective for many *pornai* (on prices for sexual services, see 3.9 below).

3.5 Musicians and dancers

A more expensive type of prostitute is to be found in the form of the various musicians and dancers who were hired to entertain the guests at symposia (drinking parties) in classical Athens. The type of 'entertainer' found most commonly in our sources is the *aulētris* (plural *aulētrides*), that is girls who played the *aulos* (conventionally translated 'flute', but which in fact comprised two reeded pipes, played simultaneously, and which would probably have sounded more like an oboe). In our literary sources we also find references to harp-players and cithara-players (the cithara was a type of lyre) as well as dancers (e.g. **Aristophanes BK** and **Aristotle B**). These female entertainers, who often feature in vase-paintings of symposium scenes, all found work at symposia entertaining the guests (sexually and otherwise): in **Fig. 20**, for instance, a naked woman reclining with a youth can be seen clutching an *aulos*, while in **Figs 21** and **22** female musicians can be seen entertaining symposium guests. Even when no musical instrument is to be seen, it seems reasonable to assume that women we find depicted drinking in male company are to be thought of as hired prostitutes, since 'respectable' Athenian wives and daughters would not normally have dined alongside their menfolk (although some scholars have challenged the assumption that the women we find engaged in sympotic and sexual scenes on Greek vases are routinely to be regarded as prostitutes: see e.g. Llewellyn-Jones 2002b, 176, for discussion, and Blazeby 2011). The flute-girl would have come into her own during the part of the symposium known as the *kōmos*, or 'revel', when the drunken guests would parade round the streets to the accompaniment of the *aulos* (as shown in **Fig. 23**). Whilst these entertainers are regularly called *hetairai* (especially by modern scholars in their discussions of the institution of the symposium), their lives as jobbing entertainers must have been very different from those of the live-in lovers and 'big-fee hetairai' we will meet later on (thus serving neatly to demonstrate the problems posed by the *hetaira/porne* divide, as outlined above).

Flute-girls and other musicians were a sufficiently ubiquitous feature of Athenian life to attract legislation concerning their pay. A maximum fee of two drachmas per night was fixed by statute (although it is unclear whether this fee included sex, which perhaps cost extra: Loomis 1998, 93–4 and 173; Hamel 2003, 12; Glazebrook 2011, 47). If two clients wished to hire the same girl then Athenian law had a solution for this, too: public officials called *astynomoi* got the interested parties to draw lots, and the girl was hired out to the winner (**Aristotle B**). This was not an idle piece of legislation either, since in the 320s we hear of the prosecution of two men who flouted this law by paying over the odds (Hyperides 4.3). Fights over *aulētrides* were evidently not an uncommon occurrence (see e.g. **Demosthenes B**) and it is significant that it was the *astynomoi* who were charged with breaking up such scuffles as occurred among their clients (Davidson 1997, 82). These men were responsible for keeping the highways of the city clear, which suggests that flute-girls and other musicians mingled with street-walkers (in locations such as the Peiraeus). This, in turn, raises the question as to what the precise difference was between these entertainers (who are often called *hetairai*) and street-walkers (who are not). As Davidson points out, by the fourth century flute-girls had acquired a reputation as cheap whores (Davidson 1997, 82), and so it was perhaps only their musical instruments and their musical training that served to differentiate these women from other peripatetic prostitutes.

A final point which ought to be made in respect not only of female entertainers, but of all prostitutes with whom their clients spent a protracted period of time, is that their clients must often have looked to get more than just sex out of the transaction. As Davidson says, '[t]he careful seclusion of respectable women in Athens ceded a huge territory of feminine intimacy to the hetaera', who was able to entertain a man with flirtatious 'looks and stares, jokes and innuendo, kisses and caresses before the question of bed arose' (Davidson 1997, 95; but see also Chapters 1.10 and 5.7 on interaction between *citizen* men and women, and Chapter 4.5 on adulterous relationships). For a man, spending time with a prostitute could, then, have emotional, social and physical dimensions and so had the potential to satisfy more than just sexual needs. In this light it is revealing, too, that women who might reasonably be thought of as *hetairai* are often depicted on vases expressing affection towards their clients (see Keuls 1985, 188–91).

3.6 Sex-slaves and concubines

Something that all prostitutes had in common was the potential to capture a client's attention. A man who regularly frequented a particular brothel or red-light district might feasibly latch on to a particular girl, and such an attachment could eventually lead to a longer-term arrangement. For a prostitute, this could involve anything from accompanying a man on a trip abroad and/or to a festival to long-term co-habitation. The orator Lysias, for example, was a regular client of Metaneira, a young prostitute who worked alongside Neaera in her high-class brothel in Corinth. Accompanied by her owner, Nicarete, Metaneira was taken by Lysias to Attica (with Neaera allegedly in tow as well, who Apollodorus says had already begun prostituting herself, despite being perhaps as young as twelve or thirteen: [Demosthenes] 59.21–2; Hamel 2003, 18). Neaera herself was taken on a similar trip by Simus, an aristocrat from Thessaly, with Nicarete once again acting as chaperone ([Demosthenes] 59.24–5).

Another option for an infatuated client was to purchase a slave-prostitute from her owner. This could evidently be an expensive business, however, and it seems that it was not uncommon for two men to make a joint purchase. Neaera was bought jointly by Timanoridas of Corinth and Eucrates of Leucas, for example, for the princely sum of 30 minas (3,000 drachmas: **Demosthenes P**). Theirs seems to have been an amicable arrangement while it lasted, but other joint purchases proved more problematic. Lysias' speech *On a Premeditated Wounding* concerns a dispute over a jointly owned woman which ended in either a black eye or attempted murder, depending on which side is to be believed (Lysias 4). Boys, too, were purchased as sex-slaves, on either a temporary or a permanent basis. In the court case for which Lysias' *Against Simon* was written, part of the dispute between two rival lovers concerns the 300 drachmas that were supposedly handed over by Simon to secure the company of the Plataean boy, Theodotus (for an unspecified period of time: **Lysias I**). To buy outright the perfume-seller's son with whom he had fallen in love, a certain Epicrates was prepared to pay 4,000 drachmas (for which he also received the boy's brother and father: **Hyperides A**).

A man might also set up home with a (former) prostitute (see Chapter 1.15). Spending the rest of his life with a *hetaira* is something about which the ageing Trygaeus fantasises in Aristophanes' *Peace* (439–40), for example, and which the old man Philocleon also mentions as a possibility in *Wasps* (**Aristophanes BK**). Indeed, a man seems most often to have set up home with a *hetaira* when he was widowed or divorced and already in possession of a healthy male heir: examples include Demeas in Menander's *Woman from Samos* (see **Menander M**) and the real-life Pyrrhus in Isaeus' legal speech *On the Estate of Pyrrhus*, who chose to take in a *hetaira* only after adopting his sister's son as his heir. The legal case in which Pyrrhus features took place long after his death and originates in a claim on his estate by the woman's grown-up daughter, the allegation being that the union between Phyrrhus and the *hetaira* was in fact a marriage of which this young woman was thus the legitimate offspring (Isaeus 3.3–4). This serves to illustrate that there was potentially a fine line between marriage to a wife and co-habitation with a concubine, and indeed, it might not always have been obvious to outsiders what status the woman in a household enjoyed (although this did not prevent speculation, of course: **Isaeus F**). To be sure, a sex worker who was a slave or metic could never aspire to become a citizen wife – at least not after of Pericles' citizenship laws in 451 BC had come into force, which dictated that a male citizen (*astos*) could enjoy a full legal marriage only with a citizen woman (*astē*: see Chapter 1.1 and 1.15). However, for a citizen woman who worked in the sex industry, the fact that she had worked as a prostitute did not in itself disqualify her from citizen status (and thus marriage). That is not to say that such women (e.g. the girl mentioned in **Antiphanes A**) would have enjoyed the same rights as other, more chaste citizen women, however: women who had prostituted themselves were evidently precluded by law from participating in certain religious activities (see e.g. [Demosthenes] 59.75).

Another category of citizen choosing to purchase and/or co-habit with *hetairai* are men yet to be married. Neaera's youthful purchasers, Timanoridas of Corinth and Eucrates of Leucas, fall into this category: indeed, it is the fact that they both decide to marry that finally prompts them to sell her (**Demosthenes P**: they offer her her freedom for 2,000 drachmas). We also find a number of professional soldiers in the comedies of Menander who take prostitutes as partners, such as the young soldier in *The Hated Man* who complains about his mistress' failure to return his affection (**Menander D**). There are even men who take (non-citizen) *hetairai* in preference to wives, though this could easily be characterised as an affront to family values, since a man thereby forfeited the possibility of having legitimate heirs (**Demosthenes K**; see also Bakewell 2008/9). Others kept mistresses in addition to their wives (although not in the same house: see Chapter 1.15). In a legal speech by Isaeus (Isaeus 6, *On the Estate of Philoctemon*), for example, we hear of the elderly and wealthy Euctemon, who had an affair with a former slave-prostitute of his before eventually abandoning his family and setting up home with her (**Isaeus J**). In a speech by Demosthenes, Apollodorus (the same man who prosecuted Neaera) is accused of freeing one *hetaira* and 'giving another away', despite being married (Demosthenes 36.45).

The appeal of co-habiting with a *hetaira* was obvious. Unlike 'respectable' women, *hetairai* could be true 'companions' and drink and dine with men, and they had experience of (and often specific training in) the arts of sex and conversation (hinted at in **Demosthenes O**, for example). It is also significant that the position enjoyed by a *hetaira*-concubine was far more precarious than that of a wife: the fact that she could be turned out of the house with relative ease (or sold, if a slave) would presumably have acted as an incentive for a live-in *hetaira* to behave well towards the man (E. Cohen 2006, 112; see **Amphis A**). This said, some of the *hetaira*-concubines we meet co-habiting with older men in New Comedy seem to feel extremely secure in their positions. In Menander's *Woman from Samos*, for example, Demeas' live-in *hetaira*, Chrysis, is confident enough of her status to risk passing off a newborn baby as her own – although Demeas is clearly not the father (*Woman from Samos*, 132–6). Demeas is far from under-standing, however, and his reaction is to throw her out of the house, making it clear to her what luxuries she has enjoyed while living with him. In a highly revealing speech, he spells out what sort of a life she will now have to endure as a jobbing *hetaira* in Athens (**Menander M**).

3.7 Big-fee *hetairai*

As we have seen throughout this chapter, the category of *hetaira* is a slippery one. In contrast to *pornē*, a woman's designation as a *hetaira* carries the implication that she is a higher earner, a woman rather than a girl, probably free and self-employed – and a suitable 'companion' for a man in that she is able to amuse him in conversation (and not simply service him sexually). Neaera (who in her youth was a slave and a brothel-worker) is characterised not only as a common whore (*pornē*) but also as an expensive *hetaira* by her prosecutor, Apollodorus, in *Against Neaera* – but here it would be a mistake to think that the term '*hetaira*' carries any hint of flattery. Indeed, by labelling a woman as a *hetaira*, an orator could tap in to a rich vein of negative characteristics associated with such women, who are regularly presented in legal speeches as 'extravagant, promiscuous, available to anyone, requiring payment, excessive ... scheming and arrogant' (Glazebrook 2006a, 126; see also Miner 2003 and Glazebrook 2005, 173–83). Women iden-tified as *hetairai* in legal speeches, such as Neaera, Phile's mother (in Isaeus 3) and Alce (in Isaeus 6), were routinely demonised in Athenian courtrooms, with their supposedly extravagant lifestyles portrayed as having serious economic consequences for the families of men con-nected with them. Stephanus (Neaera's 'husband') allegedly resorted to extorting money from gullible foreigners whom he conveniently caught in bed with his 'wife' (**Demosthenes S**); in another speech, Olympiodorus is said to have squandered his money on a *hetaira* while his sisters and niece live in poverty (**Demosthenes K**); and in Isaeus 3, young men are said to ruin themselves by falling in love with such women (3.17; on the portrayal of prostitutes in comedy and other literary genres, see Henry 1988, esp. 2–31, 47–8 and 112–14).

The image of the high-living and demanding *hetaira* conjured up in the law courts was certainly a convenient stereotype for speakers to employ in attacks on their opponents, and it was a stereotype based, at least in part, on a social reality. Whilst '*hetaira*' was a label that could be applied to a whole host of sex workers, many of whom were no doubt modest earners, a small minority of *hetairai* were very well reimbursed indeed for their services: a group often referred to as the *megalomisthoi* or 'big-fee' *hetairai* (see e.g. Davidson 1997, 104–7). According to some accounts, the going rate for a night with these legendary *hetairai* of Athens – women like Phryne and Gnathaena – was a mina (i.e. 100 drachmas: **Machon A**), but whatever rewards they received for their services in reality, our sources certainly concur that these high-class *hetairai* were well off. Theodote, for example, the *hetaira* visited by Socrates in Xenophon's *Memorabilia*, is described as well dressed (as is her mother) and has not only maids but also a lavishly appointed house at her disposal (**Xenophon F**). And the description of the Sicilian-born *hetaira* Laïs in a fragment of the fourth-century comic playwright Epicrates is also testimony to the riches to which an exclusive courtesan could aspire in her youth – although as perhaps befits the title of the play, *Anti-Laïs*, the speaker cruelly chooses to stress the depths to which this *hetaira* has now sunk in her old age (**Epicrates A**: cf. also **Figs 24** and **25**, where older women, presumably to be thought of as prostitutes, are variously threatened and beaten while engaging in oral and group sex). Nor was Laïs the only *hetaira* to feature in a comedy: a whole string of courtesans such as Gnathaena, Nannion, Phryne, Thaïs and Clepsydra ('Water-Clock', who supposedly got her nickname from timing her sex sessions) featured in comedies in the fourth century (Athenaeus 13.567c; **Eubulus A**), which can only have served to increase their fame and reputations in the city. Indeed, in classical Athens these *hetairai* enjoyed a celebrity status quite unparalleled by that of any 'respectable' citizen wife or daughter of the day.

Naturally there is far more to exclusive *hetairai* than a capacity to demand large fees and the negative reputation they enjoyed in Athens' courtrooms. These courtesans were also celebrated for their wit, charm and attractiveness. Xenophon tells us that Theodote's beauty is 'beyond description' (*Memorabilia* 3.11.1) and that she is often painted by artists. What is more, she participates in some clever repartee with Socrates, who singularly fails to get out of her the source of her income (**Xenophon F**). Instead she will only say that she supports herself through the generosity of friends (one of whom, according to Athenaeus, was Alcibiades: Athenaeus 13.574e). This avoidance of talking directly about sex and money is another characteristic ascribed to big-fee *hetairai*. In a fragment of a comedy by Anaxilas, for example, the speaker complains that *hetairai* (whom he calls *pornai*, 'whores') neither specify the nature of their services nor make direct requests for payment: instead, they choose to employ euphemisms and hints (**Anaxilas B**).

Certain scholars have seized on the allusive way in which *hetairai* conduct their business, receiving 'gifts' and bestowing 'favours', as central to their definition: this is what ultimately separates *hetairai* from *pornai* who charge fixed fees for individual sex acts (a point seemingly made in **Anaxilas A**). Davidson, for example, stresses the importance of *choice* in the image that *hetairai* project to the world. It is the *hetaira* who chooses whom she sleeps with, and when to return a 'favour' – or indeed whether to demand a favour in the first place, since it is also in her gift to offer her services for free (Davidson 1997, 123–7; the granting of a 'favour' is elsewhere associated with boys rather than women: see Chapter 2.2). In a similar vein, Edward Cohen stresses the importance of *freedom* to a *hetaira*'s self-definition: unlike a slavish *pornē*, she is free to associate with whom she pleases and avoids any impression of being constrained to work 'out of economic necessity' (E. Cohen 2006, 110). What Davidson calls the 'avoidance of economic definition' also means that these high-class *hetairai* presumably avoided paying Athens' *pornikon telos* (prostitution tax; cf. **Aeschines K**) or having their fees capped in the manner of a flute-girl's (see 3.5 above). On a number of levels, then, a *hetaira* resists classification or quantification – which is also, of course, part of her allure.

As with other types of sex workers, the category of 'big-fee *hetairai*' is highly permeable. For example, women who were once exclusive courtesans move on to new pastures: if the stories about her original profession are correct then Aspasia, reportedly a big-fee *hetaira* hailing from Miletus, did just this when she settled down with Pericles in the late fifth century. Not all *hetairai*'s middle and old age were spent in the comfortable houses of Athenian citizens, however. Whilst some no doubt became brothel-keepers or procurers, if the portrait of Laïs in Epicrates' comedy has any grain of truth in it then other high-class prostitutes could fall on hard times (**Epicrates A**) – and certainly it is plausible that an ageing prostitute would struggle to earn the fees which she had demanded in her youth and be forced to take on less glamorous work. The case of Neaera is also instructive. At one stage in her life she could no doubt have claimed to have been a big-fee *hetaira* and yet in many ways she fits the mould rather poorly – she was, after all, a slave for much of her life, a brothel-worker (albeit in a high-class establishment), and evidently beholden to her liberator, Phrynion, after he had purchased her freedom. But just like Aspasia, she later co-habited with an Athenian citizen, Stephanus, either legally as his wife (which is always a possibility, if she was in fact born of Athenian citizen parents), more informally as his concubine, or as a foreign woman masquerading as an Athenian wife, depending on which side in the court case is to be believed. Neaera's experience of working in a brothel in Corinth cannot have been wholly atypical, either: big-fee *hetairai* (who were characteristically foreign-born) presumably gained experience of working in the sex industry when young in their native cities before moving to Athens.

3.8 Male prostitution

Scholars tend to agree that male sex workers were far less prevalent than their female counterparts, and certainly the organisation of male prostitution seems to have differed somewhat from its female equivalent. There is no indication that Athens could lay claim to such a thing as a large-scale male brothel, for example – although there is evidence to suggest that rent-boys worked out of private houses. In addition, we have evidence of youths being bought as sex-slaves and of contracts for the exclusive use of a boy for a prolonged period (**Lysias I**; Hyperides 3.4 and 3.9; cf. Aeschines 1.165: on male prostitution contracts, see also E. Cohen 2003, 228–9, and de Brauw and Miner 2004). In all likelihood, too, male street-walkers also mingled with female prostitutes in Athens' red-light districts. One of the more curious features of male prostitution is the existence of individual 'stalls' or 'cubicles' (*oikēmata*) opening onto the street, in which youths would evidently entertain their clients. These are described in Aeschines, *Against Timarchus*, for example (**Aeschines G**), and while these did exist for women, too, such cubicles would appear to be more characteristic of the male sex industry (on *oikēmata* as possible features of female brothels, too, see Glazebrook 2011, 41–2: the picture here is confused by the fact that *oikēma* is regularly translated as 'brothel'). According to a late anecdote, Phaedo, one of Socrates' close associates, had once worked in such a cubicle as a slave following the capture of his native Elis (Diogenes Laertius 2.105). A line in Aristophanes' *Frogs* brings home one occupational hazard that many prostitutes must have faced, but to which these solo cubicle-workers must have been particularly susceptible: in one of the grimmer parts of the underworld, alongside perjurers and mother-beaters, are to be found men who 'steal a boy's money while screwing him' (*Frogs* 148).

As with female prostitutes, the vast majority of male sex workers would have been slaves or metics, although some Athenian boys evidently worked as prostitutes, too. As outlined in Chapter 2, while there was no law explicitly forbidding citizen boys from working in the sex industry, what did contravene Athens' laws was for a former rent-boy to hold public office or address the Assembly (**Aeschines C** and **Demosthenes C**; see Chapter 2.8). The mid-fourth century saw at least one (politically motivated) prosecution under this law, namely the case brought against Timarchus by his arch-rival Aeschines in 346–345 BC, and threats to bring similar prosecutions were evidently something of a rhetorical commonplace amongst politicians (E. Cohen 2005, 205–6). Timarchus was found guilty as charged and suffered the prescribed penalty: *atimia*, the loss of his citizen rights. In this same speech, Aeschines mentions the case of another citizen prostitute, an orphan named Diophantes, who appealed to a magistrate to help him recover the four drachmas owed to him by a client (1.158). The fact that he was an orphan might help to explain why he was driven to prostitution, of course. And the fact that he was a citizen might also account for what seems like a large sum if it was indeed paid for a single sex act. Perhaps free-born Athenian youths could charge a premium (just as a premium could be charged for hiring a free-born daughter or citizen wife: **Demosthenes O** and **S**).

How did a free boy ply his trade? Earning a living as a street-walker or touting for trade in bath-houses were no doubt two options (as perhaps was working in a cubicle), but there were evidently other possibilities, too, as Aeschines' speech *Against Timarchus* demonstrates. Given that the account of Timarchus' sexual career was found convincing enough by a jury to convict him (regardless of its veracity), the details of his life sketched out by Aeschines must have had the ring of truth about them – yet this speech offers a very different model of prostitution from anything we find ascribed to a female sex worker. Timarchus' life as a youth (*meirakion*) was allegedly spent residing with a series of different men as a live-in lover, while he simultaneously took numerous

opportunities to hire himself out as a rent-boy, the sexual acts themselves seemingly taking place in private houses (Aeschines 1.137–73).
But despite Aeschines' lengthy description of Timarchus' deeds, his
career as a prostitute would have been short compared to that of most
female sex workers. Since youths were generally considered attractive
only as long as they had smooth skin, the advent of a beard (along with
hair on his buttocks and thighs) would have typically spelt the end of a
boy's career (see e.g. *Greek Anthology* **B** and Chapter 5.5).

Whilst there is no evidence to support the notion that women
frequented prostitutes, we do at least gain a glimpse of a poor, youthful gigolo in Aristophanes' *Wealth* consorting with a wealthy older
woman (**Aristophanes BN**). In the play, poverty is banished, and so
the Old Woman is now rejected by the youth, and the economic basis
of the relationship is laid bare.

3.9 Expenditure on sex

The price of commercial sex in Athens could evidently vary greatly
depending on the type of prostitute that was selling his or her services,
the sex act being requested and/or the length of time a girl's or boy's
services were required. As we have seen, some sources put high prices
on the services of Athens's top courtesans – e.g. a mina (100 drachmas)
demanded as a fee by Phryne (**Machon A**); 1,000 drachmas for a night
with Gnathaenion, the granddaughter of Gnathaena (Machon 340);
or even 10,000 drachmas for the attentions of Laïs (Aulus Gellius
1.8) – but given, as we have seen, that exclusive *hetairai* were often at
pains to avoid the impression of selling their services to clients, it is
doubtful whether these sums represent reality (**Anaxilas B** and even
Aristophanes BN may give some indication of the kind of gifts which
hetarai demanded, however). In establishing the cost of sex we have a
certain amount of evidence from classical Athens itself (conveniently
collected by Loomis 1998, 166–85), which is supplemented by more
abundant evidence that post-dates the classical era (Roman Comedy
providing a particularly rich seam of evidence). Whilst certain patterns
emerge, the figures we find quoted are not always consistent with one
another: here we no doubt have to contend with the fact that prices
varied greatly depending on what exactly was on offer from whom,
and that the sums cited in comedies (our major source) may often be
exaggerated for effect. A further factor to consider here is the effect of
inflation and deflation on the classical Athenian economy (the cost of
a large painted vase, for instance, seems to have risen from about 4–6

obols in the early fifth century to around 12–18 obols by 440 BC, only to fall again in the fourth century: Johnston 1991, 228). While an average wage in classical Athens is difficult to arrive at, the much-quoted figure of one drachma a day at least serves as a guide: this was the wage paid to both skilled and unskilled labourers working on the Erectheion in the late fifth century BC, whereas public office holders might be paid anything from 3–9 obols a day, depending on their role (see Loomis 1998, 232–4, for an overview).

The lowest fee we hear of for sex is one obol (a sixth of a drachma) – a figure which crops up several times (e.g. **Philemon A**), but which many scholars think sounds too low to be a realistic price (e.g. Halperin 1990, 107, who makes the equation with English expressions such as 'two bit whore'). Perhaps a standard fee at the cheap end of the market was instead three obols (half a drachma: e.g. Antiphanes, fr. 293 KA). In a comic fragment this is the fee for the sexual position known as *kybda* (**Plato Comicus A**), for which the woman bends over and is penetrated from behind (a position that was evidently thought ideal for a 'quicky', since in vase-painting it is often depicted as taking place with one or both of the participants still clothed, and which may therefore have been favoured by street-walkers when having sex out of doors: see **Fig. 19**). In the same fragment, one drachma (another commonly occurring sum in our sources) is the price of the position known as *lordō*, where again the woman is penetrated from behind, but this time while standing upright, bending backwards. At the top end of the range was the *kelēs* or 'racehorse' position, for which the man lay down and was straddled by the woman. No source quotes a price for this position, but one anecdote describes a bronzesmith who supposedly spent a vast sum of money ('a large sum of gold') on an act of *kelēs* provided by the celebrated *hetaira* Gnathaenion (Athenaeus 581c–f).

A further sum that crops up regularly in our sources is two drachmas, which, as we have already seen, was the maximum sum an *aulētris* could charge for the evening (**Aristotle B**): not that this is the only price we find charged for the company of female entertainers. In Menander, for example, we hear of 12 drachmas being paid for a harpist (albeit per day, rather than simply for an evening: **Menander E**) and in *Woman from Samos*, *hetairai* are said to be able to earn 'just' 10 drachmas for 'running off to dinner parties' in Athens (**Menander M**: a high-sounding sum, which has generated a certain amount of discussion amongst scholars: see Loomis 1998, 177–8).

We touched earlier on some of the prices involved in buying a sex-slave – the 3,000 drachmas paid for Neaera (**Demosthenes P**);

the 4,000 paid for the perfume-seller's son and his family (**Hyperides A**) – or for hiring a sex-slave under contract (the 300 drachmas spent on Simon for Theodotus, the Plataean boy, for an unknown period of time: **Lysias I**). We have touched, too, on allegations in legal speeches that expenditure on prostitutes has brought ruin on a man (e.g. **Isaeus O**; cf. Lysias 3.17). Such complaints are also to be found on a smaller scale in New Comedy, when older men complain of young men's expenditure on prostitutes (e.g. **Menander E**).

In brief, sex could be bought for relatively small sums of money in classical Athens and more or less standard fees do seem to have operated at the cheaper end of the market. However, buying or freeing a (sex-)slave, keeping a mistress, or purchasing the attentions of one of Athens' more celebrated courtesans could prove a very costly business indeed – and in the case of *hetairai*, the amount of expense a man incurred would not always have been easy to put a figure on.

3.10 Ideology of prostitution

The bulk of this chapter has been given over to a survey of the sex industry in classical Athens; that is, to establishing, as far as possible, what was done, by whom, and for how much. But how can the nature of the sex industry in classical Athens inform us about the society in more general terms? What does it tell us about gender relations and the importance of sex in defining societal roles? In this section, we shall look at four different scholars' takes on Athenian prostitution: a feminist account, a 'constructionist' account, and finally the accounts of two writers who in different ways reject key aspects of previous scholars' understanding of classical Athenian sexual practices.

One of the best-known feminist accounts of classical Athenian sex and sexuality – prostitution included – is Eva Keuls' *The Reign of the Phallus* (Keuls 1985), where the emphasis is placed firmly on the exploitation of women in Athens' sex industry. As mentioned at the beginning of the chapter, Keuls rejects the notion of the glamorous *hetaira*, calling it 'a fabrication of the male mind' (199), a convenient myth whereby Athenian men could 'gloss over the fact that their principal sex outlets were debased and uneducated slaves . . . who were almost certain to end their lives in misery' (200). She chooses to draw attention to the more unpleasant aspects of prostitutes' lives, such as the working conditions in brothels (which she assumes were very poor: 156) and the violence we sometimes see perpetrated on women in vase-paintings (e.g. **Figs 24** and **25**; see also Chapter 5.6). She also sees the symposium as fulfilling an educative purpose sexually: it was here, she suggests, that youths gained their (hetero)sexual initiation and learnt 'male supremacist behaviour' (176). Key to her interpretation of vase-paintings which depict men having sex with prostitutes is her understanding of the significance of penetration from the rear, the sexual position most often depicted on Greek vases. This, she claims, is 'humiliating to the recipient' and so was, along with anal intercourse (which we also find depicted on occasion), 'a suitable culmination of initiatory sex' (176; see also Chapter 5.6).

The power dynamic established by penetrative sex acts is also central to the 'constructionist' account of Athenian prostitution offered by David Halperin in *One Hundred Years of Homosexuality* (Halperin 1990, 88–112: see also Chapter 2.10). In particular, Halperin discusses a belief which was evidently widespread in the fourth century that Solon, Athens' legendary law-giver, had established public brothels in the city in the early sixth century BC (**Philemon A**). Important to Halperin is the idea that the provision, via public brothels, of sex that was affordable even to the poorest citizens can be viewed as 'an intrinsic part of the democracy' (101). And what makes it democratic, he suggests, is that it ensured 'that there would always be a category of persons for every citizen to dominate, both socially and sexually' (100). This bold expression of the notion that penetration *equals* power gives prostitution a vital role in the self-definition of (male) Athenian citizens.

The main focus of Halperin's discussion, however, is on male prostitution and in particular the law according to which a former prostitute could be disenfranchised if he sought to play a role in public life (see Chapter 2.8 and 3.8 above). Halperin sets himself the task of explaining why male prostitution incurred this penalty of *atimia* (loss of one's citizen rights) when other crimes punished in this way, such as failing to repay debts, shirking military duties, and so on, all represent what he calls 'a dereliction of *civic* duty' (95). His answer once again revolves around the power relationship established by a penetrative sexual act: by allowing himself to be penetrated, Halperin suggests, a man 'positioned himself in a socially subordinate role to his fellow citizens . . . and joined instead the ranks of women, foreigners and slaves' (97). By letting himself be penetrated a man has, then, effectively chosen 'to surrender [his] phallus' (97) and thereby forfeits his status as a citizen, who by definition not only owns a phallus but uses it to penetrate others. Furthermore, a prostitute is also uncitizenlike inasmuch as he lets others treat him as they please and allows himself to be degraded by submitting to oral and anal sex (95–6).

The next approach to Greek prostitution we shall consider is that of James Davidson in *Courtesans and Fishcakes* (1997). In this and later work, Davidson questions many of the conclusions reached by scholars working in feminist and above all constructionist traditions concerning not just ancient prostitution but sexuality in general. For example, Davidson rejects the idea that penetration from behind is degrading for the woman (178–9), and far from dismissing the notion of the 'refined hetaira' (as Keuls does), he explores how Athens' big-fee *hetairai* differ from other prostitutes by examining the nature of the public images they fashioned for themselves (109–36). As for the law concerning male citizens who had formerly prostituted themselves, Davidson offers an assessment of the famous prosecution of Timarchus under this law (see Chapter 2.8) which differs from Halperin's reading in crucial respects. Davidson argues that what worries Athenians about citizen prostitutes is that they can be bought and can therefore become subject to another man's power, both socially and economically. Sexual subordination, he suggests, is merely one symptom of this: '[w]hat is happening is a problematization of political friendship in sexual terms, not the problematization of penetration in political terms'. He adds, 'the crucial point about prostitutes is not what they get up to in bed, for ultimately that is speculation; it is that they are for sale' (277).

The last treatment of prostitution we shall look at is that of Edward Cohen, who in a series of publications has also challenged some of the assumptions that he sees as underpinning many scholars' views of sex and prostitution in Athens. In his 2000 article '"Whoring under Contract"', for example, he labels as 'an academic fantasy' the idea that 'the majority of the residents of Attica were wantonly exploited sexually by the adult-male citizen minority', which, he claims, is the 'prevailing dogma' of contemporary scholarship (E. Cohen 2000a, 116). In defence of this view, he marshals evidence to suggest that slaves and foreigners – prostitutes included – were meaningfully protected from sexual exploitation or abuse by Athenian legislation concerning *hybris* ('outrage' or 'insolence': E. Cohen 2000a, 116–23, and 2005, 213–19). Furthermore, he also challenges the assumption that citizen sex workers were such a rarity (2003, 228–31), compiling a catalogue of known citizen prostitutes (E. Cohen 2000b, 167–77; for reception of this idea see e.g. de Brauw and Miner 2004, 308–9, and Glazebrook 2006b, 36–8). Davidson maintains that 'consensual arrangements for sexual services did not evoke moral outrage at Athens' (2000a, 131) and discusses the practice of drawing up prostitution contracts – evidently more prevalent in the case of male prostitutes – which, he claims, provide evidence of 'mutuality and market egalitarianism' between service-provider and client (2000a, 115). This is not to say that Cohen thinks that prostitution was stigma-free, however. Echoing Halperin's 'constructionist' views, he states that the sexual submission involved in prostituting oneself would have been a source of dishonour and humiliation for a citizen prostitute (2000a, 127; cf. **Demosthenes W**). Nevertheless, Cohen's work raises provocative questions about how prostitutes were regarded by the Athenian public at large, how they were treated by their clients, and the sections of society from which sex workers were drawn.

3.11 Conclusion

The aim of this chapter has been to provide an outline of the sex industry in Athens. As we have seen, prostitution was both socially and legally sanctioned in the city and the range of options available to a male consumer of sex was certainly large: from affordable brothel-workers and street-walkers to the pricier options of sex-slaves and live-in lovers and the expense and allure of high-class courtesans. While living and working conditions for prostitutes were no doubt often poor, employment in the sex industry could also bring significant financial rewards for women as well as a degree of social independence unparalleled in classical Athens. At one end of the scale, a fair number of brothel-workers appear to have bought their freedom from their owners, for example; at the other, high-class courtesans are to be found in luxurious surroundings, keeping company with some of the most important men of the day in a way which would be unthinkable for 'respectable' Athenian wives and daughters. For figures like Neaera's owner, Nicarete (and perhaps Aspasia, too), the sex industry provided a rare opportunity in the ancient Greek world to become a business-woman and entrepreneur. Prostitution, then, represents something of a paradox to modern eyes in that it is both an arena in which women were exploited by men and yet also, in some cases at least, a means by which women were able to gain a level of independence unavailable by other routes. And just as the different categories of sex workers in Athens often overlap and are difficult to define with precision, so does the institution of prostitution itself resist easy analysis, raising as it does challenging questions about the role it played in society in shaping not only relations between the sexes but also the lives of the individual women (and boys) involved.

CHAPTER 4

Sex and the Law: Adultery and Rape

4.1 Introduction

Classical Athenians had a curious mixture of laws regulating their sexual behaviour. As we have seen in previous chapters, legislation served to protect boys from sexual interference whilst outside the supervision of their immediate family (Chapter 2.8; as well as being hired out for prostitution by their kin: **Aeschines A**), and the state also played a role in regulating the sex industry, with prostitutes registered and taxed, and rules laid down governing the hiring of female musicians-cum-courtesans (**Aeschines K**; **Aristotle B**: Chapter 3.1 and 3.5). Further statutes served to curtail the rights of members of the citizen class who had formerly prostituted themselves (**Aeschines C** and **N** and **Demosthenes C**: Chapter 2.8 and 3.6). However, when it comes to areas where the law impinged on sexual behaviour in classical Athens, it is two further topics which tend to dominate modern discussions. These are adultery and rape.

The legal position on adultery and rape in classical Athens, as well as social attitudes towards these two crimes, will form the subject matter of the current chapter. Not that these two misdeeds obsessed ancient Athenians equally. Whilst Athens could boast a whole series of laws which pertained either directly or indirectly to the crime of *moicheia* ('adultery') and its punishment, the situation for rape was quite different. Indeed, Classical Greek famously had no word equivalent to the English 'rape', and there is no reason to suppose that rape or sexual assault formed the subject of specific legislation in the city. Instead, the crime that we would recognise as 'rape' most likely fell under the remit of more generic legislation in Athens concerning violent attacks and insolent behaviour, as we shall see. Strikingly, too, forced sex is not universally condemned in our sources and even surfaces regularly as a motif in popular genres. Greek myth, for instance, contains numerous instances of young women being pursued and impregnated by gods and, in the late fourth century, full-blown rapes often form the backdrop to the plots of New Comedy – plays which in other respects are largely genteel.

The structure of this chapter is as follows. We shall first consider the topic of *moicheia* ('adultery'), examining what this word meant to ancient Athenians, the legal penalties which men and women engaging in illicit sex might suffer, and the social realities of adultery, such as the reasons why men and women might indulge in *moicheia* and the opportunities that existed to commit it. A key text here is Lysias' legal speech, *On the Murder of Eratosthenes*, which concerns the death of a *moichos* ('adulterer') who, we are told, was caught in the act and killed by the wronged husband – supposedly in accordance with Athenian law. We shall then go on to look at rape, examining how this crime is portrayed in our sources – sometimes condemned, sometimes condoned, and only rarely viewed from a woman's perspective (and note that in this chapter the word 'rape' will be routinely used to denote forced, non-consensual sex, notwithstanding the difficulties in applying this term to the world of the ancient Greeks; the discussion will also focus on the rape of women: see Chapter 2.8, Shapiro 1992, 64–70, and Kilmer 1997b, 132–7, on male rape). The legal procedures available for prosecuting rape will also be considered, along with other ways in which ancient Athenians might have handled this crime and the possible consequences for both the perpetrator and victim. The nature of our sources is such that ancient authors often discuss *moicheia* and sexual assault alongside each other, sometimes comparing and contrasting the two crimes. And so, one theme considered at the end of this chapter is how adultery relates to rape in the minds of ancient Athenians, and in particular, the question as to whether – as is famously claimed by the speaker of *On the Murder of Eratosthenes* – adultery was indeed regarded as a worse crime than rape.

4.2 *Moicheia* and adultery

The conventional translation of the Greek term *moicheia* into English is 'adultery'. However, as most scholars agree, *moicheia* meant something quite distinct in Athenian law, differing from our concept of 'adultery' in a number of crucial respects. In most legal and religious codes, 'adultery' means the wilful violation of the marital bond and is committed when a man or a woman has sex with someone other than their spouse. To be sure, marital infidelity was a key element of *moicheia*, and the act of sleeping with a citizen's wife – and in all likelihood his concubine (*pallakē*) – would have been classed as *moicheia*. However, the way in which this crime seems to have differed most strikingly from 'adultery' is that *moicheia* could also be committed in respect of unmarried women, such as a citizen's daughter, sister, or any other female relative living in his house and who therefore fell under his legal protection.

So, *moicheia* was a crime committed when a woman had sex with a man without the permission of her *kyrios*, i.e. the male citizen under whose legal guardianship she fell (her husband, father, brother, and so on: see Chapter 1.1). The woman also had to be 'respectable', that is to say, not a prostitute: women who offered their services for money were, it seems, expressly excluded from laws covering *moicheia* (**Demosthenes U**; D. Cohen 1984, 164–5). It should also be stated that the laws of which we are aware essentially concern citizens and their families and so it is unclear to what extent the laws on *moicheia* extended to the wives and female dependants of non-citizens. What is more, unlike their womenfolk, husbands were under no legal obligations to be sexually faithful. Since *moicheia* could only be committed in respect of a citizen's female relatives, a married man who had pederastic relationships with boys, who frequented brothels and/or who had sex with *hetairai* was no more guilty of *moicheia* than one who had sexual relations only with his own wife. And since the question of whether a sexual act constituted *moicheia* depended solely on the status of the woman – and not on the marital status of the lover – a *moichos*, 'adulterer', could as easily be an unmarried man as a married one. The consequences of this are striking: since an act of *moicheia* could be committed in respect of a single woman, it would be theoretically possible for 'adultery' to take place despite the fact that neither partner was married.

Not every scholar is comfortable with the notion that *moicheia* could take place where there was no marital bond to violate. David Cohen, in particular, has challenged this view, pointing out that, if *moicheia* could be committed in respect of unmarried women, this 'would render Athens unique among ancient, medieval and modern legal systems' (D. Cohen 1984, 149, and 1991, 102; see also Carey 1995, 408 and 413). Numerous scholars have defended the 'traditional' view that *moicheia* takes in the sexual activities of not just married but also unmarried female relatives, however. Ogden, for example, points to examples of words like *moichos*, 'adulterer', and *moicheuō*, 'to commit adultery', being used in respect of liaisons with unmarried women in

New Comedy (Ogden 1997, 27) and, as we shall see below, we also find an example of *moicheia* alleged to have taken place in respect of an unmarried woman in the legal speech *Against Neaera*. What Cohen's discussion of *moicheia* neatly highlights, however, is that when classical Athenians used the word *moichos* or *moicheia* it was generally (although not, as we have seen, exclusively) illicit sex with a married woman that they envisaged. In summary, then, while *moicheia* could be committed in respect of a range of women, the archetypical act of *moicheia* for classical Athenians was one that took place between a married woman and her lover.

4.3 *Moicheia* and the law

Unravelling the law on *moicheia* in classical Athens is a far from straightforward task. Classical Athenians could evidently boast a whole host of statutes pertaining either directly or indirectly to *moicheia* and its punishment, with different laws having been laid down in different periods of the city's development. So rather than there being a single law on *moicheia* in Athens, it is more accurate to talk of a patchwork of laws, the wording of some of which is known to us, others not. The purpose of this section will be to paint a picture of the various statutes that are cited, referred to or alluded to in the classical era and which, taken as a whole, served to regulate the punishment of this crime in Athens.

The earliest law which has a bearing on this topic is a statute concerning justifiable homicide (**Demosthenes D**), variously credited to Draco (**Xenarchus A**) and Solon (**Plutarch E**; see also **Aristotle D** and **Lysias G**). This law permits the killing of a man caught having sex with (literally 'on': *epi*) another man's 'wife, mother, sister, daughter, or with a concubine kept for the purpose of begetting free children'. This is evidently the statute evoked by Euphiletus, the speaker of *On the Murder of Eratosthenes*, who claims that the law of Athens compelled him to kill Eratosthenes, the man he caught in bed with his wife (**Lysias F.26**). Euphiletus' claim is clearly untrue: the law merely sets down the circumstances under which a man may be absolved from criminal responsibility for another man's death – it does not counsel the wronged party to kill a *moichos*. Nevertheless, it is noteworthy that the law-maker sees the death of the wrongdoer as a possible and reasonable outcome for a man who has engaged in illicit sex. It should also be noted that whilst this statute touches on the topic of *moicheia*, it is not a law specifically *about* adultery. Indeed, as has been pointed out by David Cohen, since the word '*moicheia*' is neither mentioned nor defined here, this law does not, in and of itself, provide evidence that *moicheia* extended to female dependants other than wives (D. Cohen 1984, 151–2, and 1991, 103). That said, the grouping together of female dependants in such a way that wives and concubines are listed alongside sisters, daughters and mothers is certainly suggestive and has been taken by many scholars to add weight to the view that Athenians regarded the infidelity of female relatives by marriage and female relatives by blood in a similar light. Importantly, too, this statute would appear to make no distinction between rape and adultery; or in other words, no account is taken of whether the woman is a willing or unwilling participant in the illicit sexual act.

A further law we find cited evidently envisages the situation whereby a *moichos* is not killed but imprisoned by the woman's aggrieved relative – and in order to secure his release, the *moichos*' family must either pay a ransom immediately or otherwise provide sureties that the *moichos* will pay the aggrieved man at a later date (**Demosthenes U**). This is the scenario we find described in the legal speech *Against Neaera*, where Stephanus is accused of trying to extract money from a foreigner, Epaenetus, on grounds of *moicheia* after catching him with his 'daughter', Phano (who, we are told, is divorced at the time of the incident: *Against Neaera* 51, 55–6 and 63; cf. **Demosthenes S**). Epaenetus evidently refused to make any payment to Stephanus, however, claiming that he had not committed *moicheia* since the woman he slept with was neither Stephanus' daughter nor respectable. Rather he alleges that Phano is the daughter of the Corinthian prostitute Neaera, and that Stephanus' house is a brothel (**Demosthenes U**). The law cited in *Against Neaera* outlines the legal procedures to be followed in the event that an alleged *moichos* denies his crime after being released (the very existence of such procedures suggesting that the imprisonment and ransom of *moichoi* was an established practice in Athens). If the alleged *moichos* is able to prove his innocence he is released scot-free; but if he is found guilty of *moicheia*, the man who caught him is allowed to inflict whatever punishment he pleases, as long as it is 'without a knife'.

This phrase 'without a knife' has caused much discussion amongst modern scholars. Perhaps, if the punishment was to be exacted in the courtroom itself, it amounted to a prohibition against the shedding of blood (Harris 1990, 374); or possibly it suggests that the wronged party was not permitted to kill or castrate the *moichos* (Ogden 1997, 28). A further possibility is to link it with another set of punishments

we find connected with *moicheia* in popular literature which involve
the humiliation of the wrongdoer. In Old Comedy and certain later
sources, we find some seemingly extraordinary acts mentioned as punishments for *moicheia*, such as the singeing off of the *moichos'* pubic
hair and the insertion into his anus of a radish (**Aristophanes AM**: in
some, less reliable traditions a scorpion fish is mentioned). Whilst it
has been argued that these are simply popular jokes and that such punishments would not have been meted out in real life (Roy 1991), others
think they have the ring of truth about them and emphasise their
potential to degrade and feminise the *moichos* and to stand as vicarious
sexual attacks (Devereux 1970, 20; Dover 1978, 106; Carey 1993). The
circumstances in which these punishments might have found use is
something about which we can only speculate, but one of the contexts
to which they have been linked is the revenge the wronged man was
allowed to wreak 'without a knife' on the *moichos* whose guilt has been
exposed in court (Kapparis 1996, 64).

One further legal provision linked to *moicheia* concerns a category
of criminal known as *kakourgoi*, or 'evil-doers'. From the Aristotelian
Constitution of Athens we can glean that this group comprised 'thieves,
kidnappers and clothes-thieves' and that the law allowed for such
criminals to be apprehended and brought before one of a group of
public officials called the Eleven (**Aristotle C**: on *kakourgoi*, see esp.
Hansen 1976, 44–5). If the alleged *kakourgos* denied his crime to the
official, he was tried in court; but if he confessed, he could be summarily executed. The implication of a passage in Aeschines' *Against
Timarchus* (**Aeschines H**) is that *moichoi* also belonged to this category
– although not all scholars are convinced that this was in fact the case
(e.g. Harris 1990, 376–7; Carey 1995, 411; cf. D. Cohen 1984, 156–7:
crucial here is that the word *kakourgos* does not appear in the passage,
though the other criminal-types listed would appear to qualify as
such). If *moichoi* did qualify as *kakourgoi*, however, then at least two
courses of action were immediately available to a man who surprised
an 'adulterer': either to restrain him and take him to be executed as a
kakourgos; or to keep him imprisoned and seek a financial settlement.
The existence of the law on justifiable homicide also meant, of course,
that the householder had something of a free rein when restraining or
imprisoning a non-compliant *moichos*, since he could always plead justifiable homicide if the man died in the struggle. But while the acciden-
tal killing of the *moichos* was clearly pardonable, most scholars agree
that the summary execution of a *moichos* by the aggrieved husband was
not one of the options expressly offered by Athenian law. This, in turn,

makes Euphiletus' actions in *On the Murder of Eratosthenes* puzzling, since he clearly states that he killed Eratosthenes naked and bound, after the struggle was over (**Lysias F**).

So did adulterers fall into the category of *kakourgoi*, and would Euphiletus therefore have been in his rights to take Eratosthenes to one of the Eleven to be executed? Many scholars see this as likely – and certainly in *On the Murder of Eratosthenes* Euphiletus presents his killing of Eratosthenes in a similar light to the execution of a *kakourgos*. Indeed, David Cohen even makes the suggestion that part of the law pertaining to *kakourgoi* was originally cited after section 28 of the speech, where there is a pause for a statute to be read out to the court, the text of which is not preserved (D. Cohen 1984, 155, and 1991, 110; followed by Todd 1993, 276). Potentially revealing here is that, both before and after the law was read out, Euphiletus emphasises certain details about what went on between him and the alleged *moichos*. These include the presence of witnesses in the house; the fact that Eratosthenes was discovered naked and lying on the bed with his wife; and the fact that Eratosthenes admitted his guilt. Particularly striking is the parallel between the way in which this *moichos* is made to admit his guilt in front of witnesses before he is killed and the procedure whereby a *kakourgos* was executed upon confessing his guilt to a public official. Plausibly, then, Euphiletus' tactic is to present the killing as essentially the same as an execution of a *kakourgos* by a public official – only cutting out the middle man. And in one sense, for Euphiletus' case to be successful it hardly mattered whether or not *moichoi* were specifically included in the Athenian law concerning *kakourgoi*, as long as it seemed reasonable to the jurors for *moichoi* to be treated in a similar way to robbers, kidnappers and the like (i.e. by being executed once they had been apprehended and had confessed: see **Aristotle C**). The trickier case for Euphiletus to make is that he was justified in taking the law into his own hands, instead of delivering the alleged *moichos* to a public official. Potentially revealing here is that Euphiletus concentrates on the details of Eratosthenes' capture and thereby deflects attention from the execution itself in this speech. Indeed, he even fails to specify what form the execution took (**Lysias F**).

There is one further possibility concerning the punishment of *moichoi*, namely that the law really *did* allow a householder to execute a *moichos* who was caught in the act. Should Euphiletus in fact be taken at his word when he says that the law ordains death for the *moichos* (**Lysias F.27**)? After all, there are some passages that seem to support the view that execution of *moichoi* was sanctioned by law in Athens (see e.g. **Aeschines H** and **Lysias J**; cf. **Xenophon B**). There are two reasons why it is less than likely that the law expressly permitted the wronged party to kill a *moichos*, however. First is the fact that if a private individual were to kill a *moichos* this might bring about a blood feud between the two men's families – an eventuality that Athenian law was often at pains to prevent (hence, for example, the requirement for a *kakourgos* to be executed by a third party in the shape of a public official). Secondly, the rhetorical strategy of Euphiletus' defence speech is likely to have been somewhat different if the law regarded the killing of a *moichos* in an unequivocal light. Ultimately, the precise nature of the legal provisions according to which a *moichos* could be punished in classical Athens is destined to remain something of a mystery, owing to the incomplete nature of our sources. Regrettably, too, *On the Murder of Eratosthenes* is the only documented legal case from the classical era where sexual infidelity takes centre stage (and it has even been suggested that this speech is a rhetorical exercise based on fictional data and was never delivered in a real Athenian courtroom: Porter 1997).

There is one final piece of legislation about which we would dearly love to know more: this is the *graphē moicheias*, or 'adultery indictment', mentioned in the Aristotelian *Constitution of Athens* (59.3). The term *graphē* ('indictment') indicates that, in contrast to a *dike* ('suit'), this law provided for the public rather than private prosecution of the wrongdoer – that is to say, the alleged offender could be taken to court by anyone who chose, and not just the wronged party, since the offence was deemed to be a matter of public concern (murder also fell into this category). However, we do not know what the *graphē moicheias* covered. Possibly, Aristotle is referring to a piece of legislation we already know about (this may have been the official name of the charge that an alleged adulterer could bring for unlawful imprisonment, for example: D. Cohen 1991, 122–3). Or possibly, it was part of the *graphē moicheias* that was read out at section 28 of *On the Murder of Eratosthenes* – in which case, maybe the law did indeed permit the wronged party to kill a *moichos*, albeit under certain prescribed conditions (Carey 1995, 412). But more likely, perhaps, is simply that the *graphē moicheias* allowed for the public prosecution of a *moichos*. If so, it would have provided yet another remedy for a wronged party – an alternative to restraining a *moichos* and demanding a ransom (and/ or taking him to one of the Eleven as a *kakourgos*). Indeed, perhaps the *graphē moicheias* was specifically designed to bypass the need for the householder to wrestle with the wrongdoer and to ensure that a *moichos* who had not been captured could still be punished. Most *graphai* fell into the category of *agōnes timētoi*, which meant that, if the accused man was found guilty, each side could propose their own punishment. Plausibly, then, a man convicted under the *graphē moicheias* could face the death penalty, if this was the punishment that the prosecution proposed (which in turn might help us makes sense of passages such as **Lysias J** and **Aeschines H** which link *moicheia* with the death penalty).

4.4 Punishing the adulteress

It takes two to commit *moicheia*, and the law also laid down sanctions for the woman guilty of colluding in illicit sex (interestingly, Classical Greek had no word in general use for 'adulteress' equivalent to *moichos*, 'adulterer'; cf. **Plato N.191e**). We hear rumours of severe punishments in operation before the classical era: under Solon, for example, it was supposedly possible for a man to sell into slavery an unmarried sister or daughter who had lost her virginity (**Plutarch E**; or perhaps pimp her out as a prostitute: thus Glazebrook 2006b) and there is a further legend of an archon who bricked up his disgraced daughter with a horse (**Aeschines O.182**). Laws quoted in legal speeches in the fourth century suggest that a different set of punishments were in operation in the classical era, however.

In Aeschines' *Against Timarchus* a law of Solon's is cited which forbade the guilty woman from wearing jewellery and attending public sacrifices and prescribed that she could be beaten with impunity if she defied these prohibitions (**Aeschines O**). This law is referred to in [Demosthenes'] *Against Neaera*, too, where we also learn that a man was obliged to divorce a wife he had taken in adultery on pain of *atimia* (i.e. loss of his citizen rights: **Demosthenes V**). *Moicheia*, then, threatened to deprive a woman of her home, of her status as a citizen wife (including the fundamental right extended even to slaves of attending religious festivals) and of her social life, too, which depended in no small part on her involvement in religious activities. In these passages the speakers variously highlight the need to keep an adulteress away from other women, for fear she corrupt them; the fact that adulteresses carry religious pollution; and the role that these severe punishments provide in discouraging acts of *moicheia*. In a passage from Euripides, we also learn that women who had been 'corrupted' once were thought more likely to stray again (a passage which also suggests that a *moichos* could be compelled to marry the woman with whom he had committed adultery: **Euripides D**).

To modern western eyes, it is not just the seriousness of the punishments meted out to adulteresses (as well as *moichoi*) that is striking, but also their public nature. Adultery is not just a private matter, to be resolved between husband and wife (although the fact that adultery marks the destruction of a couple's mutual trust is highlighted as important, too: **Xenophon A**). Adultery is also a matter for state intervention, with the law prescribing the termination of the marriage if the wife has been unfaithful. The fact that the *graphē moicheias* allowed for a public rather than private prosecution may also be relevant here: if this law provided for the indictment of a *moichos* (as many scholars assume), then the fact that the state allowed this crime to be prosecuted by anyone who chose to (and not just a wronged *kyrios*) implies that it took a particular interest in exposing *moicheia* and therefore dissolving marriages in which *moicheia* had occurred. This certainly makes sense in the context of the Athenian democracy: when citizenship is so closely guarded, marital infidelity risks bastards being born into citizen households and being brought up (either with or without a husband's knowledge) as Athenian citizens (see Chapter 1.15). What is more, the fact that adultery has occurred potentially brings into question the paternity of all the children born to a woman, since there is likely to be uncertainty as to when the relationship with the *moichos* began – and the question also arises, of course, as to whether the wife has strayed before. Revealing here is the fact that Euphiletus, in *On the Murder of Eratosthenes*, is at pains to stress his wife's fidelity prior to the birth of their son: in other words, he is keen to put the paternity of his son beyond question (**Lysias B**).

4.5 Behind closed doors: the reality of *moicheia*

Legal provisions are one way of getting to grips with *moicheia* in classical Athens, but what were the realities of the crime? There may have been a vast array of legal procedures that could be taken against *moichoi*, but since more than one passage refers to husbands covering up their wives' infidelity it seems reasonable to suppose that these were not always followed (**Euripides F**; cf. **Aeschines I**). The reasons for this are, perhaps, obvious enough. For example, a husband might be unwilling to break up his home and divorce his wife (a process which would also entail the return of her dowry: see Chapter 1.4); or he might be ashamed to make the crime public and/or not wish to drag his private life through the courts – especially as this might lead others to speculate about the paternity of his children. There is mention of money changing hands, too, as a result of adultery – in addition to captured adulterers having to pay for their release, we also find a reference to wives being paid for adulterous liaisons (**Plato C**) and, perhaps more puzzlingly, to a *moichos* practising adultery for financial gain (**Aristotle E**). So there is reason to suspect that, where at least some adulterous relationships were concerned, a deal was struck between the husband and the adulterer to the mutual benefit of both parties. Ogden even suggests that an infertile man might encourage his wife to take a lover in order to provide him with an heir (Ogden 1997, 36). Certainly, too, it would seem a reasonable course of action for a *kyrios* to keep the seduction of one of his unmarried relatives quiet, rather than advertise her infidelity to the world – especially in the case of a young woman whose marriage prospects might thereby be ruined.

The extent to which *moicheia* occurred is, of course, something about which we can only guess, and estimates that a significant proportion of children born in classical Athens were likely to have been adulterine are purely speculative (Ogden 1997, 25). But what opportunities existed for citizen women to have extra-marital affairs? David Cohen is surely right to point out that there were numerous contexts in which 'respectable' women might leave the house and come into contact with men in classical Athens: most notably, for purposes of work; visiting (female) friends, neighbours and family; and organising and attending religious festivals (D. Cohen 1991, 150–4). In Old Comedy we also gain glimpses of how women might have flirted with men and cheated on their husbands (e.g. **Aristophanes BA** and **BG**), as well as the suspicions that men harboured about their wives (e.g. Aristophanes, *Women at the Thesmophoria* 396–417). The classic scenario, however, is for a woman to be spotted by a man at a religious festival, wedding or funeral. Euphiletus' wife, for example, is spotted by her future lover, Eratosthenes, at the funeral of her mother-in-law (**Lysias C**) – whose death also removes a major obstacle to the relationship taking place, since the wife is now no longer supervised in the family house (Lysias 1.7; see Porter 1997, 436). The ensuing affair is then conducted with the help of a slave-girl intermediary (**Lysias C** and **E**), a feature we also find in adulterous liaisons in Old Comedy (e.g. **Aristophanes BE** and **BG**). The (theoretical) examples of adultery we find outlined in two passages in Aristotle, however, suggest that women may sometimes have met lovers closer to home: he variously talks of men sleeping with the wife of a neighbour and a friend (*Nicomachean Ethics* 1137a5; *Magna Moralia* 1188b17).

The reason why men and women chose to commit adultery has also been the subject of speculation by scholars. Given the difference in age, education and life experience which must have often existed between husband and wife, plus the fact that many marriages were probably arranged with minimal consultation of the bride (see Chapter 1.2), it is probably fair to say that not every marriage in classical Athens was a happy one – and unlike her husband, a woman had no socially sanctioned extra-marital outlet to meet her emotional and sexual needs (see Chapter 1.10). As for *moichoi*, it has been pointed out that, given the young age at which women were married, *moicheia* would have provided a rare opportunity for a citizen man to court and have a relationship with a woman who was a social equal (and not a prostitute: D. Cohen 1991, 168). Cohen also argues, on the basis of sociological evidence from other traditional Mediterranean cultures, that a *moichos* 'increases his own status [and] accentuates his masculinity, by dishonoring other men by seducing their women' (D. Cohen 1991, 168). This view is most likely mistaken, however, since classical Greeks, far from viewing *moichoi* as macho or virile, routinely condemn the practice of *moicheia* (Carey 1995, 417) and characterise *moichoi* as womanish men – ineffectual, weak-willed and effeminate dandies (see e.g. Davidson 1997, 164–6; Patterson 1998, 175–6).

We have already seen one major disincentive to commit *moicheia* in the form of the legal punishments which the adulterous couple could expect to suffer. A further potent force in ancient Athens which must have acted both to prevent *moicheia* and to expose it when it happened was no doubt the watchfulness and chatter of the household and wider community. We get a glimpse of the Athenian gossip network in action in *On the Murder of Eratosthenes* when Euphiletus is approached by an old woman who informs him of his wife's adultery (**Lysias E**). Elsewhere, we see girls trying to avoid the scrutiny of other women, such as the young girl we encounter waiting for her boyfriend in Aristophanes' *Assemblywomen* while her mother is away (**Aristophanes AF**). What is particularly interesting to note here is the role that other females play in policing a woman's behaviour. The assumption is often made that it is men who control and restrict women's activities in the ancient world, but as David Cohen suggests, it was more likely that 'women were the primary agents of social control in regard to their sex' (D. Cohen 1991, 160). His arguments here are strong. After all, it would have been from their mothers and other female relatives that girls would primarily have received moral instruction in their childhood and learned what behaviour was expected of them. And whereas men were regularly absent from the home, women would routinely have lived and worked alongside other female relatives in a household, putting them in a position to keep an eye on each other's actions. Euphiletus' young wife makes for an interesting case study here: presumably she found herself under the supervision of her husband's mother in the early days of her marriage and it is, revealingly, only after the older woman's death that the affair begins. Outside the household, too, women's activities no doubt came under the watchful gaze of their neighbours when leaving the house or receiving visitors, which would have made conducting illicit liaisons highly risky. Presumably, even unfounded gossip could affect a girl's reputation adversely.

4.6 Rape: a modern crime in an ancient setting

There can be few better illustrations of the differences between ancient and modern attitudes towards sex than the fact that Classical Greek possessed no term equivalent to the English 'rape'. In modern western cultures rape is a central concept both in sexual politics and in law: it represents the fundamental violation of a woman's (or man's) right to make choices about her (or his) own sexuality and is therefore considered the most serious of sex crimes. The absence not just of a word but also of a legal or moral category of 'rape' in ancient Greece suggests a value system very different from our own and one which it takes careful observation to understand. Yet the very lack of a concept of 'rape' presents a major complication for any investigation of sexual assault in the Greek world, since it is not always easy to determine whether an act we find described in an ancient source (or, indeed, depicted in art) qualifies as what we would call 'rape'. Girls are regularly seized and abducted in myths; pursued by gods on Greek vases; or made pregnant by strangers in Greek comedies – but our sources regularly skirt over what to us is the crucial fact: was the girl a willing or unwilling participant in the sexual act?

In any modern definition of rape the key issue is, then, consent. In western legal codes, rape is characterised by the *absence* of consent and takes place when the victim is coerced into a sexual act against her (or his) will, typically by force or violence. Laws also protect from predatory sexual behaviour those thought unable to provide consent, such as legal minors (sex with someone below the age of consent is termed 'statutory rape'). When the crime that we would recognise as rape is described in ancient sources, however, the unwillingness of the victim is mentioned only rarely (**Herodotus A** is a rare exception here, where the victim is specifically described as unwilling). Instead, 'rape' is typically described as an act of violence or outrage. Most commonly, Greek uses words cognate with *bia*, 'force', 'violence' (e.g. *biasmos*, 'a forcing'; *biazesthai* 'to force': e.g. **Lysias G.32–3**, **Menander F** and **Pausanias A**) or *hybris*, 'insolence', 'outrage' (e.g. *hybrizein*, 'to commit an outrage, humiliate', e.g. **Aeschines B** and, again, **Pausanias A**). Words such as *damazesthai*, 'subdue', *aischynein*, 'shame' and *adikēma* ('wrongdoing') also feature in descriptions of forced sex (Cole 1984, 98; **Euripides C** and **Lysias G.32**).

So, the act that we would call 'rape' is generally described by ancient Greeks using words which connote that a sex act involved force and/ or humiliation and shame. For a woman who was raped, the shame and dishonour engendered by the act could evidently be acute: we hear of more than one woman in ancient Greece committing suicide after being raped, for example (e.g. **Herodotus A** and **Pausanias B**). Crucially, too, the shame and dishonour of rape also affected the woman's *kyrios*, a striking example of which comes in the story told by Pausanias of a Boeotian man whose virgin daughters are raped by two Spartans. The girls commit suicide and their father, unable to obtain justice for the crime, subsequently kills himself, too (**Pausanias A**; cf. Xenophon *Hellenica* 6.4.7).

It is worth dwelling for a moment on the nature of the dishonour suffered by this man since it illustrates an important, broader principle. As we saw in the earlier discussion of *moicheia*, the sexual activities of a respectable woman came under the control of her *kyrios* – a fact which in turn explains the scant interest taken by the Greeks in whether a woman was a willing or unwilling participant in a sexual act: the decision is not hers to make. Of prime importance, then, was the consent of the *kyrios*, and when this was bypassed – be it by an act of rape, seduction or adultery – it was a matter of grave concern to him: he was the one ultimately responsible for the chastity of his womenfolk, his role being not just to control but also to protect. Indeed, this way of viewing rape – as an attack on, and an insult to, a woman's *kyrios* – makes frequent appearances in our sources and there are numerous examples of a *kyrios* apparently conceiving the rape of a female relative under his protection as primarily a crime against himself (e.g. **Menander A** and **Euripides H**). To modern western eyes, this conception of a crime – as an insult inflicted on one man by another – may appear to bypass the woman's experience, making it resemble a dispute over an 'infringement of property rights' (T. Harrison 1997, 189); but this is perhaps to belittle the deep sense of honour felt by the *kyrios* in respect of the chastity of his female dependants.

Needless to say, with an act capable of rousing such strong emotions, rape did not go unpunished. In Herodotus, for example, we find stories such as the killing of the Persian envoys who dared to fondle the wives of the Macedonians at the court of Amyntas, king of Macedon (Herodotus 5.18–21). In myth and literature, too, rape is punished. In Euripides, for instance, Theseus takes revenge on his son, Hippolytus (in the play of the same name), whom he believes to have raped his wife, Phaedra (who is Hippolytus' stepmother: **Euripides G and H**). In the everyday world of the city-state, rape would also have been actionable in law: we know of extensive legislation covering forced sex in the Cretan town of Gortyn, for example (see e.g. Cantarella 2005b), and various legal provisions in Athens could also have been pressed into service to prosecute a rapist (see below).

But rapes are neither always punished nor routinely condemned – in myth and myth-history at least. In an important study of ancient Greek attitudes towards rape, 'Did Rape Exist in Classical Athens?', Harris considers not only instances in our sources where rapes are punished, but also cases where rape is either treated leniently or condoned (Harris 2004). The abduction of a woman by one group can, for example, be viewed as a justifiable retaliation for an abduction committed by another group, providing no real cause for protest. This is at any rate the view taken by Herodotus in the account he gives at the beginning of his *Histories* of the various abductions of women which sowed the seeds of conflict between East and West (Herodotus 1.1–5; Harris 2004, 56). In myth, too, the abductions and rapes of young women by gods regularly go unpunished. What is more, as Harris' analysis of various literary retellings of such stories demonstrates, the abducted or raped girls are routinely shown to have no grounds for complaint about their treatment, part of the reason for which, he suggests, is that their own status and that of their children are enhanced by their association with a god (Harris 2004, 69–71). Persephone, for example, becomes queen of the underworld (*Homeric Hymn to Demeter*), whilst Creusa bears Apollo a son who is destined for a glorious future (Euripides' *Ion*).

The feature shared by instances where rape is condoned is that none of the rapists is presented as guilty of *hybris*, 'outrage', 'insolence'. Either such rapes are presented as a reasonable retaliation for a previous wrong, or alternatively, in myth the girl and her family derive some benefit from her union with a god. So, examples of what we in the modern western world see as a single category of crime – 'rape'

– are viewed in very different ways in our sources, on the one hand smiled on or treated leniently; on the other hand strongly condemned, punished, and capable of rousing a deep sense of shame and dishonour. Ultimately, the act tends to be judged according to its effect on, and implications for, the girl's *kyrios* and family, with any feelings of revulsion a victim may have overshadowed by other considerations. The intention of the aggressor is also important. If a rape is committed with no aim to insult the girl's *kyrios* or clan, then the attack is judged far more favourably than an unprovoked assault designed to bring harm and humiliation to the woman's family. In short, some rapes are 'merely' pardonable misdemeanours in Greek eyes, whereas others constitute *hybris* – outrageous, insolent behaviour, intended to humiliate.

This discussion of ancient attitudes to rape invites us to consider how women were regarded in Athenian society and law. Where, in particular, does female consent feature in all this? As Harris has pointed out (Harris 2004, 61), the existence of the concept of *moicheia* – an act which requires the willing participation of a woman for it to be distinguished from, say, forced sex – suggests that ancient Athenians did recognise that women were capable of giving consent to sex (and therefore capable of withholding it, too). However, the issue of female consent is only rarely brought to the fore in descriptions of rape and, as Omitowoju states, when it comes to viewing sexual assaults as *hybris*, 'there is no situation which is termed *hubristic* where we can see such a definition resting on the lack of consent of the woman alone' (Omitowoju 1997, 6). Tom Harrison, too, makes some deliberately provocative points about consent. As he notes, respectable women's sex lives were controlled by men in classical Athenian society, and since it was a girl's *kyrios* who ultimately decided whom she would marry, there is a sense in which marital sex, too, might also be considered non-consensual (in modern western terms, at least). And so, he suggests, '[t]he scale along which sexual relations were judged and controlled (if we can reduce it to a single scale) was not one that ran between non-consensual intercourse and romantic, reciprocated love, but between one form of non-consensual intercourse and another' (T. Harrison 1997, 197; see also D. Cohen 1993).

4.7 Rape in myth, art and comedy

According to Keuls, classical Athenians were 'obsessed' with rape (Keuls 1985, 47), an act which both she and other feminist scholars have seen as playing a central role in the ideology of sex in the male-dominated society of classical Athens. Paradigms from Greek myth are regularly drawn on to illustrate the points that feminist scholars make. In her study of the *Homeric Hymn to Demeter*, for example (which recounts the story of the abduction of Persephone by Hades), Passmann comes to the conclusion that, in the man's world of ancient Greece, rape represents an idealised form of marriage: '[i]n the patriarchal world . . . the only proper marriage will be rape, because it must be against the desire of the woman; the only proper bride is the intact virgin; the only proper motherhood is that which comes about as a result of rape' (Passmann 1993, 58). For Keuls it is not a rape but Semele's seduction by Zeus and eventual death which serve as a 'mythological blueprint of the relationship between the sexes in Classical Athens'. She explains: 'Translated into societal terms, the male has the power, marries [the woman] at his choice solely for the purpose of reproduction . . . and destroys her' (Keuls 1985, 51). The underlying premise of both scholars' work is that male power – enacted through the phallus – serves to repress women and hold them in check, with rape, seduction and marriage all playing a similar role in female subjugation. Here there is perhaps an echo of Susan Brownmiller's famous statement to the effect that rape 'is nothing more or less than a conscious process of humiliation by which *all* men keep *all* women in a state of fear' (Brownmiller 1975, 15).

Doubtless not all scholars would wholeheartedly endorse these feminist analyses of the Persephone and Semele myths, or the assertion that classical Greeks were obsessed by rape (see esp. Lefkowitz 1993, who argues that mythological 'rape' should in fact be understood as seduction). Nevertheless, the fact remains that the themes of lustful pursuit and sexual coercion recur in Greek myth, art and literature in a way that is true of few other cultures. The case of vase-painting demonstrates an important point, however, namely how the subject could rise and fall in popularity in an artistic genre. We possess over 750 vases depicting scenes of amorous pursuit, spanning roughly the period of 550 to 425 BC. These are initially mythical scenes in which the victim is a girl or young woman, the aggressor usually a hero or god. Interestingly, though, the focus of artists subtly shifts over time, with heroic pursuits in vogue from 500 to 475 BC, pursuits by gods most popular from 475 to 450 BC, and 'ephebic' pursuits (where the aggressors are simply young men, 'ephebes') coming to prominence from 450–425 BC, at a time when the genre was already in decline (Stewart 1995, 74). The dwindling popularity of pursuit scenes from the mid-fifth century onwards has variously been accounted for:

Zeitlin suggests that popular morality in Athens at this time is beginning to stress 'love over lust' (Zeitlin 1986, 131); whereas Stewart emphasises the growing importance in the Periclean age of *sōphrosynē*, 'prudence', 'self-control' (Stewart 1995, 87).

The scenes themselves can be read in competing ways. Commonly the pursuer is reaching for his victim, sometimes managing to grab her, sometimes not. In **Fig. 26**, for example, Apollo reaches for the sleeve of the woman (possibly Creusa) with his left hand and in his right clasps a branch, which lies suggestively across his groin and points between the woman's legs. The woman throws her hands in the air with a gesture that suggests surprise or perplexity, but which simultaneously serves to open her body up to her attacker. Here as typically in pursuit scenes, the woman turns to look her attacker in the eye, her glance thus cast in a different direction from her moving body. The sexual undertones and eventual domination of the woman by the man are perhaps clear enough in images such as these, but scholars have also detected a tension in the two parties: curiosity and even flirtation on the part of the woman; apprehension on the part of the man, caught in the moment before he seizes his victim (e.g. Stewart 1995, 83, who also suggests, however, that such images are less about sex and more about the 'girl's capture and acculturation': 79). When Carson states that these scenes of amorous pursuit are 'ideal representations of normal wedding rites' (Carson 1985, 25), there is an allusion once more to the idea that marriage and rape share the same goal, the subjugation of the woman by the man. But this may not be the whole story. It is, after all, possible to read such scenes as exploring the hopes and fears of both parties as they approach the point of sexual contact – and not simply as a celebration of man's domination of woman. Indeed, some scholars have interpreted the rape myths on which scenes like these are based as being 'about' marriage in a very different way from Keuls, Passman and Carson, seeing them not as triumphalist, wish-fulfilling accounts of sexual conquest, but as largely encapsulating female (as well as male) anxieties about sex and marriage (e.g. Robson 1997). Either way, scholarly approaches to artistic and mythical representations of rape tend to share common ground, in that they see rape stories as providing a vehicle through which ancient Greeks conceptualised and explored the relationship between the sexes.

Rape surfaces in various literary sources throughout the classical age, notably in the *Histories* of Herodotus (see T. Harrison 1997) and in fifth-century tragedies, such as Euripides' *Hippolytus* and *Ion* (see Scafuro 1990 and Rabinowitz 2011). Rape also occurs in the comedies of Aristophanes, where it is often presented in a celebratory light – a form of rough sex where the woman might even be portrayed as a compliant partner (**Aristophanes AA** and **AZ**; but cf. **Aristophanes AH**). In Aristophanic drama rape is 'always projected, never accomplished' and thus 'belongs to an off-stage imaginary world where men can fulfil their urges without causing hurt to anyone' (Robson, forthcoming) – an assertion both of male power and of youthful vigour (Sommerstein 1998, 109).

Perhaps the most striking treatments of rape in classical literature are to be found in New Comedy, however, the best-known proponent of which was Menander, whose plays date from the late fourth century. Whilst it never occurs either on- or offstage, rape nevertheless plays a key role in a number of Menandrian comedies (and this is also true for the Roman playwrights Plautus and Terence, whose works are largely based on Greek originals). The usual pattern is that, at some point prior to the action of the play, a young unmarried woman is raped, usually whilst participating in an all-female religious festival, such as the Tauropolia (*Epitrepontes*) or Adonia (*Woman from Samos*). She then marries, but bears a child which is obviously not the product of the marriage. Naturally enough, this has enormous implications for the relationship: in *Epitrepontes*, for example, Pamphile is left by her husband Charisius when she gives birth to a child after just five months of marriage. However, the couple is always reunited when it is discovered – without either of them realising before – that it is the husband who was the rapist. A variation on this theme is for the couple to get married only after the identity of the rapist has been discovered (Pierce 1997, 163).

Naturally, the nature of these conventional plotlines raises enormous questions about the way rape was regarded in classical Athens. After all, to modern eyes a scenario whereby a woman discovers that her new husband is the man who raped her several months previously is the stuff of nightmares – and certainly not a fitting resolution to a light comedy. So how are we to understand the recurrence of rape in New Comedy? One tack taken by scholars has been to stress the usefulness of rape in plot terms to comedy. If a play's plot is to revolve around a misunderstanding connected to the identity or parentage of a baby (and this was a popular theme in comedy throughout the fourth century), and if the play is to have a happy ending, then the child needs to have two free-born Athenian parents who are married at the time of its birth, since only then will the child grow up to be a legitimate Athenian citizen. Moreover, an anonymous rape (rather than, say, a seduction) allows for a misunderstanding to occur in the first place. And lastly, rape permits the girl to remain respectable in the eyes of the audience in a way that would not be true if she had been seduced and willingly had sex outside wedlock. So, rape can thus be seen as a convenient plot device – although for the happy ending to satisfy it is, in Sommerstein's words, 'essential that the trauma of rape is played down as much as possible' (Sommerstein 1998, 105).

The way in which rapes are portrayed and regarded in these plays certainly merits attention. Whilst rapes are often quickly forgiven and forgotten by the victim (**Menander I**), they are nevertheless presented as distressing to women (e.g. **Menander G**). Rapists, too, often castigate themselves for their actions (**Menander H** and **L**; cf. **Euripides C**). However, the attacks are rarely described in great detail (which has led some scholars to speculate that, in certain plays at least, it is seduction rather than rape that has occurred: e.g. D. Cohen 1990, 148 n. 3; Brown 1993, 197). Crucially, too, it is not that the young woman has been raped that causes her the most concern, but rather the fact that she falls pregnant with what she assumes is a bastard child (no rape in New Comedy, it seems, fails to result in a pregnancy). And this is a problem that can be neatly resolved by her marriage to the child's father – who, as luck would have it, invariably turns out to be a solvent Athenian citizen.

Is the way in which rape is portrayed in New Comedy – and, in particular, the scenario whereby a woman marries her rapist – merely a matter of convention, a 'plot device [which] would have borne no relation to real life' (Pierce 1997, 178)? Whilst many scholars choose to emphasise the stylised nature of New Comic rapes and the standard excuses which rapists proffer (love, intoxication, etc.: see Scafuro 1997, 246–59 and Harris 2004, 43–4, for references), Harris takes a different line. As he points out, until relatively recently a number of legal codes in Central and South America allowed a rapist to escape punishment if his victim would agree to marry him (the law in Peru changed only in 1997, for example: Harris 2004, 50–1). The logic here is that the girl's loss of virginity greatly reduces her chances of finding a husband, and thus the law provides the rapist with an incentive to give back to the girl an important opportunity of which he has robbed her: the chance to get married. Given that New Comedy is often singled out for its realism by ancient writers, Harris suggests that the same remedy may have been made available to rapists in classical Athens, too, and for similar reasons. An offer of marriage would also indicate to the girl's family something all-important about the act in Greek eyes, namely that the rape was not intended as an act of *hybris* (in *Woman from Samos*, for example, Moschion readily admits his fault and makes his offer of marriage to the girl's mother immediately: **Menander L**). Importantly, then, by asking for the girl's hand, the rapist demonstrates that he does not intend to dishonour the girl's *kyrios* and family by leaving them with a female dependant who has lost her virginity and is thus unmarriageable (thus also Scafuro 1997, 239–40).

4.8 Rape and the law

There seems to have been no law which exclusively covered forced sex in classical Athens and, furthermore, there is no example recorded in our sources of an act that we can unequivocally point to as 'rape' being prosecuted in an Athenian courtroom. But this has not prevented scholars from speculating over the legal mechanisms available to punish this crime. As we saw earlier, an act which we would regard as rape is regularly described by Greek writers with words cognate with *bia*, 'force', 'violence', and *hybris*, 'outrage', 'insolence', and so the two legal remedies which immediately suggest themselves for the prosecution of rape in the courts of Athens are the *dikē biaiōn*, 'suit for violence', and the *graphē hybreōs*, 'indictment for *hybris*'.

Neither *bia* nor *hybris* is in any way equivalent to what we would term 'rape'. Indeed, both terms were more commonly used to refer to physical assaults than to rape per se, with *hybris* reserved for an act which, as outlined earlier, had the intention and effect of humiliating the victim. In the Athenian legal system, a female could not prosecute a case herself, so any action taken on behalf of a citizen woman would have been managed by her *kyrios*. Prosecution under the *dikē biaiōn*, 'suit for violence', involved a private action (since a *dikē* was a civil suit) and if it was successful, the wrongdoer would be required to pay a fine to his accuser (not the victim). In Plutarch's condensed account of Athenian legislation on sex crimes he may well be referring to the *dikē biaiōn* when he states that the penalty for rape (*biazesthai*) was 100 drachmas (**Plutarch E**), though this does not wholly square with the puzzling description of this law that we find in Lysias (**Lysias G**).

In contrast to a *dikē*, a *graphē* involved a public prosecution, and so it was technically open to any male citizen who so chose to bring a charge against a wrongdoer under the *graphē hybreōs*, 'indictment for *hybris*'. The possibility that someone other than the raped woman's *kyrios* might prosecute for rape has interesting consequences, of course, since a third party might thus be encouraged to expose a crime of rape that had been hushed up (and exposure of the crime would certainly have been in the state's interests in the case of a married woman who had been raped, since she might otherwise foist a bastard on the city). Many *graphai* fell under the category of *agōnes timētoi*: this meant that, if the accused man was found guilty, each side proposed a penalty between which the jury was then required to decide. Quite plausibly, the prosecution could propose the death penalty, which calls into question the claims made by the speaker of *On the Murder of Eratosthenes*, and later by Plutarch, that Athenian law treated rapists more leniently than adulterers (**Lysias G** and **Plutarch E**).

How could *hybris* be proved? Presumably *hybris* lay largely in the eye of the beholder, and the absence of a judge in the Athenian courtroom to interpret the law meant that both parties in the case were at liberty to construe the alleged crime in whatever way they saw fit. However, the judgement as to whether *hybris* had been committed ultimately lay with the jurors, who, in the context of a trial, effectively 'decided what was Athenian law, at least on that particular day' (Hansen 1976, 47). Since *hybris* was a term that could be applied to all manner of crimes, we cannot always be certain whether any given act of *hybris* we hear of in our sources involved rape. Indeed, sex does not feature at all in Aristotle's definition of *hybris* (**Aristotle L**; cf. Aristotle *Rhetoric* 1374a13–15 and Fisher 1992, 1) and it is adultery rather than forced sex that Euphiletus describes as *hybris* in *On the Murder of Eratosthenes* (**Lysias A**). Intriguingly, we find the word *hybris* used twice in the context of crimes connected with non-citizen women – a Rhodian cithara-player and a flute-girl (**Dinarchus A** and **Demosthenes B**) – but given the broad range of misdeeds that could be described as *hybris* there is no way of knowing whether these were prosecutions for rape (see Fisher 1992, 39–40, and 1995, 69–70, 74–5; Omitowoju 1997, 12–13). Interestingly, the drunken gang bang (gang rape?) of the Corinthian prostitute Neaera is only described as *hybris* once in the speech that bears her name, and since this is in a passage paraphrasing the complaints she herself makes about her treatment (**Demosthenes R**; cf. **Demosthenes Q**), these words (which are, after all, spoken by Neaera's prosecutor) may well constitute a slur – namely that, as a foreigner and a prostitute, as she is alleged to be, she has no right to appeal to the concept of *hybris*. Certainly there is no compelling evidence to suggest that the rape of a non-citizen woman was ever prosecuted in Athens as *hybris*. But furthermore, it is also worth bearing in mind that, for all the persuasive arguments made by scholars that the rape of a *citizen* woman was actionable as *hybris*, we have no evidence to confirm that the law was ever used in this way.

Aside from the *dikē biaiōn* and *graphē hybreōs*, a number of laws already encountered in this chapter in the context of *moicheia* could plausibly be brought into service in respect of rape. For example, the law on justifiable homicide quoted in Demosthenes' *Against Aristocrates* (**Demosthenes D**) does not distinguish between *moichoi* and rapists, and so presumably a householder who killed a rapist he had caught having sex with his 'wife, mother, sister, daughter, or with a concubine kept for the purpose of begetting free children' could claim immunity for prosecution under this law. It is possible, too, that rapists, as well as *moichoi*, could be restrained and taken to one of the Eleven as *kakourgoi*. Indeed, if rapists and *moichoi* discovered in the house were to be treated differently, this would put the householder in the invidious position of having to establish in the heat of the moment what sort of sex crime the man he had caught was committing (a task made none the easier by the fact that the wrongdoer would doubtless protest that he had committed whatever he considered to be the lesser offence). It should be added that, since there was no age of consent in Athens, there was no crime of statutory rape (see D. Cohen 1993, 14–15), just as there was no crime of marital rape (which is even alluded to in a light-hearted context in Old Comedy: **Aristophanes AV**; cf. *Lysistrata* 973–9).

Finally, we come to the issue of what happened to the raped woman. Some scholars have suggested that the law required a citizen husband to divorce a wife who had been raped (e.g. A. R. W. Harrison 1968–71 36 n. 1). There is no evidence either to support or to disprove this claim, but if the law did indeed demand that a raped woman be divorced then it was, as Ogden says, 'unspeakably cruel' and presumably conceived with the aim of ensuring that a bastard child resulting from the rape was not foisted on the state (Ogden 1997, 30). But what was the fate of an unmarried woman who was raped? If the scenarios we find in New Comedy owe anything to real life, then the victim may well have been pressured into marrying her rapist (at least if they both were citizens). For married and unmarried women alike, then, the incentive must have been great to hush up a rape (especially if there was no resulting pregnancy) since little good could result from the rape becoming public knowledge. Not only would the raped woman attract scandal and scrutiny by reporting the crime, but she was also thought to carry religious pollution and risked being seen as 'damaged goods' (in Menander's *Epitrepontes*, for example, Charisius abandons his wife when he discovers that she was raped before their marriage – ignorant of the fact that he himself was the rapist). What Stewart describes as a 'low rape' society, then, may turn out to be a society where rape is regularly brushed under the carpet; and the lack of prosecutions to which he points to support his claim that rape was uncommon may equally constitute evidence that both raped women and their *kyrioi* chose to keep the crime to themselves (Stewart 1995, 77). After all, a *kyrios* might have good reason not to prosecute a rapist, if doing so meant bringing shame and censure on his family, possibly having to divorce his wife and/or ruining the marriage prospects of his female relative.

4.9 Conclusions: *moicheia* and rape

The incomplete nature of our sources means that the precise scope of legal provisions covering the crimes of *moicheia* and forced sex in classical Athens is destined to remain something of a mystery. A particular cause of frustration is that, among the hundred or so legal speeches that have come down to us, none directly concerns a prosecution for adultery or rape. Nor do the scraps of evidence we have paint a picture that is easy to interpret – indeed, in the case of *moicheia* in particular, it seems that Athenians could lay claim to a number of laws, seemingly dating from different periods in the city's social and political development, which offered a whole host of different legal remedies to the wronged party. Perhaps many Athenians of the classical era were, like us, unclear as to what exactly the city's laws on *moicheia* comprised.

Social attitudes towards illicit and forced sex are also challenging to unravel. Perhaps this is less so in the case of *moicheia*, which, with the exception of some scurrilous jokes in Old Comedy, is routinely condemned. However, the crime we would recognise as 'rape' could be viewed in startlingly different ways depending on factors such as the identity of the attacker, his motivation, and the outcome for the girl's family. Here, it seems, the motivation of the rapist and his actions subsequent to the attack are all-important.

This leads us to the vexed question of whether classical Athenians did indeed view adultery as a more serious crime than rape. This is the much-quoted claim made by Euphiletus in *On the Murder of Eratosthenes*, where he states that Athenian law treats *moicheia* more harshly than rape, his reasoning being that, unlike the rapist, the *moichos* corrupts the woman's soul, weakens the bond between husband and wife and throws the paternity of all her children into question (**Lysias G.33**). Harris amongst others has argued the legal claims made here do not stand up to scrutiny, pointing out that Euphiletus' assertion that *moichoi* were punished with death, whereas rapists were only fined, represents a highly selective view of Athenian law (Harris 1990). Yes, the *dikē biaiōn* seems to have prescribed a fine as the penalty for rape, but this was not the only punishment a rapist might suffer – indeed, he could plausibly face the death penalty if prosecuted under the *graphē hybreōs* (and his killing was also permitted, if not encouraged, under the law on justifiable homicide). *Moichoi*, on the other hand, were not always punished with death: indeed, the restraining and ransoming of *moichoi* seems to have been a well-worn course of action in classical Athens, as we have seen. However, this is not to say that Euphiletus' arguments are completely disingenuous. There is, after all, the very real possibility that *moichoi* were routinely punished more severely than rapists (indeed, if the plots of New Comedy reflect real life, then a rapist's 'punishment' might simply be to marry his victim). And even scholars who are suspicious of Euphiletus' rhetorical claims in this passage tend to agree that his arguments (which, we note, focus on marital infidelity rather than *moicheia* more broadly defined) would have struck a chord with the jury. As Harris himself puts it: 'the *moichos* did in a way pose a greater threat to [the jurors'] authority in the household and thereby to their honour, than did a rapist. While the rapist exercised power over a woman's body for just a short time, the *moichos* could win a long-lasting mastery over her soul' (Harris 1990, 375).

It is this ability of marital infidelity to throw a household into confusion which leads it to occupy the position of the 'paradigmatic sexual offence' in classical Athens (D. Cohen 1990, 148). Both rape and *moicheia* can cause an affront to the honour of the woman's *kyrios*; and both, arguably, represent acts of coercion – one through physical force and/or threats; one through mental persuasion. But whereas rape constitutes what Ogden describes as 'a defined and prospective threat' (Ogden 1997, 33), marital infidelity casts a longer shadow for classical Athenians, since it has the potential to undermine the very fabric of the household by casting doubt on the paternity of its children – and ultimately, through the introduction of bastards into the ranks of citizens, threatens to undermine the democracy itself.

What is sidelined in all this, however, is what for us is the all-important issue of consent. As Omitowoju comments, female consent in our sources is 'never prioritised as the central concern for the regulation of sexual behaviour' (Omitowoju 1997, 3), and what instead come to the fore in Greek accounts of rape and adultery are concepts such as *hybris* and (largely male) honour. In this chapter, then, we have seen once again just how fundamental the differences can be between classical Athenian and modern western views of sexual behaviour. The differences between the value systems of the two cultures will be in evidence in the next chapter, too, as we turn to the very different topics of beauty, sexual attraction, fantasy and taboo.

CHAPTER 5

Beauty, Sexual Attractiveness, Fantasy and Taboo

5.1 Introduction

For the Greeks, beauty was evidently a two-edged sword. As we saw in Chapter 2, boys' beauty is regularly praised in archaic lyric, for example (e.g. **Solon A** and **Theognis C**), but we also hear of beauty's downside in poetry of this era: the youthful allure of which pretty boys are possessed can lead a man to lose himself to Eros, leaving him helpless and overwhelmed (**Ibycus A**, **Pindar A**). As for female beauty, while good looks are admired, of course, there is also a long tradition of a woman's attractiveness being viewed as capable of bringing danger to herself and destruction to others (Hawley 1998). Mythical figures such as Helen and Pandora are prime examples of beautiful women who bring ruin and death to those around them – attracting male scorn into the bargain (see e.g. **Aeschylus A**). And another archetype in myth and literature is the alluring woman who derails her lover's plans by distracting him with sex, such as Hera, who distracts Zeus with love-making at *Iliad* 14.161–223, and Circe and Calypso in the *Odyssey*, who delay Odysseus' homecoming. Indeed, these Homeric figures form part of a long line of women whose sex appeal is capable of getting the better of men (with sexiness often seen as going hand in hand with greed and deceit; see esp. Hesiod's succinct warning about money-grabbing, beautiful women: **Hesiod A**). This femme fatale tradition is drawn on and reconfigured in the classical era, too, emerging in the form of the beautiful prostitutes of New Comedy who consume young men's fortunes; the wanton mistresses of oratory; and the irresistible sex appeal of the women of Aristophanes' *Lysistrata*, which they use to use against their menfolk when they stage a sex strike to force an end to the war (**Aristophanes AT**). Furthermore, as Hawley demonstrates in his essay on 'The Dynamics of Beauty in Classical Greece', by the late fifth century, beauty can also be placed in direct contrast to virtue and good reputation. A neat illustration of this comes in Euripides' *Andromache*, where the eponymous heroine lives as a concubine in the house of Neoptolemus alongside his wife, Hermione. As the two argue, Andromache reminds her envious rival that it is virtue which pleases a husband rather than good looks (**Euripides A**; cf. Xenophon, *Oeconomicus* 7.43). By the late fifth century, then, there is evidence to suggest that anxieties about the power of female beauty have developed a moral dimension, the implication of sentiments we find expressed both in *Andromache* and elsewhere being that, for a woman, excessive reliance on, and attention to, her looks can be detrimental to the development of her character (Hawley 1998, 42).

This chapter takes a broad look at what beauty and sexiness comprised for classical Athenians. It aims to paint a picture of the aspects of physical appearance and behaviour which classical Athenians found attractive, seemly, seductive and arousing – as well as sexual behaviour that was considered perverse and morally questionable. Not that this is a straightforward proposition, of course, since we are faced with the challenge of delving into aspects of the personal lives and private fantasies of ancient Athenians which many of them would routinely have avoided discussing in public. The body beautiful was much on display in classical Athens – in statuary, in vase-painting and also in real life, since boys and men trained and practised sport in the nude (on nudity in Greek life and Greek art, see Bonfante 1989 and Hannah 1998). But nudity had its place. It may have been open to a male citizen to show off his physical condition in the gymnasium, but less acceptable for him in other situations – and certainly if a 'respectable' woman should appear in public, her wifely, motherly or daughterly virtues were best displayed through unobtrusive dress and modest conduct. This is a world where both gender differences and appropriate behaviour matter.

In our search for notions of beauty and sexual attractiveness in classical Athens, our sources naturally limit what we can reconstruct. Since literary texts and artistic works were produced almost exclusively by men and predominantly for male consumption, it is (elite) male tastes about which we are best informed. As we shall see, we find clear indications as to which physical qualities were prized in citizen girls, wives and boys, in particular, as well as the type of modest behaviour that these groups were expected to exhibit. Different qualities were often looked for in prostitutes, of course, and the professionalism and exclusivity of big-fee *hetairai* served to make these women in particular the stuff of allure and sexual fantasy (see Chapter 3.7). Not that the line between the citizen wife and the prostitute is always easy to draw. In

vase-painting, for example, the bride becomes an increasingly eroticised figure in wedding imagery as the fifth century progresses (Sutton
1992, 19–20), and many scholars have challenged the assumption that
the women we find engaged in sexual exploits on Greek vases are all
to be regarded as prostitutes (see e.g. Llewellyn-Jones 2002b, 176, for
discussion, and Rabinowitz 2002, 134, on the problems inherent in
the term 'respectable'). In the late fifth and early fourth centuries, we
also see citizen women portrayed in a sexual light in Aristophanes'
comedies (e.g. **Aristophanes AT**, **BG** and even **AD**) – though these
do, admittedly, differ from the full-blown sexual fantasy figures of Old
Comedy who are often conceived of as submissive slaves or prostitutes
(e.g. **Aristophanes AA**, **AZ** and **BK**).

The structure of this chapter is as follows. We will first look at the
cultural ideals of female beauty and sexual attractiveness that prevailed
in classical Greece and then go on to consider topics such as make-up,
clothing and nudity as well as notions of 'appropriate' and flirtatious
female behaviour. Next we will examine male physical attractiveness
and again consider which forms of behaviour in boys were considered
seemly and which seductive. The topic of erotic fantasy will also be
explored and, lastly, sexual practices which were deemed perverse and
taboo.

While vase-painting and the comic dramas of Aristophanes (and
other fragments of Old Comedy) are two especially significant sources
for this chapter, a range of other evidence will be drawn on, too, from
across the classical era and beyond. The chronological spread of our
sources is worth bearing in mind here, since it is doubtless the case that
trends and fashions concerning sexual attractiveness, eroticism and
taboo came and went in Athens in a way that it is now difficult for us
to capture. Certainly artists' and poets' engagement with erotic themes
varied over time. As touched on previously in Chapter 1, sexually
explicit scenes on Attic vases, which enjoyed relative popularity in the
sixth and early fifth centuries, begin to peter out after 475 BC and then
all but disappear by the middle of the fifth century – a full generation
before the plays of Aristophanes, with *their* sexual content, begin to be
staged (see Chapter 1.2). Significant cultural forces were also at play
in the city during the classical era, and attitudes towards institutions
such as marriage and homosexuality undergo significant shifts, as we
have seen (see e.g. Chapters 1.17 and 2.6). These changes no doubt
impacted on other aspects of sexual life in Athens, including the ideals
of physical beauty, appropriate behaviour, fantasy and taboo addressed
here.

5.2 The ideal woman: female beauty and the sexualised body

What did female beauty comprise for classical Athenians? If we turn first to literary texts, what is perhaps surprising is how little attention these pay to facial features, such as the shape, colour or size of a woman's eyes, lips, and so on. Notionally attractive women in Aristophanes' comedies, for example, might simply be described as 'beautiful' (*kalos*: e.g. *Knights* 1390; *Lysistrata* 955) or 'blooming'/'youthful' (*hōraios*, *hōrikos*, e.g. **Aristophanes AA** and **AO**), or as having a 'beautiful face' (*euprosōpos*, e.g. *Frogs* 410). But since the women's facial features are not described the audience is essentially left to project their own ideas of beauty onto these figures (which were, of course, played by masked male actors).

A further feature highlighted in comedy as a characteristic of female beauty is pale skin – a quality which has positive connotations in Greek culture as a whole (see e.g. Thomas 2002). White skin is sometimes simply a characteristic of youth (e.g. Aristophanes, *Assemblywomen* 699), but is perhaps more often used to mark out women as upper-class. Numerous examples can be found in tragedy of the adjective 'white' (*leukos*) being used to describe the neck, throat, cheek, hands or feet of a noble woman (in Euripides' *Medea*, the Corinthian princess, Glauce, has a 'white cheek' and an 'all-white foot', for example: *Medea* 1148 and 1164). Importantly, the pallor of these body parts – all of which were exposed when a woman was fully dressed – was a sign that she spent her life indoors: ostensibly, a modest and chaste upper-class woman had no need to expose herself to the sun by straying from the house or working outside. This notion that upper-class 'good girls' had pale skin seems to have had a flipside, too: in a fragment by the comic playwright Xenarchus we find a description of a brothel where girls bask topless in the sun (**Xenarchus A**) and in another comic fragment, the complexion of street-walkers is unfavourably compared with that of young girls, whose skin is not only of a superior colour but also soft (**Timocles A**; cf. **Aristophanes AE**). In other words, a suntan potentially marked a woman out as a 'bad girl' (a notion that was already present in Homer: see Thomas 2002, 2–6, for example, who discusses how the epithet 'white-armed' is used of co-operative and sympathetic women in the *Odyssey*, but never of seductresses like Calypso and Circe). The positive associations of pale skin even creep into Aristotle's theories of sex and reproduction: light-skinned, feminine women are said to be more likely to feel pleasure and secrete more fluid during intercourse than dark-skinned, manly-looking women, thus making them more likely to conceive (*On the Generation of Animals* 727b33–728a4).

Another way to explore the question of feminine beauty is by examining the many idealised images of women that appear in statuary and vase-painting. Llewellyn-Jones neatly sums up the presentation of female figures in classical Athenian art when he observes that '[w]omen in Attic art . . . are well-groomed, exquisitely dressed, perfect and desirable beings with slim figures, full breasts, pale skins, languid gestures, and straight noses' (Llewellyn-Jones 2002b, 177). Slim women with pale skin and even features emerge as the notional ideal here, then, which essentially chimes with what we can glean from literary sources, one important caveat being that slim does not mean 'skinny': whereas a plump woman may be regarded as lascivious (see e.g. **Xenophon C**), a thin woman was not (Pomeroy 2006, 363). Importantly, too, artistic representations of the female form also routinely lay emphasis on women's sexuality. Clothing is often represented (quite unrealistically) as transparent or figure-hugging, for example, serving to highlight women's breasts and genitalia in what Llewellyn-Jones describes as 'genital maps' (Llewellyn-Jones 2002b, 181). The garment routinely sported by women on Athenian vases is the peplos, which in real life would have covered a woman's chest in a double fold of fabric (Sebesta 2002, 130). In addition, underwear was regularly worn in the form of a breastband that would have served to flatten rather than lift the breasts (Stafford 2005). Yet on vases the outline of women's breasts is regularly visible through the fabric of their garments: indeed, breasts are often to be seen projecting prominently, sometimes with the areola in evidence, too, and sometimes with the nipple erect (Sebesta 2002, 129–30; Llewellyn-Jones 2002b, 185; see **Figs 2** and **21**, and cf. **Fig. 27**, where the flute-player and girl dancer wear see-through clothes). Such representations stand in stark contrast to the way in which respectable women would have appeared in public, dressed in opaque clothing, often swathed in a mantle, and routinely wearing a head-covering to veil or obscure the face (Sebesta 2002, 128; Llewellyn-Jones 2003, esp. 23–83).

This eroticisation of the female breast is evident in literary sources, too. In Aristophanic comedy, for example, we find two dancing-girls praised for their firm breasts, which are compared to quinces (**Aristophanes AC**; cf. **Aristophanes AE**), and elsewhere in Aristophanes breasts are likened to apples, turnips, salted olives and nuts (**Aristophanes AU**; Aristophanes, *Women at the Thesmophoria* 1185 and frs 148 and 664 KA). These comparisons suggest that ideal breasts are compact and firm to the touch, a conclusion confirmed by Gerber's study of breasts in Greek erotic literature, in which he remarks on the emphasis placed by Greek writers on their 'smallness, firmness and roundness' (Gerber 1978, 208). In sexual scenes on Greek vases, breast-play also features commonly enough to suggest that the female breast was a focus of male erotic interest (Kilmer 1993, 26; see e.g. **Fig. 20** where a youth fondles a flute-girl). The exposure of the single breast of an otherwise draped female figure, a common motif in classical statuary, presumably carried erotic overtones, too – whilst also allowing the artist to express ideas such as the weakness and vulnerability of the women depicted (Bonfante 1989, 544–5, and B. Cohen 1997).

Another area of erotic interest revealed in vase-painting is female genitalia. In the case of clothed figures, folds of material commonly form a triangular shape between the woman's thighs (Sebesta 2002, 129) or, alternatively, a dark patch of pubic hair might be in evidence beneath transparent garments (Llewellyn-Jones 2002b, 188). In more explicit scenes, we find numerous examples of what Kilmer calls 'genital display', that is to say, the deliberate positioning of the female body by the artist so that the genitals are on show to the viewer of the pot and/or to a male onlooker on the vase (Kilmer 1993, 141–54; see e.g. **Fig. 18**). Some vases which focus attention on female genitalia give us particular pause for thought. Occasionally we find women involved in what seems to be an erotic dance, clutching dildos: in **Fig. 28**, for example, a naked woman holds one dildo at the opening of her vagina and another to her mouth. Is this purely a product of male fantasy or some form of erotic entertainment put on, say, for symposium guests? On a handful of vases, we also find images of naked women urinating (Kilmer 1993, 109 and 146). Does the genital exposure depicted in these scenes mean that these images would have been considered erotic? Or are these vases best thought of as playful? Playfulness would certainly be an obvious way to read the picture painted on the inside of one wine cup (ARV^2 404 Berlin 3757: R531 in Kilmer 1993): this depicts a woman urinating into a wine bowl – that is to say, a bowl presumably similar to the one from which the drinker's cup will just have been filled. But perhaps on this vase – and others, too – playfulness and eroticism go hand in hand.

Depictions of naked women on vases inevitably raise the subject of pubic hair. We know from literary sources that unkempt pubic hair was considered unsightly: one old women in Aristophanes' *Lysistrata*, for instance, boasts that despite her age her 'man-bag' is not hairy, but rather 'singed clean with the lamp' (*Lysistrata* 824–8). So, singeing with the flame of a lamp was one way in which pubic hair was removed, another favoured method being plucking (e.g. **Aristophanes AO**). Scholarly discussion of pubic hair has largely centred on whether women practised total or only partial depilation. When female genitalia is visible in classical statues, there is routinely no pubic hair on display, whereas in vase-painting, while many women have no pubic hair, others have a neat triangle. So, did women aim for complete depilation or not? In *Greek Erotica on Attic Red-Figure Vases*, Kilmer suggests that pubic hair in vase-painting acts as an age marker for female figures, with adolescent girls' lack of pubic hair contrasting with the neatly plucked or singed hair of older women (Kilmer 1993, 133–41; cf. Chapter 2.2). Literary evidence can be complex to interpret and is ultimately unable to settle the argument satisfactorily. What does 'singed clean with the lamp' mean exactly? Does the description 'mint shoots neatly plucked out' at *Lysistrata* 89 imply complete or partial depilation? The fact that many women on vases *do* have pubic hair, however, plus the fact that Lysistrata envisages that men will be aroused by their wives being 'plucked in a delta-shape' (**Aristophanes AT**) – which surely implies a neat triangle of pubic hair – probably suggests that partial depilation was the norm. To be sure, the absence of pubic hair on sculpted female figures in particular may hint at an alternative fashion for total depilation, but hairless genitalia in art is perhaps best understood as an artistic convention (and one which could also suggest youthfulness).

A further feature of erotic interest is the buttocks. Pomeroy probably overstates the case when she claims that 'buttocks, not breasts, were the most attractive feature of a female figure' for Greek men (Pomeroy 1975, 47), but women's bottoms do nevertheless receive sufficient praise in our texts to suggest that they could hold considerable sexual appeal (see e.g. Aristophanes, *Lysistrata* 1148 and *Peace* 875–6). Pomeroy ascribes male interest in buttocks to what she calls 'the homosexual context of Greek antiquity', but perhaps of more relevance here is the predominance of rear-entry vaginal sex in Athenian sexual culture, which would regularly serve to make a woman's buttocks an important focus of her partner's sexual attention. Certainly rear-entry positions are those in which we find heterosexual couples most commonly engaged in vase-painting (Kilmer 1993, 33–43: see **Figs 19** and **24**) and they also seem to have been favoured by prostitutes (see Chapter 3.9). In sexual images on vase-paintings, female buttocks are depicted from a variety of angles – or are sometimes obscured depending on the precise position adopted and the placing of the couple in relation to the viewer. An area adjacent to the buttocks and genitalia, the thigh, also receives attention in our texts (e.g. **Aristophanes AE**), and legs are frequently shown in outline beneath folds of women's drapery on both statuary and vase-painting (e.g. those of the reclining woman in **Fig. 22** and the dancing-girl in **Fig. 27**).

One thread that runs through this study of the beautiful and sexualised female body is the strong connection between desirability and youth. The ideal woman is 'blooming' or 'youthful' (*hōraios, hōrikos*) with a good complexion and soft skin; she has small, pert breasts and is slender, with firm flesh and either no pubic hair or a tidy, well-tended triangle. Since these are attributes at least as likely to be possessed by a teenage girl as by a full-grown woman – indeed, probably more so – it seems a reasonable inference that the age at which Athenian girls were married (perhaps fourteen to eighteen) roughly coincided with the time of life at which they were considered to be at their physical peak (see Chapter 1.6). Tellingly, we also find these ideals of natural, youthful beauty contrasted with contrived beauty or – somewhat cruelly – with the unattractiveness of old age. As far as contrived attractiveness is concerned, a fragment of a comedy by Alexis details the various deceits that can be practised by prostitutes to disguise their physical shortcomings and to enhance their more saleable qualities: short women wear thick-soled shoes, tall ones stoop; thin girls wear padding, fat ones corsets, and so on, while attractive features like good teeth can be shown off by laughing (**Alexis A**). As for old age, in Aristophanes' *Wealth*, an old woman is mocked for her grey hair, wrinkles, missing teeth and heavy make-up (**Aristophanes BO**; cf. **Aristophanes AE** and *Greek Anthology* **A**). A rare hint that men's tastes in women sometimes differed from the cultural ideal of the slim, young girl comes in a fragment of a comedy by Xenarchus, however. Here clients in a brothel are said to be able to choose from a range of women of all shapes and ages, including prostitutes who are old, middle-aged and curvy (**Xenarchus A**).

5.3 Making up the Athenian woman: the role of cosmetics

Youthfulness, pale skin and firm breasts may have been qualities possessed by some women some of the time, but what of women who failed to live up to expectations? Our sources are generally silent as to what women made of these physical ideals and how much they felt under pressure to conform to socially accepted norms (cf. **Aristophanes AW**, where the negative consequences of growing older are at least voiced). This said, we have ample evidence of women seeking to alter their appearance either with make-up or by other means. At one extreme we find the prostitutes of the Alexis fragment, who are said to go to great lengths to appear more attractive to clients (**Alexis A**), but citizen wives evidently used cosmetics and enhanced their appearance through clothing, too.

The extent to which Athenian housewives used make-up has been the subject of a certain amount of scholarly debate. Much of this centres on the interpretation of a passage in Xenophon's *Oeconomicus*, where Ischomachus rebukes his young wife for wearing cosmetics and raised shoes, saying that he prefers to see her unadorned and with a colouring gained through being actively engaged in household chores (**Xenophon K**). Some have taken this passage as evidence that the use of make-up by citizen women was frowned upon (e.g. Grillet 1975, 97–100), though perhaps what we are presented with here is simply Ischomachus asserting control over his young wife (Pomeroy 1994, 103), or, as one scholar has suggested, a key stage in Ischomachus' transformation of the girl from someone with potential to be idle and deceptive into an active and productive co-worker (thus Glazebrook 2008/9, 233–4). Evidence from Old Comedy certainly suggests that citizen women did wear make-up: it is applied liberally by old women in an attempt to disguise the signs of old age, for example (e.g. **Aristophanes BO** and Aristophanes, *Assemblywomen* 878, 928 and 1072), and in *Lysistrata* it is envisaged as part of the armoury of younger women looking to arouse their husbands sexually (**Aristophanes AT**). A further instance of the use of make-up by an Athenian housewife is to be found in Lysias 1, *On the Murder of Eratosthenes*, where we learn that Euphiletus' wife wears cosmetics – ultimately, it turns out, to make herself more attractive for her lover (Lysias 1.14 and 17; cf. **Hyperides B**). Brides, too, wore make-up on their wedding day (Hawley 1998, 43). In short, while Glazebrook may be right that 'cosmetic use was very much part of the ordinary woman's adornment' (Glazebrook 2008/9, 244), younger women were perhaps most likely to wear make-up when they aspired to be the object of a man's attention and wanted to look their seductive best, whereas older women may have used it to conceal the signs of ageing.

What did classical Greek make-up comprise? The most common cosmetic seems to have been white lead (*psimythion*, i.e. lead carbonate) which was applied to the face and perhaps other exposed body parts to give a pale appearance (remains of white lead have even been found in jars in women's graves, which may well hint that its use was not uncommon: Thomas 2002, 11). White lead is the substance that Euphiletus' wife uses to enhance her complexion and which Aristophanes' old women supposedly smother onto their dry, wrinkled skin in *Wealth* and *Assemblywomen* (see above). The other standard cosmetic was *anchousa*, a red substance made from alkanet root (Walton 1946, 68–9; Glazebrook 2008/9, 235–6). This was rubbed into the cheeks as a form of blusher.

Women made themselves up in other ways, too. *Melan* (a black dye), or even soot, could be used to highlight eyelashes and eyelids or to paint a line under the eyes. In a fragment of a comedy by Eubulus, for example, we meet the image of a black stream emanating from the eyes of an over-made-up older woman on a hot day (**Eubulus C**). We also hear of prostitutes using soot to darken their eyebrows, white lead to lighten dark skin and rouge to give colour to pale skin (**Alexis A**: the opposite of the skin tone to which respectable, upper-class women aspired). It is particularly noteworthy that added emphasis on the eyes is a look associated with prostitutes. Working girls were not expected to behave in the same way as modest women, who lowered their heads and averted their eyes in the presence of men: rather, they drew attention to their eyes and attracted men's gaze. In short, elaborate make-up in general – and eye make-up in particular – is the hallmark of the prostitute (Hawley 1998, 50; see also **Xenophon L**, where again, it is lack of make-up which characterises the citizen wife). Presumably when citizen women did use make-up, then, the onus was on them to apply it sparingly.

Further negative associations of make-up for classical Athenians include idleness and deception. We have already seen how the made-up look of Ischomachus' young wife is contrasted with a more natural look (**Xenophon K**) and she is later given a long list of chores which will aid her appetite and help her acquire genuine beauty (Xenophon, *Oeconomicus* 10.9–11). Instructively, too, the alluring housewives of Aristophanes' *Lysistrata* are also envisaged as sitting idly at home in their finery, rather than engaging in housework (**Aristophanes AT**). As Thomas has suggested, the strategies used by women to protect or enhance the pallor of their skin – namely remaining indoors or applying white lead – can both be viewed as deceptive stratagems, too (Thomas 2002, 11). Predictably enough, perhaps, we also find connections made between women who wear make-up and over-obsession with appearance – a negative quality that women develop at the expense of more appropriate wifely virtues (Glazebrook 2008/9, 244–6; see also the description of Vice personified in **Xenophon C**).

Relevant in this connection is the mirror, which in the classical era becomes a potent symbol of obsession with one's own looks. These objects are associated primarily with women (but also feminised men) and in tragedy, most notably, they frequently portend doom (Frontisi-Ducroix 1996, 53–250; Hawley 1998, 46–8). Once more, then, we find evidence of beauty – whether natural, contrived or merely aspired to – being viewed as potentially harmful both for the woman herself and those around her.

5.4 Clothes and deportment: dressing to impress and walking the walk

Women had other decisions to make about their appearance, of course, aside from those surrounding make-up. A woman's clothing and deportment could also speak volumes about her character. Once more, there are distinctions to be made here between the way in which respectable women dressed and behaved and the clothing and conduct of prostitutes.

The standard garments worn by Athenian women were the traditional peplos and – more commonly in the classical era – the chiton, both loose-fitting garments formed from large rectangles of material, gathered at the waist with a belt. Vase-paintings regularly depict scenes of female dressing and/or undressing (the fact that paintings represent 'a frozen moment of action' often makes it impossible to tell which: Blundell 2002, 145), as well as numerous 'adornment scenes' in which companions help a bride to dress for her wedding (see Chapter 1.5 and **Figs 1** and **2**). The wedding dress, plus the scent, jewellery and distinctive shoes worn by the bride on her special day, stand in marked contrast to the everyday and unexceptional nature of the clothes that women wore at other times, however. The clothing of citizen women receives relatively little mention in our literary sources, unless an unusual garment is being sported, such as the see-through shifts of *Lysistrata*'s seductive wives (**Aristophanes AT**; cf. **Fig. 27**), the man's cloak that Praxagora steals from her husband in Aristophanes' *Assemblywomen* (**Aristophanes AD**), or the saffron-coloured dress called a *krokoton* which an over-made-up old woman dons in the same play in hopes of snaring a young man for sex (*Assemblywomen* 879; according to Dalby, these dresses mark a woman out as 'fun-loving': Dalby 2002, 114). In Xenophon's *Oeconomicus* there is a tantalising mention of 'the decorative attire that women wear for festivals' (9.6). On a day-to-day basis, however, respectable Athenian women seem to have dressed modestly and unobtrusively.

The situation with prostitutes is somewhat different. When specific mention is made of the attire of high-class *hetairai*, the impression given is that they wear opulent clothing and fine jewellery. When Socrates visits the sophisticated courtesan Theodote, in Xenophon's *Memorabilia*, for example, it is not only the woman herself who is well-dressed, but also her mother and her female attendants (**Xenophon F**). In a fourth-century comic fragment we also learn of a *hetaira* called Nannion, who wore gold jewellery and expensive cloaks – a look which supposedly drew attention away from her less than perfect body (**Athenaeus A**; cf. **Xenophon C**). It seems a fair assumption, too, that the street-walkers, flute-girls and other working girls who paced Athens' streets dressed in ways to hint at their trade and appeal to prospective clients. And if showy, eye-catching clothes were associated with prostitutes, most respectable Athenian housewives would presumably think twice before dressing ostentatiously themselves (on the attire of prostitutes in comparison to that of other women, see Dalby 2002).

High-class courtesans may be associated with opulent clothing, but prostitutes are also associated with nudity and exposure. In comedy, we find mention of nude women on display in brothels, for example (**Eubulus A** and **B**, **Philemon A** and **Xenarchus A**), and there are copious examples of male characters in comic drama discussing the naked bodies of prostitute figures (e.g. **Aristophanes AC** and **BL**; whether these figures were represented on stage by costumed male actors or by naked slaves or prostitutes has been the subject of some discussion: see e.g. Zweig 1992, 78–81 and 85). On vases, too, we find images of men inspecting naked or partially clad women in what are apparently brothel scenes (e.g. **Fig. 18**). Relevant here is the debate mentioned in the introduction of this chapter as to whether naked women on vases should automatically be thought of as representing prostitutes (see 5.1 above). There is inevitably uncertainty here, but where there is a symposium context evoked and/or an indication that the women pictured in male company are musicians or dancers, it is perhaps a reasonable assumption that a client–prostitute relationship is being signalled (see Chapter 3.5). The wearing of jewellery by a number of women in explicit sex scenes – a hint of showy opulence? – has also been taken by some to hint at their status as professional sex workers (see Kilmer 1993, 154; in **Fig. 20**, for example, the naked woman not only holds a musical instrument but is also wearing a necklace).

Our sources also provide insights into how women were expected to conduct themselves. A notional ideal was that respectable women took dainty steps, kept their heads and eyes lowered in the presence of men and showed respect to their husbands by remaining silent (see e.g. **Euripides E** and **K**; Bremmer 1991, 22–3; Cairns 2002a, 134; Llewellyn-Jones 2002a, 86–8; Glazebrook 2008/9, 236–7). In public a woman was expected to veil her head and sometimes her face, an action we sometimes see portrayed in vase-painting, where women might adjust their veil or lift a portion of their sleeve to obscure themselves from the gaze of others (Llewellyn-Jones 2002a, 87, and 2003, esp. 85–120 on veiling gestures). Indeed, clutching at clothes is a common gesture in vase images, where women also adjust skirts, fasten (or loosen) belts, bind (or untie) hair in a hairband and stoop to put on, take off or adjust a sandal (Blundell 2002). As has been noted, these gestures serve to underline the figures' industriousness and femininity by showing them occupied in delicate, womanly activities (Llewellyn-Jones 2002a, 89), but the fastening and unfastening of clothes can also have erotic connotations, of course. In particular, the donning or removal of clothing can hint at sexual activity and, as Colin MacDowell notes, the 'constraining effect' and 'promise of release' implicit in the act of the tight lacing of a shoe – or, presumably, the fastening of other items of clothing – easily lends itself to sexual interpretation (C. MacDowell 1989, 73). Interestingly, it is in wedding imagery from the later fifth century that the erotic overtones of shoe-touching are made most explicit, since an Eros figure is often to be found by the feet of a bride bending down to adjust her sandal (Oakley and Sinos 1993, 18). The belt is also an object closely associated with the wedding and the loss of female virginity. Girls traditionally dedicated their belts to Artemis or Athene just prior to marriage – an act which prefigured the removal of the new bride's belt on the wedding night and the opening up of her body to her husband (Blundell 2002, 156–7 and 161). As if to confirm that hair-binding, sandal-lacing or belt-fastening could engender erotic interest in men, when these activities are depicted on vases we occasionally find the presence of a male onlooker (Blundell 2002, 161; see e.g. **Fig. 29** where a woman adjusts her belt in the presence of a youth [not pictured]).

The modest and restrained deportment expected of respectable women, and even the subtle eroticisation of female interaction with clothing in art, can once more be usefully contrasted with more brazen behaviour associated with prostitutes. We have already noted, for example, how make-up was used by prostitutes to draw attention to the eyes, which in turn invited the kind of direct eye-contact routinely associated with bold and shameless behaviour (Cairns 2002a, 128 and 134; see also 5.6 below on the importance of the gaze in conveying *erōs*). In comedy we find further indications of the kind of flirtatious and erotic behaviour that prostitutes practised in order to snare or arouse their clients. We hear of brothel-workers enticing men by calling them pet names (**Xenarchus A**), for example, and in Aristophanes' *Women at the Thesmophoria*, we find a particularly elaborate act of seduction when a prostitute arouses a Scythian archer by dancing, stripping, sitting on his knees, removing her sandals, letting herself be fondled and kissing him (*Women at the Thesmophoria* 1172–201; and while kissing is perhaps mentioned more in our sources in relation to boys, this was clearly an erotic activity that men enjoyed with women, too, e.g. **Aristophanes AC** and **Plutarch B**).

As for the explicit sex scenes we find in vase-painting, it is not just the nudity of the females depicted and their participation in sexual acts that set them apart from respectable women. These women often adopt splayed postures, their limbs outstretched in positions which could not differ more from the closed silhouette expected of a citizen woman in public (Llewellyn-Jones 2002a, 91; see e.g. **Figs 24** and **25**). On rare occasions, some of these eroticised women might even return the gaze of their lovers (as on the cover of this book; also **Figs 20** and **30**). But before taking direct eye-contact in scenes like this to indicate that the women depicted are prostitutes, we would do well to recall that one further context in which we find women meeting men's eyes is in wedding imagery on red-figure pottery – yet another example of the eroticisation of the bride in late fifth-century vase-painting (see **Figs 5** and **6**).

It is in fifth-century comedy, however, where we find the most provocative blurring of the line between citizen women and prostitutes: in Aristophanes' *Lysistrata*, for example, the citizen wives engaged in the sex strike are portrayed as tantalising their sex-starved husbands by means of seductive clothing and sensual deeds (**Aristophanes AT** and **AX**). And in a long scene later in the play, one citizen wife, Myrrhine, teases her husband with the promise of sex, constantly running off to fetch items supposedly to aid their imminent lovemaking, like a bed, mattress, pillows and perfume (*Lysistrata* 870–953; cf. **Aristophanes AD**, where perfume is also mentioned in connection with sex).

5.5 Male beauty: sexy boys and the citizen body

When it comes to male beauty, the important distinction to make is between adult men on the one hand and boys and youths on the other. As far as adults were concerned, there was a clear premium on fitness and athleticism, as the lithe and slender frames of men depicted on Greek vases and in Greek statuary bear witness. Paleness and flabbiness are conditions suitable for slaves and foreigners, not for Greeks, the connection often being made between physical fitness and military valour (see Bonfante 1989, 555; Xenophon, *Agesilaus* 1.28). Indeed, in Xenophon's *Memorabilia*, Socrates chides his out-of-shape companion, Epigenes, for being unpatriotic, since his poor physical condition is unsuited for defending his homeland by military service (**Xenophon G**). Like other Greek states, Athens held its own (male) beauty contests to determine which men would head up religious processions and also staged the much-vaunted Euandria as part of its annual Panathenaia festival. The Euandria was a contest of 'manliness' for Athenians only, and seems to have placed at least as much emphasis on bodily strength and ability as on beauty, promoting Athenian ideals of what one scholar calls 'aesthetic and physical excellence' (Wilson 2000, 38; see also Hawley 1998, 39).

In classical Athenian culture, it was not generally as adults that males were considered sexually attractive by other men, but rather as pubescent boys and youths, with a boy's sexual allure diminishing at the point when he started to grow facial and body hair (see also Chapter 2.2). Since the period during which a youth was desirable was so short (as few as four or five years according to one late source: *Greek Anthology* **B**; cf. **Theognis B**), it was a seller's market, the supply of suitable boys never destined to meet the demand of potential admirers (*erastai*). One pin-up boy of the late fifth century was Charmides, the effects of whose beauty on his many fans are described in Plato's dialogue of the same name (**Plato A** and **B**). As with notionally beautiful women, it is noteworthy that physical descriptions of ideal youths such as that offered here by Plato do not include specifics such as the shape and colour of Charmides' eyes, his hair colour or even his height – readers are merely informed of his 'stature' and 'beauty' and the perfection of his naked body, with the rest left to the imagination (for a rare discussion of facial features, see Xenophon, *Symposium* 5, the mock 'beauty contest'). Charmides' body, which is portrayed as so mesmerising, would no doubt have been the product of training in the gymnasium. Although, as Osborne discusses in *The History Written* *on the Classical Greek Body*, body-building is unlikely to have been the primary aim of exercise (Osborne 2011, 27–54), the ideal youth might nevertheless be expected to have a well-developed chest, shoulders and buttocks (**Aristophanes AL**; cf. [Demosthenes] *Erotic Essay* 10, where a boy's 'beauty', 'colouring' and shining skin are the qualities singled out for praise). Interestingly, while in homoerotic pairings in black-figure vase-painting the muscularity of the younger partners is often marked (see **Figs 8** and **9**), in red-figure this is less the case – although the boys depicted remain 'what we would call "fit"', as one scholar puts it (Lear and Cantarella 2008, 63–4; see e.g. **Figs 12**, **13** and **16**). Such are the erotic associations of the gymnasium that the smell of olive oil rubbed onto the skin by athletes and the sweat of male exertion also seem to have had their own allure (**Xenophon M**).

Among the body parts mentioned most often in connection with beautiful boys are their mouths and thighs (**Aeschylus B**, **Anacreon B** and **Solon A**). Mouths are connected with the erotic act of kissing, of course (**Aristophanes AG**, **Aeschylus B** and **Athenaeus B**), an activity regularly depicted in homosexual courtship scenes (e.g. **Fig. 7**). Thighs, on the other hand, are connected with intercrural sex (i.e. the position we find adopted most often by same-sex partners in vase-painting, where the older partner inserts his penis between the younger partner's thighs, e.g. **Figs 9**, **10** and **11**: see Chapter 2.3). Boy's testicles also come in for praise in comedy (**Aristophanes AQ**), the act of fingering a boy's balls featuring in one particularly elaborate seduction fantasy in Aristophanes' *Birds* (**Aristophanes AG**) – a passage which offers striking parallels with some of the courtship scenes in vase-painting where *erastai* similarly reach for boys' testicles (see Chapter 2.3 and **Fig. 8**). Aside from touching, there is pleasure to be had simply in looking at a boy's genitalia (**Aristophanes BJ**), the mere imprint of which in the sand can be arousing (**Aristophanes AK**). As for the ideal Greek penis, it is funnel-shaped, uncircumsised – and small (see e.g. **Aristophanes AL** and **Figs 8**, **9** and **15**; cf. Aristotle, *Generation of Animals* 718a23, where a large penis is linked with male infertility). In vase-painting, large penises are associated with the kind of lack of control displayed by sexually voracious satyrs (animal-like human figures with horse's tails: **Fig. 31**), or with old or ugly men (see Bonfante 1989, 551; Lear and Cantarella 2008, 64–5, and Stafford 2011, 346) – the very antithesis of the ideal of the attractive boy possessed of self-control (*sōphrosynē*). The small penis was a potent symbol of youth and modesty to such an extent that not only boys but adult men, too, are often depicted on vases with 'idealised' immature genitalia (Beazley 1950, 321: Lear and

Cantarella 2008, 64–5). In scenes of homosexual courtship and sex, the courted boy is nearly always portrayed with a flaccid penis, his lack of erection emphasising once again the qualities of modesty and self-control that ideal youths possess (Lear and Cantarella 2008, 65, who note only two exceptions to this rule: see also Chapter 2.3; see **Figs 8** and **10**, but cf. **Fig. 9** where the central youth's penis is, arguably, semi-erect).

It is noteworthy, too, that desirable boys and youths are regularly described in similar ways to notionally attractive women and girls. The fact that, in Aristophanes' comedies, we find adjectives such as 'blooming'/'youthful' (*hōraios*, e.g. **Aristophanes AG**) and 'beautiful' (*kalos*: *Assemblywomen* 626–8) applied to males may not be particularly surprising (cf. also **Aristophanes BN** and Chapter 2.4), but more unexpected perhaps is the description of a strapping youth's hand praised as 'soft' (*Wasps* 554). The association of beautiful boys with feminine characteristics is particularly apparent in sympotic poetry, where we find examples of attractive boys described as having a 'maidenish glance' (**Anacreon A**) or 'smooth cheek' (**Theognis C**). In their modest behaviour, too, boys resemble women in that – on courtship scenes on red-figure vases, for example – they are frequently depicted as casting their eyes to the ground, unlike the lover/admirer (*erastēs*), who looks directly at the object of his affection (Hubbard 2002, 273). Not that this convention is always adhered to, however, since on occasion we do find examples of the boy meeting his lover's gaze (see **Fig. 7**, where the level of visual interaction between the different couples varies considerably). As Hubbard indicates, eye-contact is highly suggestive in the context of homoerotic flirtation, where a number of things might thereby be signalled, such as 'reciprocated interest and admiration, contemptuous or fearful rejection, hope of material gain, or a superior self-assurance grounded in knowledge of his control over an insecure fan' (Hubbard 2002, 280). As Cairns shows, the gaze plays a key role in conveying *erōs* in both homosexual and heterosexual contexts (Cairns 2002a, 132–3; **Plato I**): the lover is inflamed by desire at the site of the beloved (**Pindar A, Sappho A**), whose reciprocated glance – as we learn in the case of Charmides – can have a devastating effect on an admirer (**Plato B**; cf. Xenophon, *Symposium* 1.9–10). Other forms of flirtatious behaviour we find connected with boys include the softening of the voice, giggling, crossing one's feet and eating phallic-shaped vegetables (**Aristophanes AK**; cf. **Aristophanes AX**).

While we are relatively well placed to judge what characteristics men prized in youths, we have very few indications as to what women looked for in men. Some rare insights come once again in Aristophanes, where, for example, one older woman describes her former toy boy (*meirakion*) as 'attractive (*euprosōpos*), handsome (*kalos*) and decent' (**Aristophanes BN**), while in *Assemblywomen*, Praxagora differentiates between 'good-looking' (*euprepēs*) 'youths' (*meirakia*) and men who are more 'plain'/'vulgar' (*phaulos*), 'snub-nosed' (*simos*) and 'ugly' (*aischros*) (*Assemblywomen* 702–5). Aristophanes also provides us with an indication of which characteristics were considered inappropriate in an adult man. The supposedly effeminate tragic poet Agathon, for example (**Aristophanes BB**), is said to be beardless, fresh-faced, pale, high-voiced, soft-skinned – and, interestingly, 'attractive' (*euprepēs*) (**Aristophanes BC**; cf. **Aristophanes BH**). Good looks aside, the qualities he possesses are certainly unmanly, but most of them would nevertheless be prized in a boy.

5.6 Erotica and sexual fantasy: the case of red-figure pottery

Glimpses of the sexual proclivities and erotic fantasies of Athenian citizens are perhaps best gained by studying vase-painting and comic drama. The context of these two media could hardly be more different, of course. While Aristophanes' plays, and the sexually suggestive scenes they commonly contain, were performed to audiences of over 10,000 in the Theatre of Dionysus at Athens, vase-painting was a more private medium, the vast majority of pots with erotic themes being produced for use at the symposium. These explicit sexual scenes have been much discussed by scholars over the years, but in fact account for only a fraction of the total output of Athenian vase-painters. Of the 30,000–40,000 pots which survive up to the modern day, only about 150 show figures engaged in sexual activity (Sutton 1992, 7). These few vases nevertheless depict a broad range of sexual activities from group sex and sadism to fellatio, anal sex and masturbation, in both heterosexual and homosexual contexts.

Kilmer's 1993 book on *Greek Erotica* looks specifically at the sexual scenes on red-figure vases (which begin to be produced in Athens from about 525 BC onwards). His analysis of these paintings shows some important trends, such as the prevalence of rear-entry sex in heterosexual couplings, the general absence of eye-contact achieved between partners, even when the man penetrates the woman from the front, and the failure of these vase-painters to represent cunnilingus (although there is a possible example on an earlier black-figure vase, Florence V 34; see Kilmer 1993, 2, and Kurke 1997, 133–5). Kilmer also highlights the predominance in group sex scenes of the trio comprising one woman and two men – never the other way round – and the fact that in red-figure the males depicted as engaged in group sex tend to be youths rather than bearded men (orgy scenes are more characteristic of earlier black-figure vases, where bearded men regularly feature; **Figs 24** and **25** feature both men *and* youths). Interestingly, in group sex scenes there is often a symposium setting evoked through items such as wine cups or wine containers (Kilmer 1993, 57–8). The extent to which sexual acts such as these took place at real-life drinking parties is open to debate, however: as Stafford suggests, athletic couplings may have happened on occasion at symposia, but these images most probably contain 'a large element of fantasy' (Stafford 2011, 355; cf. Dover 1974, 206, who concludes that it would have been shameful to be seen having sex in public).

A notable feature of sex scenes on vases is the frequency with which apparently sadistic acts are portrayed. In a number of vase-paintings, we find a man poised to strike a woman with a slipper or sandal, for example (as Blundell points out, the fact that Greek had a verb, *blautoō*, meaning 'to beat with a slipper' implies that this was not such an uncommon occurrence: Blundell 2002, 150). As Kilmer observes, the sandal features most commonly in what he calls 'heterosexual foreplay' when three-way sex is taking place, and it regularly finds use as a 'persuader' to coerce the woman into an act of fellatio (a flute occasionally finds use as a weapon, instead: Kilmer 1993, 110, 109 and 124–5). Whilst no doubt enjoyable for the man, oral sex was evidently seen as unpleasant for the giver, and women are nearly always depicted as performing the act under compulsion or with the threat of violence (Kilmer 1993, 71). On one vase, sympotic youths are fellated by a trio of apparently middle-aged women, all of whom are arguably depicted as being coerced into the act (one is beaten by a slipper, another has her head held in place by a youth's arm: **Fig. 24**), and all of whom are simultaneously penetrated by another man from behind. The stretch marks clearly visible around the women's mouths seem to indicate their discomfort as they try to accommodate the oversized penises.

Scholars tend to agree that not just oral but also anal sex was seen as degrading for the partner being penetrated (in homoerotic contexts, vase-painters only rarely portray anal sex and scrupulously avoid depicting oral sex between human males: Sutton 1992, 14; Lear and Cantarella 2008, 115–27; cf. **Fig. 31**). In practice, owing to the small scale of the images it is often difficult to tell when anal rather than vaginal sex is being portrayed in heterosexual scenes, though in one painting where a man is telling his partner to 'hold still' (*heche* *hēsychos*), it would certainly appear that it is the act of anal sex that is causing the woman discomfort (**Fig. 32**). But even if anal sex is to be viewed as 'demeaning' for the woman (thus Sutton 1981, 88–96; Keuls 1985, 174–5; Shapiro 1992, 58; Zweig 1992, 84; cf. Henderson 1991, 51–4), that is not to say that it was an act that women never engaged in willingly. As Kilmer points out, 'anal copulation was one of the most reliable birth-control methods available', which may plausibly have led to it being performed not only between prostitutes and their clients but also by some married couples (Kilmer 1993, 34).

In addition to acts of copulation, we also find solo performances on vases. Women are to be seen clutching dildos, sometimes more than one at a time, in scenes which seem to be catering to male fantasy (see also **Aristophanes AS** and Rabinowitz 2002, 145–6; women are only very infrequently to be found engaging in acts of clitoral stimulation: see Kilmer 1993, 64–6 and 99–101). Curiously, dildos in vase-painting are regularly depicted with a scrotum, testicles, retractable foreskin and even an eye painted on the glans (**Fig. 28**, for example, displays all of these except the scrotum). We also find examples of object insertion (e.g. a flute-girl straddling an up-turned amphora, the tip of which disappears inside her vagina: the now lost ARV² 65 = R114 in Kilmer 1993). Interestingly, vase painters tend to avoid depicting explicit lesbian sex acts (Kilmer 1993, 26–30; **Fig. 17** is perhaps a rare exception here), although scenes showing physical contact and affection between women are common enough (Rabinowitz 2002).

Male homoerotic imagery, by contrast, features regularly on Athenian vases. As outlined in Chapter 2, the focus here tends to be on the pederastic courtship of a youth or boy (the *erōmenos*) by an older partner (the *erastēs*: see Chapter 2.2 and 2.3). The sexuality of such scenes is characteristically restrained, however, with fewer than 5 per cent of surviving homoerotic scenes portraying acts of consummation (Lear and Cantarella 2008, 106). In pederastic couplings, intercrural sex is the norm, the *erōmenos* generally depicted as impassive and almost never as sexually aroused (as noted in 5.5 above, Lear and Cantarella 2008, 65, count only two instance of *erōmenoi* with erections; cf. DeVries 1997, who identifies images where boys display affection towards their lovers). Indeed, only very rarely do we find 'rule-breaking' scenes of anal sex between males, or of wild orgies between revelling youths, or any hints of sadism, to compare with the content of the heterosexual images discussed above (see Chapter 2.3 and **Figs 10** and **13**).

Interestingly, then, there seem to be protocols governing the depiction of sex acts between men and boys which do not apply in respect of sex between men and women, and this in turn has implications for how we read sexual images. Many scholars emphasise the way in which mutuality is often lacking in heterosexual scenes, for example, and how hostility is displayed towards women, who are frequently 'used impersonally, as mere sexual tools' (Sutton 1992, 11). For Frontisi-Ducroix, the rear-entry position adopted in heterosexual pairings is significant, too, in that it generally results not only in a lack of eye-contact between the couple but also, she claims, 'a lack of comfort for the woman' (Frontisi-Ducroix 1996, 84). And as for sadistic and group-sex scenes, Shapiro talks of the 'explicit abuse and degradation of the women involved' (Shapiro 1992, 54).

As numerous scholars have suggested, then, there is good reason to see in images of heterosexual sex the pornographic objectification of women. But this said, it is probably unwise to cast all of our images in exactly the same light: that is to say, pornographic objectification may sometimes be black and white, but it arguably comes in a number of shades of grey, too. To nuance our picture a little, it is worth bearing in mind that mutuality between men and women *is* occasionally expressed on our vases, for example (e.g. in the image on the front of this book). And importantly, some of the assumptions lying behind the degradation model have been questioned, too. Davidson, for instance, challenges the notion of rear-entry sex being impersonal or degrading for the woman; instead, he suggests that 'rear-entry sex was not bestial or humiliating, but lewd' – that is to say, sexy rather than sexist (Davidson 1997, 179). As for sadistic scenes, Kilmer even proposes that a man's use of a slipper to strike his partner during sex would not just enhance his own pleasure, but 'might also contribute to the woman's enjoyment of the occasion' (Kilmer 1993, 115). On a more mundane level, if painters were minded to convey female discomfort, they might have been less keen to paint women as lying, kneeling or supported on cushions during sex, as is often the case (see e.g. **Fig. 30**). Relevant, too, when considering images of heterosexual sex is the reputation that women enjoyed in ancient Greece for being, as one scholar puts it, 'sexually insatiable once aroused' (Carson 1990, 138). This may be a sexist stereotype catering to male fantasy (and one that can no doubt conveniently be called upon by men to condone abusive behaviour) but it is also, significantly, an image of women that sees them as active and enthusiastic participants in sexual acts rather than as passive victims of male sexual desire (cf. **Aristophanes BG**). Lastly, Sutton raises some particularly thought-provoking questions about the nature of pornographic images (if this is how we choose to categorise sexually explicit vase-paintings) when he points out the existence of two distinct models for understanding pornography's effects. One is what he calls the '*peitho*' model, which essentially sees viewers persuaded to emulate what they see; the other the '*catharsis*' model, which sees pornography as providing a release for potentially dangerous fantasies and passions (Sutton 1992, 6–7). He leaves it to his readers to judge what kind of viewers the ancient Athenians might have been.

Other, less explicit aspects of sexual fantasy that surface on Greek vases also merit brief mention. One is the pursuit scene, which usually takes the form of a god, hero or young man chasing a girl or young woman (see 4.7 and **Fig. 26**), although we also find this theme reconfigured as the homoerotic pursuit by Zeus of the beautiful boy Ganymede, and, more subversively, as the pursuit of a young man by Eos, goddess of the dawn (see Shapiro 1992, 61–9 and esp. Osborne 1996). The full or partial nudity of idealised male and female figures on vases could be said to hold erotic potential, too, as could scenes depicting wedding and adornment imagery, or those where male onlookers observe women dressing or performing chores (Blundell and Rabinowitz 2008, 128–35; Keuls 1985, 235–59; Blundell 2002, 130). In a more obviously sexual vein, satyrs form a special category on Greek vases, regularly to be found stalking maenads (female followers of Dionysus) or engaged in athletic and/or 'rule-breaking' sexual activities, such as homosexual anal sex or fellatio (**Fig. 31**). Satyrs are characterised by their sexual incontinence and oversized penises – the very antithesis of the modest and moderate, ideal youth (see Lissarague 1990).

5.7 Wish fulfilment and sexual fantasy: the case of Old Comedy

The comic plays of Aristophanes, dating from the late fifth and early fourth centuries, are a particularly rich repository of sexual fantasy. Aristophanes' comedies are generally built around the premise of a low-status figure – most commonly a disgruntled old man – coming up with a brazen scheme which allows him radically to change his own personal circumstances, and sometimes those of the broader community, for the better. Dicaeopolis in *Acharnians* and Trygaeus in *Peace*, for example, both secure peace in time of war – Dicaeopolis just for himself and his family, Trygaeus for Greece as a whole. Dicaeopolis and Trygaeus are both poor, uneducated rustics, who in the theatre would have been played by actors wearing grotesque masks with padded bellies and rumps. Yet despite the fact that such figures would possess none of the charms of youth, wealth, culture or beauty, in Aristophanes' comedies they come to enjoy all manner of sexual benefits as reward for their efforts. Dicaeopolis is able to enjoy the company of two sexually compliant dancing-girls in the final scene of the play, for example (**Aristophanes AC**), whilst Trygaeus gets to marry the beautiful young Harvest (Opōra). These fantasies are highly unrealistic, to be sure, but in one sense this makes their appeal all the more broad: no man in the audience – however old, poor or ugly – is precluded from imagining himself in Dicaeopolis' or Trygaeus' position. The formula of 'old man *plus* young girl' was evidently popular with theatre audiences, since Aristophanes presents us with reinvigorated old men enjoying the attentions of sexually submissive young women in a number of his plays.

Dicaeopolis' dancing-girls; Trygaeus' enticing bride, Harvest; the figure of Reconciliation in *Lysistrata*; and a series of other sexually compliant women make up the category of what Zweig calls 'mute, nude, female characters' in Aristophanes (Zweig 1992). These female fantasy figures are given no personality in the plays beyond being sexually available objects, and stand by as passive onlookers while male characters discuss their physical attributes (**Aristophanes AC**), articulate sexual fantasies (**Aristophanes AZ**), ask them to perform sexual services (**Aristophanes BK**) and discuss them as if they were inanimate objects (**Aristophanes BL**; *Lysistrata* 1114–88). Zweig suggests that the episodes in which these women feature would not only have 'vividly confirmed male assertions of social supremacy and control' but also have helped to produce 'a social environment that condoned and encouraged hostile attitudes and violent actions against women' (Zweig 1992, 85 and 88). While Zweig's analysis is a useful lens through which to look at these scenes, it is also worth bearing in mind that sexual fantasies in Aristophanes are almost exclusively presented in a celebratory rather than a triumphalist light (Robson 2009, 137). That is to say, a power relationship between the men and women may well be in evidence in these scenes, but an essential part of the fantasy is that the women are presented as willing participants and not passive victims (see also Robson, forthcoming, on sexual assault fantasies in Aristophanes which are characteristically described in a similarly upbeat way, e.g. **Aristophanes AA** and **AZ**; but cf. **Aristophanes AH**). It is also worth noting that the naked, fantasy figures in Aristophanes tend to be characterised as prostitutes (e.g. Dicaeopolis' dancing-girls in *Acharnians*; the flute-girl in *Wasps*), that is, as professional sex workers with experience of dealing with men and their sexual demands.

Athenian housewives also feature in the plays in a sexual light, the comic stereotype of citizen women which emerges at the end of the fifth century being that they are fond of drink, dishonest and sex mad (Robson 2009, 82–91). In *Thesmophoriazusae*, for example, we hear of some of the outrageous sexual exploits in which Athenian wives supposedly indulge (**Aristophanes BE** and **BG**), whilst in *Lysistrata*, the women are portrayed as initially seeing the proposed sex strike as a far from appealing prospect and, once it is under way, finding it difficult to maintain (*Lysistrata* 125–44 and 717–57).

There are also more subdued sexual fantasies and sexual pleasures to be found in Aristophanes' plays. Male pleasures can range from glimpsing a woman looking out of a window (**Aristophanes BI**), to exchanging a glance with a girl whose breast is poking out of a torn dress (*Frogs* 409–12), to kissing a slave-girl while the wife is in the bath (*Peace* 1138–9; cf. **Lysias D**). Alongside heterosexual encounters, we occasionally find homosexual pleasures as the object of fantasy, too, such as looking at boys' 'private parts' (**Aristophanes BJ**) or kissing a willing boy and fondling his testicles (**Aristophanes AG**). Lesbianism does not feature in our surviving plays, however, as a topic of male fantasy or otherwise. As for masturbation, the women in *Lysistrata* discuss dildos in the context of finding sexual satisfaction in the absence of their warring husbands (**Aristophanes AS**). Male masturbation features in Aristophanes' plays and elsewhere as a 'humorous topic' which meets with 'good-humoured disdain', as Stafford puts it in her study of the topic (Stafford 2011, 356 and 343). It is an activity suited to social groups such as slaves, the old and the unsophisticated – but is occasionally indulged in by younger men in comedy, too, when they find themselves deprived of any other viable sexual outlet (e.g. *Assemblywomen* 707–9 and Eubulus, fr. 118 K-A).

5.8 Sex on the fringes: taboo and sexual perversion

In every culture there are sexual acts and practices which are subject to emotional aversion or inhibition. In this and previous chapters, we have seen how unwritten protocols govern a number of aspects of the sexual behaviour of classical Athenians, serving to guide citizen women and boys, in particular, to act in modest ways, but also prompting citizen men to behave in radically different ways towards, say, their wives, their older or younger male lovers and different classes of prostitutes. Looking at the diversity of sexual experience in the city, and dwelling on the evidence of vase-painting and Old Comedy in particular, can no doubt serve to disguise just how circumspect citizen men would have been in their behaviour much of the time where sex and sexuality were concerned. Outside the symposium (the viewing context of most of the pottery discussed in this chapter) and the theatre (where, in the case of comedy at least, a special festival atmosphere prevailed, allowing an openness of expression unparalleled in daily life), sexual topics would often have been avoided or discussed in an indirect and euphemistic way. Obscene language, sexual organs and sexual acts would all have been subject to their own taboos for classical Athenians, who would have expected them to be 'treated with respect and modesty' (Henderson 1991, 5).

The feelings of revulsion that a taboo sexual practice can inspire are perhaps best demonstrated by incest. This is a topic famously explored by Sophocles in *Oedipus the King* (where Oedipus marries his own mother, Jocasta: **Sophocles D**; cf. **Sophocles C**) and which also surfaces in other Greek myths, such as that of Thyestes (who has sex with his own daughter, Pelopeia). There appears to have been no legislation in place in Athens criminalising incest, since in *Laws*, Plato states that it is an unwritten rule that prevents parents from sleeping with their children and brothers with their sisters (**Plato G**; see also Xenophon, *Memorabilia* 4.4.20). Not that Athenians recognised quite the same moral prohibitions as modern western societies, however, when it came to which members of your family were considered out of bounds sexually. As we saw in Chapter 1, it was relatively common for a girl to marry her (paternal) uncle, for example, and marriage to a half-brother or half-sister born of a different mother was also sanctioned by Athenian custom (Chapter 1.2 and **Demosthenes L**).

Of a different order altogether are the taboos associated with specific sex acts in classical Athenian culture, such as anal and oral sex. As we have seen in this chapter, vase-painters tend to avoid depicting both of these activities in homoerotic scenes, for example, and only portray fellatio relatively infrequently in heterosexual contexts (Kilmer 1993, 71, counts six 'certain examples' of red-figure vases which depict oral sex). The few references we find to cunnilingus in comedy would appear to indicate that this form of oral sex was also considered distasteful (**Aristophanes AP** and **BN**; see Henderson 1991, 185–6).

Why are vase-painters generally so keen to avoid representing anal (and oral) sex in homosexual contexts? This is a problem we grappled with in Chapter 2, where different scholarly approaches were considered (see Chapter 2.3, 2.9 and 2.10). Whichever way this question is answered, however, it seems safe to conclude along with Lear that anal sex was seen as 'less admirable' than, say, the acts of courtship and scenes of intercrural sex that vase-painters more frequently chose to depict (Lear and Cantarella 2008, 106). In Old Comedy, a number of adult men – often real-life Athenians like the tragic playwright Agathon – are pilloried as 'wide-arsed' (**Aristophanes AN** and **BD**) and/or are mocked for their supposedly enthusiastic engagement in this form of sexual activity as the passive partner (**Aristophanes BB**; see Chapter 2.6 and 2.9 and cf. Davidson 1997, 167–82, and 2008, 52–67).

Excessive desire for sex is something that classical Athenians took a dim view of more generally. In Chapter 2, we encountered the scare-figure of the *kinaidos*, the most extreme form of sexual deviant (Chapter 2.9). As we saw, most scholars take the term *kinaidos* to connote an adult man who willingly plays the role of the passive participant in anal sex, but key to his character is perhaps also – or instead – his insatiability. In Plato's *Gorgias* the *kinaidos* is likened to someone with a persistent itch, and Socrates ridicules the notion that such a man can be said to be happy purely on the basis that he is constantly able to scratch (**Plato D**; see Davidson 1997, 171–81). The increasing importance of self-control (*sōphrosynē*) as a virtue in fifth-century Athens extended to sexual behaviour, too. The ability to control sexual appetites was a sign of manliness and strength (Dover 1973, 64) and stood in contrast to a womanish or slavish dependency on one's desires – this is not a culture in which men boast about their sexual conquests. As we have seen, then, in comedy an excessive craving for sex is a stereotype associated with women and can also be used as the basis of provocative and scurrilous slurs against men. Tellingly, too, it is not just men who thirst excessively after sex with other men who are characterised as effeminate in our sources, but also men whose sexual incontinence leads them to commit adultery with women (see Chapter 4.5). In vase-painting, sexual excess is also associated with animal-like satyrs and, in the human realm, is something to which the young are portrayed as being more prone than the old (some of our most spectacular scenes of group sex in red-figure, for example, involve the combination of youths and inhibition-breaking wine: Kilmer 1993, 58; see Chapter 2.3). In an anecdote preserved for us by Plato, we are told that the tragic poet Sophocles expressed his relief that old age had given him respite from sexual desire, which he is said to have described as 'a fierce and frenzied master' (**Plato J**).

Another sexual scare-figure is the tyrant, the subject of an article by Philip Holt, who undertakes an analysis of the various sexual perversions which are attributed to these figures in Greek literature (Holt

1998). Key to the havoc that the tyrant can wreak is his unrestricted power and lack of accountability, which means he can have sex with whomever he wants, however he wants. What Holt calls the 'perversion of sex' associated with tyrants (Holt 1998, 226) manifests itself in actions such as the shaming of their subjects' wives, sons and daughters and using force rather than persuasion to gratify their sexual desires (allegations not infrequently made in Athens against supposedly tyrannical individuals, too, e.g. [Demosthenes] 17.3; Thucydides 8.74.3, 86.3; Isocrates 4.114). In Herodotus' accounts of eastern despots, we find further tales of sexual outrageousness, such as incest (Herodotus 3.31–2) and even an incestuous rape (Mycerinus, king of Egypt, rapes his own daughter, who subsequently hangs herself: **Herodotus A**). The sexual transgressions of Athens' own tyrant, Peisistratus, may not run to incest, but are eyebrow-raising nevertheless. Unwilling to have any children by the daughter of Megacles, whom he marries for the sake of a political alliance, he eschews conventional intercourse with her in favour of sex which is performed *ou kata nomon*, in 'an unconventional way' (Herodotus 1.61). The precise method is left for the reader to guess at, but the girl's family is outraged when the truth finally comes out.

5.9 Conclusion

In this chapter we have seen a picture, painted in broad brush strokes, of the notions of beauty, sexiness and appropriate behaviour – as well as fantasy and taboo – in existence in classical Athens. Important patterns emerge here, revealing a society which prizes youthfulness; which both praises and mistrusts female beauty; and which defines fitting behaviour in strikingly different ways for different categories of citizen and non-citizen (the adult male; the citizen wife and daughter; the boy; the prostitute). Indeed, self-presentation becomes all-important in a culture whose members are prepared to make what are essentially moral judgements on the basis of personal appearance – that is to say, where paleness and flabbiness have the potential to generate an accusation that a man is unpatriotic (**Xenophon G**); or where a suntan, exposure of flesh, excessive make-up or over-opulence of dress can serve to mark a woman out as a prostitute (**Alexis A**, **Xenarchus A** and **Xenophon F**; cf. **Xenophon C**). What is fascinating to see is how vase-painters and comic poets play with these social conventions to create challenging images for their audiences. In Aristophanes, for example, we find sexually available boys and sluttish wives (e.g.

Aristophanes AG and **BG**). In vase-painting, we find not only modest boys, but also boys who are enthusiastic and responsive to their lovers; not only copious examples of young women pursued by gods, but also the occasional young man pursued by a goddess; not only industrious and dainty women, but also females energetically engaged in a whole assortment of sexual acts. The question here is whether these artistic creations are simply to be regarded as representing male fantasy, whether they are deliberately provocative and/or humorous on the part of the vase-painters, and/or whether they reflect some genuine blurring of categories in the minds – or, indeed, in the experience – of their creators and intended audience.

The survey in this chapter has sought to identify cultural norms and ideals that prevailed throughout the classical era, but it is surely the case that notions of beauty, sexiness, appropriate behaviour and so on would have been continually subject to change. After all, as we saw in previous chapters, sexual mores were in flux throughout the classical era. Marriage assumes an increased importance as the fifth century wears on, especially in the turbulent years of the Peloponnesian War (431–404 BC: see Chapter 1.1 and 1.13). Attitudes towards homoerotic relationships also undergo significant changes as pederasty shifts from being a high-prestige institution at the dawn of the classical era to one that appears to be in crisis in the fourth century (see Chapter 2.6). Throughout the classical era, too, the role of women was subtly changing, new laws were being framed governing sexual behaviour (especially marriage), and existing legislation was being cited in the Athenian law courts in the course of various causes célèbres (such as the prosecution of Timarchus in 346–345 BC and that of Neaera a few years later: see Chapters 2.8 and 3.2). It would be surprising if none of these cultural forces impacted on concepts of beauty, attractiveness, fantasy and taboo – just as it would be surprising if fashions in clothing, make-up and deportment did not alter in ways that it is now impossible for us to ascertain.

Inevitably much is lost to us, too, of the variety in individual tastes that must have existed among men in classical Athens. Counter-cultural proclivities evidently did exist, however, such as a penchant harboured by some men for older women, perhaps (**Xenarchus A**), or for prostitutes who were supposedly free-born girls (**Demosthenes O**) – or, indeed, for playing the role of the *erōmenos* in a homosexual pairing in adulthood (see Chapter 2.11). Indeed, for some of those men and women who broke the law by committing adultery, perhaps part of the thrill here even resided in its very illicitness (Neaera is supposedly able to charge more for her sexual services, for example, by pretending to be a married citizen woman: **Demosthenes S**). We are also badly informed about the darker side of human sexual behaviour. We know of no real-life example of the crime we would call 'rape' in classical Athens, for example (see Chapter 4.8), no substantiated case of incest (although we do have accusations, e.g. Lysias 14.28) – and while there is certainly evidence to suppose that domestic violence occurred in the city in the form of wife-beating (Llewellyn-Jones 2011), our sources are also silent on the subject of sexual abuse (see Fisher 1998, 94 n. 32; cf. **Aristotle K**). Indeed, on a broader level, we essentially know very little about the type and the frequency of sexual activity that went on in any Athenian home.

Taken as a whole, then, our sources are coquetteish: they reveal but they also obscure. Sometimes frank and explicit, often evasive and euphemistic, the artists, poets and writers whose works allow us to build up our picture of classical Athens lead us to pose at least as many questions as we are able to answer. Perhaps this mixture of candour and mystery is to be expected where sex is concerned, where different protocols inevitably apply in public and in private. Our story of sex and sexuality in classical Athens may never be complete, but we are fortunate at least in that our sources provide a whole array of fascinating starting points from which we can to attempt to tell it.

Part II

Documents

Introduction

The translations of passages in Part II are intended, as far as possible, to be both literate and literal. On the one hand, each translation aims to preserve something of the tone of the original – and thus a more colloquial idiom has generally been used for extracts from comic drama, for example, in contrast to the more formal or poetic idioms of philosophy and tragedy respectively. On the other, clunkiness has often been chosen over fluency where the original idea might be in danger of getting lost in paraphrase. A distinctive feature of these translations is that key words have been glossed in the text, the aim here being to provide better access to the thought world of the ancient Greeks and the all-important concepts and categories they used to describe it. In the realm of love and sexual desire, for example, words like *erōs* and *philia*, *erastēs* and *erōmenos* appear in round brackets after the English words used to translate them. Note that in general, it is the dictionary form of these glossed words that is given and not necessarily the form that appears in the text.

Within the extracts, square brackets are used to indicate where notes have been inserted to explain a reference in the text. In drama, italics are used to signal my own additions in the form of stage directions and/or contextual information. Square brackets are used as well to signal text which is dubious, i.e. where there is a line or sentiment thought not to be the work of the original author. In particular, many of the laws appearing in the manuscripts of legal speeches are thought to be later insertions by copyists. Square brackets are also used to indicate conjectures and/or gaps in the original manuscript or papyrus. Finally, when a whole text is thought not to be the work of the author to whom it has traditionally been attributed, this has been indicated with square brackets around the author's name. Scholars generally take the legal speech *Against Neaera* to be the work of Apollodorus rather than Demosthenes, for example, despite the fact that it was preserved as part of the Demosthenic corpus. This book follows standard practice in giving the author as '[Demosthenes]'.

Note that the heading of each extract contains a cross-reference in square brackets indicating the chapter(s) and section number(s) in which it is cited and/or discussed.

Aeschines

Athenian orator and politician, c. 397–322 BC. The trial at which *Against Timarchus* was delivered took place in 346–345 BC.

A Athenian laws protecting boys from sexual exploitation

Aeschines, Against Timarchus *1.9–14 [2.5; 2.8; 2.11; 4.1]*
[9] For first of all the teachers – to whom we entrust our own children out of necessity and whose livelihood depends on their behaving decently (*sōphroneō*) (and for whom the opposite would spell financial ruin) – are, despite this, evidently mistrusted by the law-maker. He expressly prescribes the time at which a free boy should go to the school-room, and furthermore how many boys should enter it with him and when he should go home. [10] And he forbids teachers from opening their school-rooms and gymnastic-trainers (*paidotribēs*) from opening their wrestling grounds (*palaistra*) before sunrise and prescribes that they be shut before sunset, evidently greatly suspicious of deserted places in the dark. He prescribes which youths (*neaniskos*) should frequent these places, what age they should be and what control there should be over them; and he lays down laws about the supervision of slave-attendants (*paidagōgos*), the festivals of the Muses in the school-rooms and of Hermes in the wrestling grounds (*palaistra*) and, finally, about the company boys should keep when going to school, and their cyclic dances [i.e. dances which boys would perform in a group at a festival, for which they would be trained by an adult instructor]. [11] For he orders the *chorēgos* – the man who is going to spend his own money on you [i.e. by funding the training of a boys' chorus to sing and/or dance at a festival] – should be over 40 years old to do this, so that he is already at an age when he is very much self-controlled (*sōphrōn*) before he comes into contact with your children.

And so [the court official] will read these laws out to you, so that you may know that the law-giver thought that a boy who was well brought up would be useful to the city once he was a man. But when a person's character has to contend with a sorry starting point to his education right from the outset, what will result from boys being badly brought up will, he thought, be citizens very much like Timarchus here. (*To the court official*) Read them these laws.

Laws
[12] [The teachers of boys shall open their schoolrooms before sunrise and shall close them before sunset. And it shall not be permitted for anyone older than the boys to enter while the boys are inside, unless he be a son of the teacher, or a brother, or a son-in-law. And if anyone should enter in contravention of these prohibitions, he shall be punished with death. And the gymnasium supervisors shall under no circumstances allow anyone who has reached maturity (*hēlikia*) to enter the contests of Hermes. And if a gymnasium supervisor allows this and does not keep such a person out of the gymnasium, he shall be subject to the law that applies to the seduction (*phthora*) of free-born youth. And *chorēgoi* who are appointed by the people shall be over 40 years in age.]

[13] What is more, gentlemen of Athens, after this he legislates about crimes which, although they are major, do actually occur in the city, I think. For it was because he did not approve of some of the things which were being done that the men of old passed these laws. At any rate, the law says explicitly that if a father, brother, uncle, guardian, or anyone at all who is responsible for a boy, hires him out as a prostitute (*hetaireō*), it does not allow a charge to be laid against the boy himself, but against the person who has acted as his pimp and the person who has hired him; against the former because he has hired the boy out for money and against the latter because, it says, he has paid for the boy's services. And he has made the penalties the same for both offenders. And he absolves a boy, once he has reached maturity, of the responsibility of looking after and providing accommodation for a father who has hired him out as a prostitute. But when his father is dead he is to bury him and see to the other customary rites. [14] Just examine how well conceived this is, gentlemen of Athens. While he is alive he is deprived of the benefits that having children brings, just as his son is deprived of his right to free speech [i.e. because men who prostituted themselves in their youth were not permitted under Athenian law to address the assembly]; but when he is dead and unaware of the good services that he is receiving – and when it is the law and the gods that are being honoured – it is now that the law orders his son to bury him and to perform the other customary rites.

B The law on *hybris* against a free child

Aeschines, Against Timarchus *16 [2.8; 4.6]*

Law

[If any Athenian should commit an outrage (*hybrizō*) against a free child (*pais*), the guardian of the child (*kyrios*) shall bring a prosecution before the Thesmothetae [i.e. the city's six junior archons] proposing a specific penalty in the indictment. And if the court condemns the accused [to death], he shall be handed over to the Eleven [i.e. the officials in charge of prisons and prisoners] to be put to death the same day. But if he is condemned to pay a monetary fine, he shall pay it within eleven days following the trial if he is unable to pay it immediately; and he shall be kept in prison until he pays it. And those who commit transgressions against the bodies of slaves shall be subject to the same process.]

C The law on male prostitution

Aeschines, Against Timarchus *1.21 [2.8; 3.1; 3.8; 4.1]*

Law

[If any Athenian has prostituted himself (*hetaireō*), he shall not be permitted to become one of the nine archons; nor assume the office of priest; nor act as an advocate for the people; nor hold any office whatsoever, either at home or abroad, whether filled by lot or elected by show of hands; nor be sent as a herald; nor speak in a public debate; nor enter into public temples; nor wear garlands at public ceremonies where garlands are worn; nor walk inside the parts of the marketplace (*agora*) purified for an assembly of people. And if anyone who has been convicted of prostituting himself should do this contrary to these prohibitions, he shall be punished with death.]

D Timarchus' sojourns at the homes of older men

Aeschines, Against Timarchus *1.39–42 [2.8; 2.10]*

[39] See, gentlemen of Athens, how moderately I mean to treat Timarchus here. For I shall pass over such wrongs as he did his own body while still a boy (*pais*) . . . . But the things he did as a youth (*meirakion*), already with the ability to think for himself and to understand the city's laws, these will form the basis of my accusations and I ask you to devote serious attention to them. [40] For as soon as Timarchus was past boyhood, he settled in the Peiraeus at the infirmary of Euthydicus

on the pretext of being a student of the art of medicine, but in reality intent on offering himself for sale, as events themselves proved. How many merchants, other foreigners, or our own citizens made use of Timarchus' body in those times I shall willingly pass over lest someone accuse me of dwelling too much on every small detail. But as for the men in whose houses he has lived, dishonouring (*kataischyneō*) his own body and the city and accepting pay for the very things that the law forbids him from doing under the penalty of losing his right to address the people – about these I shall have words to say. [41] Gentlemen of Athens, there is a certain Misgolas, son of Naucrates, a man who in other respects is a gentleman (*kalos k'agathos*) with whom one could find no fault, but who is bent on this thing like one possessed and who is always accustomed to have around him [male] cithara-singers (*kitharōidos*) or [male] cithara-players (*kitharistēs*). I say this not to be coarse, but so you might know the sort of man he is. When he realised why Timarchus here was spending his time at the infirmary, he got him to move into his home by paying him a sum of money up front; for Timarchus was in good condition, young, shameless and well suited for the thing that Misoglas proposed to do – and which Timarchus proposed to let him do. [42] And Timarchus here did not shrink from this, but submitted, despite the fact that he had everything he could reasonably wish for – for his father left him a good deal of property which he has squandered, as I shall demonstrate in the course of my speech. Rather, he did these things because he was a slave to the most shameful (*aischros*) pleasures – to gourmet treats and sumptuousness at table, to flute-girls (*aulētris*), prostitutes (*hetaira*), dice-games and other things – none of which ought to hold mastery over a well-bred and free man. And this wretched man felt no shame (*aischynomai*) at leaving his father's house and living with Misgolas, who was neither a friend of his father's, nor someone of his own age, but rather no relation at all and older than him – a boy in his prime living with a man with no restraint (*akolastos*) in these matters.

E A shameful act goes unnamed

Aeschines, Against Timarchus *1.55 [2.1; 2.8; 2.10]*
For the things that this man here was unashamed (*aischynomai*) to do in deed, I would sooner die than describe in plain words in your presence.

F Hegesandrus takes a shine to Timarchus

Aeschines, Against Timarchus *1.57 [2.8]*

[Hegesandrus] had such an abundance of money and frequently visited the house of Pittalacus, with whom he played dice; when he saw Timarchus for the first time there, he was pleased with him, lusted after him and wanted to take him to his own house, thinking that Timarchus was similar to him in nature (*physis*).

G Male prostitutes in cubicles

Aeschines, Against Timarchus *1.74 [3.8]*

Observe those males who sit in cubicles (*oikēma*: or 'brothels'?) – those who practise the profession quite openly. Yet these people, when the necessity arises, nevertheless place something in front of themselves for shame's sake (*aischynē*): they shut their doors. If, then, someone were to ask you as you were walking along the street what was this person was doing, you would immediately call the deed by its name; not because you saw or knew the man who had gone in, but because, since you know full well the nature of the person's trade, you also know the deed itself.

H The punishment of adulterers – among others

Aeschines, Against Timarchus *1.91 [4.3]*

Which of the clothes-snatchers, thieves, adulterers (*moichos*), murderers or those guilty of great crimes – if they have commited the act in secret – will be punished? For where these [criminals] are concerned, the ones caught in the act are immediately punished with death, if they confess; whereas those who have evaded notice and deny their crime are judged in the courts and the truth is determined through probability.

I Timarchus' treatment of women

Aeschines, Against Timarchus *1.107 [2.8; 4.5]*

And he [Timarchus] showed such insolence (*aselgeia*) towards the wives (*gynē*) of free men as no one else has ever shown.

J Timarchus denounced as Hegesandrus' 'woman'

Aeschines, Against Timarchus *1.110 [2.8; 2.9]*

Pamphilus of the deme of Acherdous, a decent man who was already angry and annoyed with [Timarchus] for some reason, when he became aware of the matter [i.e. that Timarchus and Hegesandrus had allegedly embezzled public money] stood up in the assembly and said, 'Men of Athens, a man and a woman are conspiring to steal 1,000 drachmas of yours.' You were amazed, wondering what he meant and in what way a man and woman were doing this. Then leaving a short pause he said, 'Don't you know what I'm talking about? The man is our Hegesandrus here, who is a man now,' he said, 'although he, too, used to be a woman – Leodamas' woman. And the woman is this here Timarchus. And I shall tell you how the money is being stolen.'

K Prostitution taxes

Aeschines, Against Timarchus *1.119 [3.1; 3.7; 4.1]*

... every year the Council (*Boulē*) farms out the tax on prostitution. And the men who buy this tax do not guess, but know precisely who it is that practise this profession.

L Praise for the right kind of boy-love

Aeschines, Against Timarchus *1.136–40 [2.2; 2.6; 2.8]*

[136] I do not find fault with honest love, neither am I saying that those who are distinguished by their beauty (*kallos*) have acted as prostitutes (*porneuomai*). Nor do I deny that I myself have been a lover (*erōtikos*) – indeed, I still am – and I do not deny that the usual rivalries and quarrels with others that result from this have also come about in my case. As for the poems that these men say I have composed, some I freely accept as my work, whereas others do not have the character which they will try to impute to them by tampering with them. [137] The distinction I make is that to fall in love (*eraō*) with the beautiful (*kalos*) and the modest (*sōphrōn*) is the experience of a kind-hearted and generous soul; but to act licentiously by hiring someone for money is the deed of an outrageous (*hybristos*) and uneducated man. And while I say that it is a fine (*kalos*) thing to be the object of uncorrupted love (*eraō*), to be induced to prostitute oneself (*porneuomai*) for pay is shameful (*aischros*). How great the divide is between each of these

two positions, and how much they differ, I shall try to teach you in my subsequent words. [138] For our fathers, when they were making laws to regulate the habits and inevitable events that stem from human nature, thought that there were certain things that ought to be done by free men but which they would forbid slaves from doing. 'A slave', says the law, 'shall neither exercise (*gymnazomai*) nor anoint himself with oil in the wrestling schools (*palaistra*).' And the statute does not continue, 'and the free man *shall* anoint himself with oil and exercise'. For when the law-makers perceived the good that derives from exercise (*gymnasia*), they forbade slaves from taking part, thinking that, by forbidding them, they were at the same time encouraging free men. [139] Again, the same law-maker said, 'A slave shall neither fall in love (*eraō*) with a free boy, nor follow him about, otherwise he shall be given fifty blows of the public lash.' But he did not prevent the free man from falling in love with a boy, associating with him or following him about, nor did he think that this harmed the boy, but rather that it is testimony to his modesty (*sōphrosynē*). But I think that while the boy is not his own master and is unable to judge who really is his friend and who is not, the law-maker encourages the lover (*erastēs*) to exercise self-control (*sōphrōnizō*) and to put off words of friendship (*philia*) until the boy is older and at an age where he can think for himself. But to follow after the boy and keep watch over him he considered to be the most robust way of looking out for and safeguarding his modesty (*sōphrosynē*). [140] And so it was that those benefactors of the state, Harmodius and Aristogeiton, men who possessed virtues in abundance, received instruction from modest (*sōphrōn*) and lawful love (*erōs*) – or we can call it by another name than love if necessary – with the upshot being that those we hear acclaiming their deeds seem to be inadequate in their praises of what those men have achieved.

M Homer's portrayal of Achilles and Patroclus

Aeschines, Against Timarchus *1.142 [2.2]*

Although [Homer] makes mention of Patroclus and Achilles in many places, he conceals their love and avoids naming their friendship (*philia*), thinking that the heightened nature of their affection is more than evident to the educated members of his audience.

N A comment on the laws on male prostitution

Aeschines, Against Timarchus *1.160 [2.8; 4.1]*

. . . first of all, call to mind the laws concerning prostitution (*hetairēsis*):
. . . [the law-giver] prescribes that, no matter how the deed is done,
the man who has done it shall take no part in the city's affairs. For he
thought that anyone who surrendered his ambition to achieve fine
(*kalos*) things when young, and instead indulged in shameful (*aischros*)
pleasures, should not enjoy full citizen rights when he was older.

O The treatment of adulteresses in law and practice

Aeschines, Against Timarchus *1.182–4 [4.4]*

[182] . . . I shall also remind you of our ancestors. They were so strict
concerning all shameful behaviour (*aischynē*), and so highly did they
regard the virtue (*sōphrosynē*) of their children, that when one of the
citizens found that his daughter had been corrupted (*diaphtheirō*), and
that she had failed to preserve her maidenhood (*hēlikia*) before marriage, he walled her up in an empty house with a horse, which he clearly
knew would kill her given that she was shut in there with it. And to this
very day the foundations of that house stand in your city, and that spot
is called 'the place of the horse and the girl (*korē*)'. [183] Solon, the most
renowned law-giver, has written in his time-honoured and solemn
manner concerning the appropriate behaviour of women. For if any
woman is caught with an adulterer (*moichos*) he does not allow her
to adorn herself, or to enter the public temples, lest she corrupt those
women who are blameless by mixing with them. And if she does enter
a temple or adorn herself, he orders whoever encounters her to tear her
clothes, strip her of her jewellery and beat her (he prohibits only killing
or maiming her), thereby depriving such a woman of her civic rights
and making her life not worth living. [184] And he orders that both
women and men who act as pimps (*proagōgos*) be indicted, and if they
are convicted, that they be punished with death, because when people
desire to do wrong but hesitate and are ashamed (*aischynomai*) to meet
one another, it is pimps who, by offering their shamelessness for pay,
allow the deed to be discussed and accomplished.

P Appropriate behaviour for male prostitutes and their admirers

Aeschines, Against Timarchus *1.195 [2.11]*

Before you listen to the speech that these men [i.e. Timarchus' support-ers] will make, call to mind their way of life; and as for those who have committed wrongs against their bodies, tell them not to bother you and to stop addressing the people. For the law does not question men who live their lives in private, but those who take an active part in politics. . . . And as for those who are hunters after such young men as are easy prey, tell them to turn their attentions to the foreigners and metics, so that they may still indulge their predilections without harming you.

Aeschylus

Tragic playwright, active in the first half of the fifth century BC. The *Oresteia* trilogy (of which *Agamemnon* forms part) was produced in 458 BC.

A Helen the destroyer

Aeschylus, Agamemnon *681–92 [5.1]*

Chorus: Who ever named her with such accuracy? Did some being we cannot see who had foreknowledge of what was fated use his tongue fortuitously, naming that spear-bride, contested by two sides – Helen? For in keeping with her name, *she* – the destroyer of ships (*helenas*), destroyer of men (*helandros*), destroyer of cities (*heleptolis*) – sailed from her luxurious enclosure [to Troy], wafted by the breeze . . .

B Achilles reproaches the dead Patroclus(?)

Aeschylus, Myrmidons, *fr. 135 Radt [2.2; 5.5]*

You did not feel reverence for the sacred honour of (my) thighs – you who are ungrateful for (my) constant kisses.

Alexis

Playwright of Middle and New Comedy, c. 375–275 BC, active from the middle of the fourth century BC.

A How brothel-keepers model prostitutes to the greatest effect

Alexis, fr. 103 KA Fair measure (Isostasion) *[3.4; 5.2; 5.3; 5.9]*
First off, everything else is secondary for them [brothel-keepers?] to
making a profit and fleecing their fellow men: they stitch up schemes
against everyone. And whenever they're doing well, they take on new
courtesans (*hetaira*) who are novices to the profession. They immediately remodel them, so that neither in their manners nor in their
appearance do they stay the same. One happens to be short. Cork is
sewn onto the bottom of her shoes. Another is tall. She wears thin
slippers and goes out drooping her head on her shoulder – this makes
her shorter. One's got no hips. She [the brothel-keeper?] fixes a pad
underneath her clothing, the upshot being that onlookers cry aloud
what a fine arse she has. If she has a fat belly, they use breasts of the
kind that the comic actors use: by attaching these just right, they hold
the garment away from her belly just like using poles. If one has light
eyebrows, they draw over them with soot. If one happens to be dark,
she is plastered over with white lead (*psimythion*). Another one is too
pale-skinned: she rubs on rouge (*paiderōs*). If she has some attractive
part of her body, it's shown off naked. If she has nicely formed teeth,
she is forced to laugh, so that those present might observe what a beautiful mouth she has. And if she doesn't like laughing, she spends the
day inside with a thin stick of myrtle between her lips, like the things
on display in butcher's shops when they've got goats' skulls for sale, so
that in time she grins, whether she wants to or not.

B Prostitution in the Kerameikos

Alexis, fr. 206 KA Pan of Coals (Pyraunos) *[3.4]*
I wanted to gain experience of another sort of life, which everyone is
accustomed to calling 'luxurious' (*hygros*). Walking in the Kerameikos
for three days, I found teachers of the life I'm talking about – perhaps
thirty in a single brothel (*ergastērion*)!

Amphis

Playwright of Middle Comedy, active in the fourth century BC.

A The advantage of a *hetaira* over a wife

Amphis, fr. 1 KA Athamas *[3.6]*

Then, isn't it easier to get on with with a courtesan (*hetaira*) than a woman you're married to (*gynē gametē*)? Much easier, of course. For to one you're attached by law and even if she despises you she stays put in your home. Whereas the other knows that she must either buy a man with her actions or go away to someone else.

Anacreon

Lyric poet, born in Teos in Asia Minor, but resident in various parts of Greece, including Athens; active in the second half of the sixth century BC.

A Ode to a heedless boy

Anacreon, fr. 360 [2.2; 5.5]

Oh, you boy (*pais*) with the maidenish (*parthenios*) glance, I am hunting you, but you pay no attention and do not know that you hold the reins of my life.

B A plea to enjoy a boy's thighs

Anacreon, fr. 407 [2.3; 2.5; 5.5]

But pledge me, dear boy (*philos*), your slender thighs . . .

C The Thracian filly

Anacreon, fr. 417 [1.6]

Thracian filly (lit. 'foal': *pōlos*), why do you look at me from the corner of your eye, stubbornly fleeing from me, supposing that I don't know what I'm doing? Let me tell you, if I put the bridle neatly on you, with the reins in my hands, I could steer you round the turning posts of the racecourse. But as it is, you graze in the meadows and frolic, lightly prancing, because you don't have an experienced horseman to ride you.

Anaxilas

Playwright of Middle Comedy, active in the fourth century BC.

A Not a prostitute, but a courtesan

Anaxilas, fr. 21 KA The Chick *(Neottis) [3.7]*

A: But if a girl is moderate and speaking [. . .] renders her service gracefully to men who make requests of her, her companionship earns her the name of 'courtesan' (*hetaira*); and now you haven't fallen in love with a whore (*pornē*), you say, but rather it's a courtesan you happen to have gone for, in fact. Well, she's uncomplicated, at any rate.

B: She's charming, by Zeus!

B The allusive nature of *hetairai*'s requests

Anaxilas, fr. 22.22–31 KA The Chick *(Neottis) [3.7; 3.9]*

You could call all prostitutes (*pornē*) the Theban Sphinx. They never talk straight, but in riddles, about how they love (*eraō*) you and are fond of (*phileō*) you and enjoy sleeping with (*syneimi*) you. Next thing: 'If only I had a four-footed [couch], or a chair', she says. Next up: 'Or a three-footed table.' Then: 'Or a two-legged maidservant', she says. The man who understands these riddles, like Oedipus, then slings his hook smartish, pretending not to have seen her, and he alone is saved – even if he doesn't quite want to be. But those who think that the women are in love with (*eraō*) them are immediately carried off and transported high into the air. In short, however many wild beasts there are, there is nothing more dangerous than a courtesan (*hetaira*).

Andocides

Athenian aristocat, politician and orator, c. 440–390 BC, active in the late fifth and early fourth centuries BC.

A Callias' relationships with a mother and daughter

Andocides, On the Mysteries *1.124–5 [1.9; 1.13]*

[124] But just consider how his son, to whom he [Callias] saw fit to award the daughter of Epilycus, was born and acknowledged by his father; it is well worth hearing, gentlemen. Callias married (*gameō*) a daughter of Ischomachus; but after living with her for not even a year, he took her own mother [as his mistress]. And this most dreadful man was living with both the mother and the daughter: he was the priest of the Mother and the Daughter [i.e. Demeter and Persephone]; and he

kept them both in his house. [125] And *he* felt no shame or fear of the Two Goddesses; but the daughter of Ischomachus thought death better than life if she had to watch such things. She tried to hang herself but was stopped half-way. Then, when she recovered, she ran away from home: the mother drove out the daughter! Then he got sick of her [the mother] and threw her out as well. She then said she was pregnant by him; but when she gave birth to a son, he denied that the child was his.

B Alcibiades' wife is driven to attempt divorce

[Andocides], Against Alcibiades 4.14 [1.4; 1.7; 1.15]
Receiving such a great dowry as none of the Greeks had, he was so shameless (*hybristēs*) – bringing into the house itself courtesans (*hetaira*), both slave and free – that he compelled his wife (*gynē*), a most modest woman, to abandon him (*apoleipō*) and go to the archon in accordance with the law [i.e. to file for divorce: *apoleipsis*]. At that he made great show of his power. He called his friends to his side, snatched his wife (*gynē*) from the marketplace (*agora*) by force (*bia*), and he showed everyone that he despised the archons, the laws and the other citizens.

Antiphanes

Playwright of Middle Comedy, active in the fourth century BC. His first play can be dated to c. 385 BC.

A A citizen *hetaira* of good repute

Antiphanes, fr. 210 KA The Waterjug (Hydria*) [3.4; 3.6]*
This man I'm talking about, catching sight of some courtesan (*hetaira*) living at his neighbour's house, fell in love (*erōs*) with her. She was a citizen (*astē*) and, although lacking a guardian or relatives, she obtained a fine reputation for goodness – a *real* courtesan (*hetaira*)! It is the others with their behaviour that damage the name [i.e. of *hetaira*] – which is actually a good one.

Archilochus

Iambic poet from the island of Paros, active in the mid-seventh century BC.

A Each to his own

Archilochus, fr. 25 West [2.10]

... man's nature, but each one warms his heart with different things:
[. . .] Melesa[nder] with a dick (*sathē*) ...

Aristophanes

The most famous and by far the best preserved of the Athenian
comic playwrights, c. 460/450–386 BC. His surviving plays (with their
production dates) are as follows: *Acharnians* (425 BC); *Knights* (424
BC); *Clouds* (423 BC; revised c. 418–416 BC); *Wasps* (422 BC); *Peace*
(421 BC); *Birds* (414 BC); *Lysistrata* and *Women at the Thesmophoria*
(411 BC); *Frogs* (405 BC); *Assemblywomen* (c. 392 BC); *Wealth* (c. 388
BC). The first nine plays belong to the phase known as Old Comedy,
whereas the final two are generally classed as Middle Comedy.

AA A fantasy of a sexual assault on a slave-girl

Aristophanes, Acharnians 271–6 [1.16; 4.7; 5.1; 5.2; 5.7]

Dicaeopolis (*singing*): For it's far sweeter, o Phales, Phales, to find a
blooming (*hōrikos*) girl sneaking off with stolen wood – Strymodorus'
Thratta from the Fell-land – and to catch her by the waist, raise her up,
cast her down, and de-pip her grape!

AB The beginning of the Peloponnesian War attributed to whoreknapping

Aristophanes, Acharnians 524–9 [3.4]

Dicaeopolis: Some young men (*neanias*), drunk with kottabos-playing,
go to Megara and steal the prostitute (*pornē*) Simaetha; and then the
Megarians, garlic-roused in their grief, stole away two of Aspasia's
prostitutes (*pornē*) in return. From that broke out the beginning of the
war between all the Greeks – from three cock-suckers (*laikastria*)!

AC Praise of female breasts

Aristophanes, Acharnians 1198–9 [5.2; 5.4; 5.7]

Dicaeopolis: Aaahhh! Aaahhh! What tits! How firm and quince-
like! Kiss me tenderly, my golden honeys, with full lip-synch and
tongue-in-groove.

AD A wife justifies her absence from the house

Aristophanes, Assemblywomen 520–42 [1.10; 5.1; 5.4]

Blepyrus:	Hey! Where have you been, Praxagora?
Praxagora:	What's it to *you*, my dear?
Blepyrus:	What is it to me? What a stupid question!
Praxagora:	You can't possibly be about to accuse me of being with an adulterer (*moichos*)!
Blepyrus:	Not just *one*, for all I know!
Praxagora:	Well, you can certainly put *that* to the test.
Blepyrus:	How?
Praxagora:	By seeing if my head smells of perfume.
Blepyrus:	What? Can't a woman get fucked (*bineō*) without perfume?
Praxagora:	Not if you're me, you can't, my dear!
Blepyrus:	In that case how come you went off in silence at the crack of dawn taking my cloak?
Praxagora:	A woman I know – a good friend of mine – sent for me in the night because she'd gone into labour.
Blepyrus:	Well, couldn't you have told me before you went?
Praxagora:	And not given a thought to my friend giving birth? She was in a bad way, my dear!
Blepyrus:	But you could have told me first! Hmmm. There's something not quite right here.
Praxagora:	No there isn't, by the two goddesses: it's just that I went straight away. The woman who came for me begged me to come out at all costs.
Blepyrus:	Well, couldn't you have taken your own cloak? . . .
Praxagora:	It was cold, you see, and I'm hardly big and strong. So I put this cloak around me to keep warm. And, my dear husband (*anēr*), I did leave you lying in the warm under the covers.

AE The appeal of youth over old age

Aristophanes, Assemblywomen 901–5 [5.2]

Girl: Don't be jealous of the young. For voluptuousness has its natural place on tender thighs and blooms upon quince-like breasts; whereas you, old woman, are plucked and powdered, a darling of death!

AF A girl pines for her boyfriend

Aristophanes, Assemblywomen *911–3 [4.5]*

Girl: (*singing*) Alas, whatever will become of me? My boyfriend (*hetairos*) hasn't come, I am left alone without him; for my mother has gone elsewhere. (*speaking*) And I don't have to say anything about what happens after that!

AG A fantasy encounter with a boy

Aristophanes, Birds *136–42 [2.2; 2.5; 2.6; 2.12; 5.5; 5.7; 5.9]*

Euelpides: I desire the same sort of thing.
Tereus: What?
Euelpides: A place where a father of an attractive (*hōraios*) boy (*pais*), when I bumped into him, would complain that I had done him wrong, saying, 'That was a fine turn you did my boy, sunshine! You met him coming from the gymnasium, freshly bathed, and you didn't kiss him, you didn't talk to him, you didn't draw him close and you didn't finger his balls. And you, an old family friend of mine!'

AH A mortal threatens a goddess with rape

Aristophanes, Birds *1253–6 [4.7; 5.7]*

Peisthetaerus (*to Iris*):   And if you annoy me in any way, then I'll first raise up this servant's legs, spread her thighs and nail her – yes, Iris herself! And she'll be amazed at the way I can stay hard for a triple-ramming!

AI A matchmaker's mismatch between a rustic and a city-girl

Aristophanes, Clouds *41–55 [1.2]*

Strepsiades: How I wish that matchmaker had met an evil end, who persuaded me to marry (*gameō*) your mother! I had a rustic life, as sweet as sweet can be, nice and mouldy and unswept, where I could stretch out as I pleased; a life full of honey bees and sheep and olive cake. Then I married the niece of Megacles . . . I a rustic, she a city-girl.
. . .

AJ The clouds change shape on seeing Cleisthenes

Aristophanes, Clouds 346–55 *[2.6; 2.9]*

Socrates: Have you ever looked up and seen a cloud that looked
               like a centaur, or a leopard, or a wolf, or a bull?
Strepsiades: Yes I have, by Zeus! What of it?
Socrates: They can assume any shape they like. So, if they see
               some hairy, wild looking guy – one of those shaggy
               fellows like the son of Xenophantus – they make fun
               of his passions by taking the form of centaurs.
Strepsiades: So what do they do if they catch sight of an embezzler
               of public funds like Simon?
Socrates: They immediately show him up for what he is by
               turning into wolves.
Strepsiades: Right! So that's why, when they saw Cleonymus the
               shield-thrower yesterday and recognised what a great
               coward he is, they turned into deer.
Socrates: And now, because they have seen Cleisthenes – do
               you see? Because of this they've turned into women
               (*gynē*)!

AK The modest behaviour of boys in the good old days

Aristophanes, Clouds 973–83 *[2.2; 2.5; 5.5]*

Better Argument: At the gym-trainer's when the boys (*pais*) sat down
they had to cover themselves with their thighs, so as not to reveal to the
onlookers outside anything . . . cruel. And when they stood up again
they had to smooth the sand down and make sure that they didn't leave
an imprint of their 'youthfulness' behind for their admirers (*erastēs*).
And in those days no boy (*pais*) anointed himself below the navel – and
so on his private parts (*ta aidoia*) there would blossom a dewy down
like on quinces. Nor would he massage his voice, softening it up for his
lover (*erastēs*), nor walk around acting as his own pimp (*proagōgeuō*)
and making eyes. Nor when he was dining was he allowed to pick up a
head of radish, nor make a grab for the older men's dill or celery, nor
eat delicacies, nor giggle, nor to have his feet crossed.

AL An ideal of male beauty

Aristophanes, Clouds *1010–19 [2.5; 5.5]*
Better Argument: And if you do these things I suggest [i.e. spend time in the gymnasium rather than in discussion] and devote effort to them, you will always have a gleaming breast, bright skin, powerful shoulders, a short tongue, powerful buttocks, a small willy (*posthē*). But if you engage in the practices of the youth of today, for a start you'll have pale skin, small shoulders, a puny chest, a big 'ham' . . . and a lengthy decree.

AM Avoiding punishment for adultery

Aristophanes, Clouds *1079–84 [4.3]*

Worse Argument: If you happen to be captured as an adulterer (*moichos*), you will say this to the man: that you've done nothing wrong. Then, refer to Zeus, saying that even he is vanquished by desire (*erōs*) and by women (*gynē*). And so how can you, a mere mortal, be greater than a god?

Better Argument: But what if someone, trusting you, gets the radish treatment (*rhaphanidoō*) and gets plucked [and singed] with ash? Will he have any good argument to offer to prevent him becoming wide-arsed (*euryprōktos*)?

AN The wide-arsed citizens of Athens

Aristophanes, Clouds *1089–1100 [2.9; 5.8]*

Worse Argument: Come on, then, tell me, what kind of people do the advocates come from?

Better Argument: From among the wide-arsed (*euryprōktos*).

Worse Argument: I agree. What, then? What kind do the tragedians come from?

Better Argument: From among the wide-arsed.

Worse Argument: You're right. What kind do the politicians come from?

Better Argument: From among the wide-arsed.

Worse Argument: Do you realise, then, that you were talking rubbish? Look which spectators are in the majority.

Better Argument: I'm looking.

Worse Argument:	What do you see then?
Better Argument:	By the gods, I see that the vast majority of them are wide-arsed. I know that this one here is *and* that one there – *and* this one here, the long-haired one.

AO The attraction of flute-girls and dancing-girls

Aristophanes, Frogs 512–21 [5.2]

Maid:	Do, please, come inside with me!
Xanthias:	I really am fine thanks.
Maid:	Oh, nonsense! I'm not going to let you go. For there's already a very attractive (*hōraios*) flute-girl (*aulētris*) inside and two or three dancing-girls (*orchēstris*) besides –
Xanthias:	What's that you say? Dancing-girls?
Maid:	In the bloom of youth and freshly plucked. So, do come in! The cook was just about to take the strips of fish off the fire and the table was being brought in.
Xanthias:	Go on, then, and quick as you like tell the flute-girls inside that the man himself is coming in. (*to Dionysus*) Slave! Follow me this way and bring my stuff.

AP The distastefulness of cunnilingus

Aristophanes, Knights 1284–9 [5.8]

Chorus: Arginotus has a brother, not akin in his ways – Ariphrades the wicked. Well, wicked is what he's resolved to be. But it's not just that he's wicked or I wouldn't have noticed him, nor is he super-wicked. No, he's discovered something wickeder still. He maltreats his own tongue with shameful pleasures, licking the abominable dew in brothels (*kasaureion*), sullying his beard and stirring up sacred hearths . . . . And so whoever does not utterly detest a man such as this, may he never drink from the same cup as me.

AQ A fantasy of sex with a boy with balls

Aristophanes, Knights 1384–6 [5.5]

Sausage-Selller (*to Demos*): On these conditions, have this folding-chair here and a boy (*pais*) with nice balls (*enorchēs*); and if the fancy ever takes you . . . turn the boy into a folding-chair!

AR The city gates as a location for prostitution

Aristophanes, Knights 1398–1401 [3.4]

Sausage-Seller: . . . at the gates, . . . when he [Paphlagon] is drunk, he will exchange foul reproaches with the prostitutes (*pornē*) and will drink the wastewater of the public baths.

AS Adulterers and dildos

Aristophanes, Lysistrata 107–9 [5.6; 5.7]

Lysistrata: There's not so much as an adulterer (*moichos*) left us [i.e. because the men of Athens are away on military campaigns]. Yes, and since the time the Milesians deserted us, I haven't even seen an eight-finger dildo (*olisbos*).

AT Lysistrata's tantalising plans for ending the war

Aristophanes, Lysistrata 149–54 [5.1; 5.2; 5.3; 5.4]

Lysistrata (*to the other women*): If we sat at home all made up and in our finest linen chitons, naked underneath, with our pubic hair plucked in a delta-shape, and our husbands started to stiffen and wanted a screw (*splekoō*), and we wouldn't approach them but kept away, they'd soon be making peace treaties, I can tell you.

AU The effect of Helen's breasts

Aristophanes, Lysistrata 155–6 [5.2]

Lampito: Certainly Menelaus, when he somehow caught sight of Helen's bare breasts (*melon*: lit. 'apples'), let his sword fall, I think.

AV The threat of forced sex in the marital home

Aristophanes, Lysistrata 160–6 [4.8]

Calonice: What if [our husbands] take hold of us and drag us into the bedroom by force (*bia*)?

Lysistrata: Hold on to the doors.

Calonice: And if they strike us?

Lysistrata: You must give in as grudgingly as you can – for there's no pleasure in this when it's done by force (*bia*) – and you should make them suffer generally. Don't you worry, they'll soon give up. For no man (*anēr*) is ever going to get any gratification unless it suits the woman (*gynē*) that he should.

AW The plight of unmarried women compared to that of men

Aristophanes, Lysistrata 594–97 [1.6; 1.14; 5.3]

Lysistrata:	I am deeply distressed about the girls (*korē*) growing old in their chambers.
Magistrate:	What? Don't men (*anēr*) grow old, too?
Lysistrata:	Really, by Zeus! You're not comparing like with like. A man comes home and even if he's grey-haired he can find a young (*pais*) girl (*korē*) to marry (*gameō*) soon enough. But for a woman (*gynē*) time is fleeting, and if she doesn't seize the short chance she's got, no one wants to marry her and she's forced to sit there, hoping against hope.

AX A husband teased during the sex strike

Aristophanes, Lysistrata 854–7 [5.4; 5.5]

Lysistrata (*to Cinesias*): Your name is well known to us, because your wife (*gynē*) always has you on her lips. Whenever she picks up an egg or an apple, she says, 'Let this one be for Cinesias.'

AY The Peiraeus as a location for prostitution

Aristophanes, Peace 164–5 [3.4]

Trygaeus: Hey you, mate, what are you doing, taking a crap (*chezō*) in the Peiraeus, where the prostitutes (*pornē*) are?

AZ A fantasy of rough sex with a willing girl

Aristophanes, Peace 894–904 [1.2; 4.7; 5.1; 5.7]

Trygaeus (*addressing various public officials*): And next, now you've got her [the prostitute Theoria], you can hold a fine athletic contest tomorrow and wrestle her on the ground, set her up on all fours, oil yourselves and fight no-holds-barred, striking and gouging with fist as well as – cock (*peos*)! And in two days' time you can hold a horse race, with *racehorse* (*kelēs*) *outriding racehorse* and chariots piling on top of each other and *thrusting* together, puffing and panting – and other charioteers will be lying on the ground, their dicks all stiff, after falling down while negotiating the curves.

BA The behaviour of adulterous women

Aristophanes, Peace 979–85 [4.5]

Slave: . . . and don't do what the adulterous (*moicheuomenos*) women (*gynē*) do. For they open the outside door a bit and peep out; and if someone turns his attention to them they go back in; and then if he goes away, they peep out again.

BB A description of Agathon

Aristophanes, Women at the Thesmophoria *29–35 [2.6; 2.9; 5.5; 5.8]*

Euripides:	This is the home of the famous tragic poet Agathon.
In-Law:	Which Agathon is that?
Euripides:	There liveth a certain Agathon who . . .
Agathon:	You don't mean the tanned, strapping one?
Euripides:	No, it's another one. Haven't you ever seen him?
Agathon:	Not the one with the bushy beard?
Euripides:	You really *haven't* seen him.
In-Law:	No, by Zeus, not that I'm aware.
Euripides:	And yet you must have *fucked* him (*bineō*) – though perhaps you're not aware.

BC Agathon's fresh-faced appearance

Aristophanes, Women at the Thesmophoria *190–2 [5.5]*

Euripides (*to Agathon*): . . . I am white-haired and have got a beard, whereas you are fresh-faced (*euprosōpos*), pale-skinned (*leukos*), clean-shaven, woman-voiced, soft (*hapalos*) and attractive to look at (*euprepēs*).

BD Agathon insulted

Aristophanes, Women at the Thesmophoria *198–201 [2.6; 2.9; 2.11; 5.8]*

Agathon:	For it is proper to bear one's misfortunes not with tricks, but by passive acceptance.
In-Law:	You certainly got wide-arsed (*euryprōktos*), you bugger (*katapygōn*), not with words, but by passive acceptance!

BE A curse on those who betray women and their sexual misdemeanours

Aristophanes, Women at the Thesmophoria *331–51 [1.10; 1.11; 4.5; 5.7]*

Critylla (*addressing the assembly of women at the Thesmophoria festival*): Everyone pray to the gods – to the Olympians and Olympianesses; to the Pythians and Pythianesses; to the Delians and Delianesses – and to the other gods. If anyone plots against the citizen body of women; or enters into negotiations with Euripides and the Medes with a view to harming women in any way; or aspires to rule as dictator or to conspire to bring back the dictatorship; or tells on a woman who is trying to pass off someone else's baby as her own; or if a slave-girl acts as a go-between and then whispers in her master's ear or is sent on a little errand and brings back false information; or if an adulterer (*moichos*) tells lies in an attempt to deceive and never gives what he promises; or if an old woman (*graus*) gives an adulterer (*moichos*) a gift; or if a courtesan (*hetaira*) receives gifts while cheating on her boyfriend (*philos*); and if an inn-keeper or inn-keeperess abuses the currency of their *chous* [three-litre] or *kotylē* [quarter-litre] measures, pray that they perish miserably, both they themselves *and* their house. But for all you others, pray that the gods grant you many blessings.

BF Old bridegrooms and young brides

Aristophanes, Women at the Thesmophoria *410–13 [1.6]*

Mica: He [Euripides] has now told slanderous tales to all the old men (*gerōn*) who used to marry young girls (*meirax*), so none of them wants to risk marriage (*gameō gynaika*) on account of the saying, 'A bridegroom (*nymphios*) who's old gets a wife (*gynē*) who's a scold.'

BG The in-law's speech about female misdemeanours

Aristophanes, Women at the Thesmophoria *466–519 [1.10; 1.11; 1.16; 4.5; 5.1; 5.6; 5.7; 5.9]*

In-Law: It's no wonder, ladies, that you're dead furious with Euripides, given that you've heard such wicked things from him – nor that your anger is boiling over. For I myself (so may I take delight in my children) hate that man – I'd be mad not to. Nevertheless, we should give the matter a proper airing amongst ourselves. For we're on our own and there's no one here to disclose what we say. Why do we insist on blaming him and get upset if he relates two or three misdemeanours of ours that he knows about, when we've committed countless thousands of them? To start with, I myself (not to mention anyone else) have all kinds of wicked things on my conscience. But the wickedest was when I was a bride (*nymphē*) of three days and my husband (*anēr*) was asleep next to me. I had this friend who had taken my virginity when I was just seven years old. He was desperate for a bit of what I had to offer and came scratching at the door. Well, I knew who it was straight away. Then I start tiptoeing downstairs. And my husband asks, 'Where're *you* off to?' 'Where? I've got these cramps and pain in my stomach, my dear, so I'm just off to the bog.' 'Off you trot, then!' And then he started busying himself grinding juniper berries, dill and wild sage [i.e. as a remedy]. And I poured water over the door hinge and went out to meet my lover (*erastēs*). And so next thing you know I was bent over (*kybda*) next to the altar of Apollo, clinging to the laurel bush and getting a good old seeing to! Euripides never mentioned *that* one – do you see? Nor does he say how, when we've no one else available, we get humped senseless by the slaves and muleteers. Nor how, when we've been shafted by someone all night long, we chew garlic so that when our husbands (*anēr*) come in from the city-walls and smell it they don't suspect we've been up to any mischief. Do you see? He never mentioned *that*! And if he reviles Phaedra, what's that to us? He's never said anything about *this* one – how the woman, while showing her husband what her mantle looked like up against the light, had her lover (*moichos*) smuggled out of the house all wrapped up: he's never spoken about that! And I know another woman who claimed to be in labour for ten days until she managed to buy a baby. And all the while her husband was going around buying birth-charms. An old woman brought it in a jar – the baby, that is – with its mouth plugged up so that it wouldn't scream. Then, when she gets the nod from the old woman, she cries out, 'Away with you! Away, husband! I think I'm giving birth *now*!' (For the baby was kicking the pot in the stomach.) *He* went running off delighted, *she* took the thing out of the baby's mouth, and *it* cried out. Then the wicked old woman, who was carrying the baby, runs to the husband, wreathed in smiles, and says, 'You've had a lion, a lion! He's the spitting image of you and resembles you in every way. Even his little todger (*posthion*) is just like yours: curved like a catkin!' Do we not do these wicked things? Of course we do, by Artemis. And then we get angry at Euripides, although the accusations we suffer are hardly any worse than the facts.

BH Cleisthenes' femininity

Aristophanes, Women at the Thesmophoria *574–6 [2.6; 2.9; 2.11; 5.5]*

Cleisthenes: My dear ladies, whose lifestyle I share: it must be obvious from my hairless cheeks that I'm a friend of yours. I'm just *mad* about femininity and have always acted as your ambassador . . .

BI Men's fascination with the 'curse' that is the female sex

Aristophanes, Women at the Thesmophoria *786–99 [5.7]*

Chorus: Everyone says many bad things about the female sex, claiming that we are an utter curse on mankind and that all manner of evils originate with us: disputes, quarrels, civil strife, sorrow, war. Come on now, if we're really a curse, why do you marry (*gameō*) us? If we're really a curse, why do you forbid us from leaving the house and from being caught so much as peeping outside. And why do you take such efforts to keep a close guard on this 'curse'? If the little lady does go off somewhere and you find that she's not at home, you have an absolute fit, whereas you really ought to be pouring libations and paying thanks if you find that your 'curse' has disappeared and is nowhere to be found at home. And if we're having a nice time round a friend's house and get tired and fall asleep, then all of you go round the couches looking for the 'curse'. And if we peep out of a window, you all seek to get a look at the 'curse'. And if she's embarrassed and retreats, then everyone is all the more keen to get a glimpse of the curse when she peeps out again.

BJ The benefits of jury service: boys' genitalia and heiresses

Aristophanes, Wasps *577–87 [2.2; 2.6; 5.5; 5.7]*

Bdelycleon:	Remind me what benefits you enjoy from your so-called 'control of Greece' [i.e. from serving on a jury].
Philocleon:	Well, we get to see the private parts (*aidoia*) of boys (*pais*) being examined for registration [the reference is probably to legal disputes emerging from boys' registrations as citizen deme-member, i.e. when boys were seventeen or eighteen]. . . . And if a father leaves behind a daughter as an heiress (*epiklēros*), having promised her to someone on his deathbed, we tell the will to go to hell . . . and give her to whoever wins us over with his entreaties. And our actions come under

no scrutiny whatsoever – which is true of no other public office.

BK An old man asks a flute-girl for sexual favours

Aristophanes, Wasps *1341–53 [1.2; 3.5; 3.6; 5.1; 5.7]*

Philocelon: Come up here, my golden little cockchafer: take hold of this rope with your hand. (*putting his leather phallus in her hand*) Here you go! Mind how you go as the rope's decayed. All the same, it doesn't mind being rubbed, though! You see how cleverly I stole you away when you were just about to suck off (*lesbiazō*) the dinner guests. Do my cock (*peos*) a favour in return for that, won't you? But you won't pay me back and won't do it, I know: instead, you'll cheat me and laugh at this thing with your mouth wide open. For you've been open mouthed for plenty of others before now. But if you're a good girl now, my little beaver, when my son dies, I'll set you free and take you as a concubine (*pallakē*).

BL Objectification of a flute-girl

Aristophanes, Wasps *1368–81 [5.4; 5.7]*

Bdelycleon:	Isn't it disgraceful that you mock me when you've stolen the dinner-guests' flute-girl (*aulētris*)?
Philocleon:	What do you mean, flute-girl? Why are you blathering on like this as if you've fallen off a tomb?
Bdelycleon:	This, by Zeus, is Dardanis that you've got here.
Philocleon:	No, it's not. It's a torch being burnt for the gods in the marketplace (*agora*).
Bdelycleon:	A torch, is it?
Philocleon:	That's what I said: a torch. Can't you see where it's split?
Bdelycleon:	So what's this black patch here in the middle, then?
Philocleon:	The pitch, of course, oozing out as it burns.
Bdelycleon:	But here, behind – this is an arse (*prōktos*), isn't it?
Philocleon:	No. It's a knot protruding from the wood of the torch.
Bdelycleon:	What are you going on about? A knot indeed! (*to Dardanis*) Come here, won't you?
Philocleon:	Hey! Hey! What are you trying to do?
Bdelycleon:	I'm taking her away from you, since I think you're worn out and incapable of doing anything.

BM Corinthian prostitutes and unscrupulous boys

Aristophanes, Wealth *149–59 [2.6]*

Chremylus: And they say that Corinthian prostitutes (*hetaira*), if it's a poor man that happens to be propositioning them, pay him no attention; but if he's rich they turn their arse(hole) (*prōktos*) towards him straight away.

Carion: They say that boys (*pais*) do just the same thing – not for the sake of their lovers (*erastēs*) but for money.

Chremylus: Not the decent ones, just the whores (*pornos*): virtuous boys don't ask for money.

Carion: What then?

Chremylus: One asks for a good horse; another for some hunting dogs . . .

Carion: Right! Because they're ashamed to ask for money, I suppose, they disguise their wickedness with a verbal deceit.

BN A toy boy rejects an old woman now he is no longer poor

Aristophanes, Wealth *975–1005 [3.8; 3.9; 5.5; 5.8]*

Old Woman: Listen then. I used to have a young boyfriend (*meirakion*); a poor lad, but attractive (*euprosōpos*), handsome (*kalos*) and decent. For if I ever needed anything, he would do everything for me properly and nicely. And I would do him any service in return.

Chremes: What was it exactly that he asked you to do each time?

Old Woman: Not a lot: he treated me with great respect. But he might have asked for twenty drachmas for a cloak or eight for some shoes. And he might have pressed me to buy a chiton for his sisters or a nice little cloak for his mother, or have asked me for the odd four bushels [145 litres] of wheat.

Chremes: (*ironically*) That's certainly not a lot, then, by Apollo, according to you! He evidently *did* treat you with respect!

Old Woman: Let me add that he said he was not asking for these things out of greed, but out of affection (*philia*), so that by wearing my cloak he would be reminded of me.

Chremes:	You describe a man who was so completely in love (*eraō*) with you!
Old Woman:	But the hateful man doesn't pay me any attention any more. Indeed, he's completely changed in every way. For when I sent him this flat-cake here and the other sweetmeats that are on the tray and said that I'd come over in the evening . . .
Chremes:	What did he do? Tell me!
Old Woman:	He sent them back to me with this milk-cake, too, adding that I was never to go there again – and on top of this he sent the message, 'The Milesians were once brave soldiers – long ago!'
Chremes:	He clearly didn't use to be a man who behaved badly. However, now that he's rich he no longer takes pleasure in lentil soup – whereas beforehand his poverty meant that he'd lick anything up!

BO Insults about an old woman's appearance

Aristophanes, Wealth *1038–65 [5.2; 5.3]*

Old Woman:	And here comes the young man (*meirakion*) I've been complaining about all this time. He looks like he is off to a revel.
Chremylus:	He does indeed, walking along with garlands and a torch in his hand.
Young Man:	Hello there!
Old Woman:	What's he saying?
Young Man:	Ancient friend, you've become grey-haired quickly, by heaven.
Old Woman:	Poor me, how insulted I am (*hybrizomai*) by his abuse (*hybris*)!
Chremylus:	He doesn't seem to have seen you for a long time.
Old Woman:	What do you mean 'a long time', you fool? He was at my place yesterday.
Chremylus:	Then the opposite has happened to him than to most people: for it seems he can see more clearly when he's drunk!
Old Woman:	No, his behaviour has always been unrestrained.
Young Man:	O Sea-God Poseidon, and ye gods of old age, how many wrinkles she has on her face!
Old Woman:	Oh, no, no, don't bring the torch near me.

Chremylus:	She is quite right. For if one lone spark hits her, she will burn like an old branch.
Young Man:	Do you want to play with me for a little while?
Old Woman:	Where, you wretched boy?
Young Man:	Right here, after taking these nuts.
Old Woman:	What game?
Young Man:	Counting . . . how many teeth you have.
Chremylus:	I will take a guess, too. I reckon she's got three or four perhaps.
Young Man:	Pay up! Because she's only one molar.
Old Woman:	You most wicked of men! I don't think you're in your right mind, making me a trough for washing dirty linen in front of all these men.
Young Man:	But you'd be better off, if someone *did* give you a proper wash.
Chremylus:	Not at all, because now she's vamped up for sale; but if that white lead (*psimythion*) gets stripped off, you will see the rags of her face all too clearly!

Aristophon

Playwright of Middle Comedy active in the fourth century BC.

A The perils of marriage

Aristophon, fr. 6 KA Kallōnidēs [1.10]

May the second man to get married (*gameō*) come to a bad end. The *first* one did nothing wrong; for he married (*lambanō*) a woman (*gynē*) without yet knowing what a disaster that was. But the one getting married after him, although he knew, threw himself into a foreseen evil.

Aristotle

Born in Chalcidice, Nothern Greece, in 384 BC, Aristotle studied under Plato in Athens until the latter's death in 348 BC. Aristotle is perhaps most famous as a philosopher and biologist, but his work spans a vast range of subject matter. He died in 322 BC.

A Pericles' 'citizenship' law

[Aristotle], Constitution of Athens *26.3 [1.1]*
... when Antidotus was archon [i.e. 451 BC], because of the multitude of citizens (*politēs*), on Pericles' proposal, they determined that a man should not have a share in the city (*polis*) unless he had been born from two citizens (*astos*).

B Laws governing the hire and pay of flute-girls

[Aristotle], Constitution of Athens *50.2 [3.1; 3.5; 3.9; 4.1]*
There are ten *astynomoi* [controllers of the city], five of whom hold office in the Peiraeus and five in the city. These men supervise the flute-girls (*aulētris*), the harp-players (*psaltria*) and the cithara-players (*kitharistria*), ensuring that that they are not hired out for more than two drachmas. If more than one man is eager to take the same girl, these men cast lots, and they hire her out to the winner.

C The procedure for dealing with certain criminals

[Aristotle], Constitution of Athens *52.1 [4.3]*
They [the Athenians] appoint by lot the Eleven to be in charge of those who are in prison and those arrested as thieves, kidnappers and clothes-stealers. If they confess, they punish them with death. But if they deny it, they take them to court. If they are acquitted, they set them free, if not, they put them to death ...

D Justifiable and unintentional homicide

[Aristotle], Constitution of Athens *57.3 [4.3]*
... if someone admits to homicide, but claims it was done in accordance with the laws, such as after taking someone as an adulterer (*moichos*), or unintentionally in war, or while participating in an athletic contest, they judge him at the Delphinium.

E Financial profit and loss resulting from adultery

Aristotle, Nicomachean Ethics *5.2.4 (1130a) [4.5]*
Moreover, if one man commits adultery (*moicheuō*) for profit, while another pays out money in the form of a fine because of his desire (*epithymia*), the latter would seem to be more

undisciplined (*akolastos*) than greedy, the former unjust (*adikos*), but not undisciplined.

F The natural affection between husband and wife

Aristotle, Nicomachean Ethics *8.12.7 (1162a) [1.10]*
The affection (*philia*) between husband (*anēr*) and wife (*gynē*) appears to arise from natural instinct. For people are by nature used to living in pairs even more than living in communities, since the household (*oikia*) is an earlier and more fundamental institution than the state, and procreation (*teknopoiia*) is a more general characteristic of living beings. For other animals, unions (*koinōnia*) are for that purpose alone, but people live together (*synoikeō*) not only for the sake of having children but also to provide the needs of life. There is immediately a division of labour between men's (*anēr*) and women's (*gynē*) work, and so they supply each other's needs by adding their own contribution to the whole. For this reason usefulness and pleasure seem to be joined together in their affection (*philia*). But it [affection] may also be based on virtue, if they are good people; for each sex has its own virtue, and this may form the basis of attraction.

G Permanent and fleeting same-sex relationships

Aristotle, Nicomachean Ethics *9.1.2–3 (1164a) [2.11]*
In erotic relationships (*erōtikē*) sometimes the lover (*erastēs*) complains that although he loves beyond measure (*hyperphileō*) he is not loved in return (*antiphileō*): maybe because there happens to be nothing likeable about him. Or often the beloved (*erōmenos*) complains that he now gets nothing when earlier he was promised everything. Such disputes occur whenever one loves the beloved (*erōmenos*) for pleasure (*hēdonē*), and the other loves the lover (*erastēs*) for profit, and these things cease to exist for both of them. For this reason, although the friendship (*philia*) remains, the relationship breaks down, since the things they loved (*phileō*) each other for do not exist. For they did not feel affection (*stergō*) for each other, but rather for attributes that were there in the beginning but were not permanent. For that reason such friendships (*philia*) are not permanent either. But friendship that is based on character and formed for its own sake lasts, as has been said.

H No word for marriage

Aristotle, Politics *1.2.2 (1253b) [1.5]*
The union (*syzeuxis*) of a man and a woman has no name.

I The governance of slaves, children and women in the home

Aristotle, Politics *1.5.1–2 1259a–1259b [1.10]*
. . . there are three parts to household management (*oikonomikos*), one the relation of master to slave (*despotikos*) mentioned earlier, one the paternal relation (*patrikos*), and the third the conjugal (*gamikos*). One rules over both one's wife (*gynē*) and children (*teknon*) as over free men, yet not with the same mode of government, but over the wife democratically and over the children monarchically. [59b] For the male (*arrēn*) is by nature better suited to command than the female (*thēlys*) . . . .

J The appropriate ages for marriage and childbearing

Aristotle, Politics *7.14.4–6 (1335a) [1.6; 1.11]*
And the mating (*syndyasmos*) of the young is bad for childbearing (*teknopoiia*). For in all living beings the offspring of the young is imperfect, and more likely to be female and small in size, so that the same thing necessarily happens in humans as well. The proof of this is that in those states where it is the custom for young men and women to have sexual intercourse (*syzeugnymi*), the people are imperfect and small in size. Moreover, young girls suffer more in childbirth and more of them die. It is for this reason, some say, that the oracle was given to the people of Troezen, because many women were dying because they were marrying (*gamiskō*) too young . . . . Moreover, giving women in marriage (*ekdosis*) when they are older also contributes to their self-control (*sōphrosynē*); for they seem to be more wanton (*akolastos*) if they have had sexual intercourse (*synousia*) when young. And the growth of men's (*arrēn*) bodies is thought to be harmed if they have intercourse (*synousia*) while their seed is growing. For it, too, has a limited time, after which it stops being plentiful. Therefore it is fitting for girls to be married (*syzeugnymi*) around their eighteenth year, and men around thirty-seven or a little later. For in these circumstances the union (*syzeuxis*) will occur at a time when their bodies are in their prime and they will come to the end of childbearing capabilities (*teknopoiia*) at the same juncture, at the appropriate time for both. And when the

children (*teknon*) take over the management of the household they will just be entering their prime of life (*akmē*) – if offspring are born promptly at the expected time – and the parents will now be coming to the end of their prime (*hēlikia*), towards the [father's] seventieth year.

K Men choose to keep quiet about *hybris* in the family

Aristotle, Rhetoric *1.12.35 (1373a) [5.9]*
And [men] commit injustices that people are ashamed (*aideomai*) to disclose, such as insults (*hybris*) against the women (*gynē*) of their household, or against themselves or their sons.

L The nature of *hybris*

Aristotle, Rhetoric *2.2.5–6 (1378b) [4.8]*
Hybris is doing or saying anything which causes shame (*aischynē*) for the victim, not for the purpose of gaining anything by it, but simply for the pleasure of it. And people seeking revenge do not commit *hybris* (*hybrizō*), but seek justice. And the reason that people get pleasure from being insulting (*hybrizō*) is that they think that treating people badly makes them feel all the more superior. (It is for this reason that the young and the rich insult people (*hybristēs*)): they think themselves superior when committing *hybris* (*hybrizō*). Dishonour (*atimia*) is characteristic of *hybris*, and the man who dishonours (*atimazō*) another slights him.

Athenaeus

A native of Naucratis in Egypt, his only surviving work, *Sophists at Dinner* (*Deipnosophistai*), was probably composed shortly before AD 200. It contains various anecdotes pertaining to figures from earlier times and is an especially rich repository of material from Athenian Middle and New Comedy.

A Nannion's nickname

Athenaeus, Sophists at Dinner *(*Deipnosophistai*) book 13, 587b [5.4]*
In *On Courtsans* (*Peri Hetairōn*) Antiphanes [i.e. a comic poet] says that Nannion was nicknamed *Proskēnion* [Front-of-Stage] because

although she had a nice face and wore gold jewellery and expensive clothes, she was particularly ugly when stripped.

B Sophocles steals a kiss from a slave-boy

Athenaeus, Sophists at Dinner (Deipnosophistai*) book 13,*
603e–604d [2.5; 2.10; 5.5]

Sophocles was fond of boys (*philomeirax*), just as Euripides was fond of women (*philogynēs*). Ion the poet says this in his work entitled *Visits* (*Epidemiai*): I encountered Sophocles [603f] the poet in Chios, when he was sailing to Lesbos as a general; when drinking wine he was playful and witty. While Hermesilaus, a guest-friend (*xenos*) of his and local representative of the Athenians, was entertaining him at a feast, standing by the fire was the slave-boy pouring the wine. Sophocles was obviously [. . .] and said, 'Do you want me to enjoy drinking?' And when the boy said yes, [Sophocles said,] 'Well, bring me my wine cup (*kylix*) nice and slowly and take it away nice and slowly.' And once the boy (*pais*) had blushed still more, Sophocles said to the man reclining next to him, 'How beautifully Phrynichus conveyed it when he said: [604a] 'The light of love (*erōs*) shines on purple cheeks' . . .

[604b] . . . Sophocles began [604c] speaking to the boy again. He was trying to pick off a small piece of straw from the wine cup with his little finger and Sophocles asked him if he could see the straw. When he said that he saw it distinctly, he said, 'Well then, blow it off so that your finger doesn't need to be washed.' And when the boy brought his face closer to the wine cup, Sophocles brought the wine cup closer to his own mouth, so that the boy's head would be nearer to his own head. When he was very close to him, he grabbed the boy with his hand and kissed him. Everyone applauded, laughed and shouted how well he had led [604d] the boy on . . . .

Cratinus

Playwright of Old Comedy, considered the great comic dramatist of the generation before Aristophanes; career dates c. 454–423 BC.

A Lust among the ruins

Cratinus, fr. 160 KA The All-Seeing Ones (Panoptai*) [2.11]*
Aristodemus, like a man behaving in an unseemly fashion (*aschēmoneō*) among the ruins of Cimon's edifices.

Demosthenes

Athenian politician and orator, 384–322 BC, to whom sixty-one surviving speeches have traditionally been attributed. *Against Neaera*, which was delivered in the late 340s BC, is now generally thought to have been written not by Demosthenes but by Apollodorus.

A Considerations when choosing a suitable groom

Demosthenes, Against Leptines *20.57 [1.2]*
. . . in our private affairs each of us considers who is worthy to marry into our families as an in-law (*kēdestēs*), or something of that sort, and these matters are also determined by certain customs and opinions . . .

B Some examples of *hybris* in Athens

Demosthenes, Against Meidias *21.36 [3.5; 4.8]*
So, someone reported to me that Meidias was going around gathering information and making inquiries about those who had been outraged (*hybrizō*), and that he is about to recount and describe them to you; such as, men of Athens, the presiding officer who, they say, was once struck by Polyzelus in your court, the Thesmothete who was recently struck while trying to wrestle away the flute-girl (*aulētris*), and other such examples. His idea is that, if he demonstrates that many others have suffered many misfortunes, your anger at him for what I have suffered would be less!

C Solon's law on male prostitution

Demosthenes, Against Androtion *22.30–2 [2.8; 3.8; 4.1]*
[30] Therefore it is worthwhile, men of Athens, both to scrutinise Solon who set up the law (*nomos*), and to contemplate how much foresight he had in setting up all the laws of the constitution, and how much keener he was on the constitution than on the matter about which he was legislating. And this is something one could discern from a number of angles, not least from the law that states that those who have prostituted (*hetaireō*) themselves are allowed neither to speak publicly nor to propose laws. For he saw that although many of you are allowed to speak you don't, so that this restriction did not seem onerous and he could have set up many harsher laws, if indeed he wished to punish these men.

D The law on unintentional homicide

Demosthenes, Against Aristocrates *23.53 [1.15; 4.3; 4.8]*

Law
[If any man kills another unintentionally during an athletic contest, or after
overpowering him [in a struggle?] on the street, or mistakenly in battle, or
when he catches him with (*epi*) his wife (*damar*), mother, sister, daughter,
or with a concubine (*pallakē*) kept for the purpose of begetting free children, he shall not be exiled as a murderer on this account.]

E Demosthenes' father betroths his wife and daughter on his deathbed

Demosthenes, Against Aphobus *I 27.4–5 [1.3; 1.4; 1.9]*
[4] For my father, Demosthenes, gentlemen of the jury, left at his death
an estate of nearly fourteen talents, a son, myself, aged seven, my sister,
aged five, and our mother, who was still alive and who had brought a
dowry of 50 minas to the household (*oikos*). He had made plans for
our welfare and, when he was about to die, put all this property in the
hands of both Aphobus here and Demophon, son of Demo. They were
nephews of his, the one the son of his brother, the other of his sister
and of Therippides of Paeania, who was not a relative, but had been
his friend since boyhood. [5] To Therippides he gave the interest on 70
minas of my property, until I should come of age, so that he might not
mishandle my affairs through greed. To Demophon he gave my sister
in marriage with a dowry of two talents, to be paid at once. And to this
man here, Aphobus, he gave our mother with a dowry (*proix*) of 80
minas, and the house to live in and use of my furniture. His thinking
behind this was that, if he bound these men to me by still closer ties,
they would be better guardians to me because of this added bond of
kinship.

F A man persuaded to marry at the age of eighteen

Demosthenes, Against Boeotus *II 40.12 [1.2; 1.6]*
And he [the speaker's father] persuaded me straight away, for I
was about eighteen years of age, to marry (*gameō*) the daughter of
Euphemus, since he wished to see children born to me.

G Marital disagreements settled for the sake of the children

Demosthenes, Against Boeotus II *40.29 [1.10]*
For surely husband (*anēr*) and wife (*gynē*) are much more likely, if they are disagreeing with one another, to make up for the sake of their children (*pais*) than, because of their hatred towards each other, to hate the children they have in common as well.

H The creation of five households from one

Demosthenes, Against Macartatus *43.19 [1.12]*
Buselus, gentlemen of the jury, was a man from the deme of Oeon, and he had five sons, Hagnias, Eubulides, Stratius, Habron and Cleocritus. All these sons of Buselus grew up to manhood, and their father Buselus divided his property among them all fairly and equally, as was fitting. And when they had divided the property among themselves, each of them married (*gameō*) a wife (*gynē*) according to your laws, and they all had children and grandchildren. Five households arose from the single one of Buselus and they lived separately, each one having his own home and creating his own descendants.

I Archiades chooses not to marry

Demosthenes, Against Leochares *44.10 [1.14]*
Archiades declared that he did not wish to marry and . . . lived by himself in Salamis.

J A law on the betrothal of women – including the heiress [1.3]

Demosthenes, Against Stephanus II *46.18*

Law
If a woman is betrothed (*engyaō*) as a wife (*damar*) in lawful marriage by her father or by her brother sired by her father or by her grandfather on her father's side, her children shall be legitimate (*gnēsios*). When there are none of these relatives, if the woman is an heiress (*epiklēros*), her guardian shall take her, but if she is not, whoever she can turn to shall be her guardian.

K A man vilified for keeping a *hetaira* in preference to a legitimate wife

Demosthenes, Against Olympiodorus *48.53–5 [3.6; 3.7]*

[53] ... For Olympiodorus here, judges, never married (*gameō*) a citizen (*astē*) woman (*gynē*) according to your laws, nor does he have children nor did he have any in the past. But he keeps in his house a courtesan (*hetaira*) he has set free, and she is the one causing us all grief and driving this man to something beyond madness. [54] For how can a man be said not to be mad who thinks he should under no circumstances do what he agreed with me, with his consent and my own, and swore on oath? And I am not only pursuing these matters for my own sake, but also on behalf of this man's sister, born of the same father (*homopatrios*) and mother (*homomētrios*), to whom I am married (*synoikeō*), and for the sake of his niece, my own daughter. For these women are being wronged not less than me, but even more. [55] For how can anyone say that they are not being wronged or not suffering grievously, when they see this man's courtesan (*hetaira*), in a most improper manner, decked out in many gold jewels and beautiful clothes, and going out in a magnificent state? They see her insulting (*hybrizō*) them, because all that was bought with our money, whilst they are completely lacking all those things themselves. How are those women not wronged more than I am?

L A man married to his half-sister by the same father

Demosthenes, Against Eubulides *57.20 [1.2; 5.8]*

I call as witnesses those of our kinsmen on our father's side who are still alive. Call first for me, then, Thucritides and Charisiades. Their father, Charisius, was brother to my grandfather, Thucritides, and to my grandmother, Lysarete, and uncle to my father – for my grandfather married (*gameō*) his half-sister (*adelphē*) by a different mother.

M A man passes his wife on to a friend and marries an heiress

Demosthenes, Against Eubulides *57.41 [1.7; 1.12]*

Protomachus was a poor man. But when he stood in line to inherit an estate by marrying a wealthy heiress (*epiklēros*), wishing to pass on my mother to another in marriage (*ekdidōmi*), he persuaded my father, Thucritus, an acquaintance of his, to take her. So my my mother was betrothed (*engyaō*) to my father by her brother, Timocrates of Melite, in the presence of both his own uncles and other witnesses. Those of them that are still living will give testimony before you.

N Athenian laws prohibiting marriages between citizens and foreigners

[Demosthenes], Against Neaera 59.16 [1.1; 1.15]

[16] . . . That Neaera is a foreigner (*xenē*) and lives with Stephanus as his wife (*synoikeō*) in contravention of the laws is something I wish to demonstrate to you clearly. And so first [the clerk] will read to you the law in respect of which Theomnastus brought this indictment (*graphē*) and this case comes before you.

Law

If a foreigner (*xenos*) shall live as a husband with (*synoikeō*) a citizen woman (*astē*) in any way or by any means, let him be indicted (*graphomai*) before the Thesmothetae by any of the Athenians so permitted who wishes to do so. And if he is convicted, he and his property shall be sold, and a third of the proceeds shall belong to the man who secured the conviction. The same principle shall also apply if a foreign woman (*xenē*) lives as a wife (*synoikeō*) with a citizen (*astos*), and any man living as a husband (*synoikeō*) with a foreign woman (*xenē*) so convicted shall be fined 1,000 drachmas.

O Nicarete buys and sells her prostitute 'daughters'

[Demosthenes], Against Neaera 59.18–19 [3.6; 3.8; 5.9]

[18] Nicarete procured these seven girls (*paidiskē*) while they were small children (*paidion*) – she was Charisius of Elea's freed-woman, and the wife of Hippias, his cook. She was skilled at recognising the comely (*euprepēs*) nature of small children (*paidion*) and knew how to bring them up and train them artfully. She made this her craft and amassed her livelihood from those girls. [19] She called them daughters (*thygatēr*), giving out that they were free women, so that she could exact the highest fees from those wishing to consort with them (*plesiazō*). When she had profited from each one's prime (*hēlikia*), she quickly sold the bodies of all seven of them: Anteia, Stratola, Aristocleia, Metaneira, Phila, Isthmias and this woman here: Neaera.

P Neaera is jointly purchased by two of her lovers

[Demosthenes], Against Neaera 59.29–30 [3.4; 3.6; 3.9]

[29] Well then, after this she had two lovers (*erastēs*), Timanoridas from Corinth and Eucrates from Leucas. Because Nicarete was extravagant in the fees she demanded, expecting all the daily expenses of the household to be paid by these men, they gave Nicarete a down payment of 30 minas as the value of (Neaera's) person, and bought her outright from Nicarete according to the law of the city to be their slave. [30] And they kept her and used her for as long as they wanted. But when they were about to marry, they told her that, since she had been their courtesan (*hetaira*), they did not want to see her plying her trade in Corinth or working for a brothel-keeper (*pornoboskos*). They said they were happy to receive less money from her than they had paid and to see her getting something to her advantage. So they said they would let her off 1,000 drachmas of the price for her freedom: 500 each. But they told her to find the 20 minas [i.e. the remaining 2,000 drachmas] to pay them.

Q Neaera's brutal treatment at various parties

[Demosthenes], Against Neaera 59.33 [3.2; 4.8]

So, after he [Phrynion] came here with her [Neaera], he treated her brutally and recklessly. He took her everywhere with him to dinners, where she would drink, and he always made her a partner in his revels: he had sex (*syneimi*) with her openly whenever and wherever he wished, making a lavish display to the onlookers of his power over her. And he took her to parties at many men's houses, including Chabrias of Aexone [. . .] and coming back from Delphi he gave a victory feast at Colias [i.e. to celebrate his victory in the chariot race at the Pythian Games, which were held at Delphi]. And there many others had sex (*syngignomai*) with her when she was drunk, while Phrynion was asleep, including Chabrias' servants.

R Neaera confides in Stephanus and entrusts herself to him

[Demosthenes], Against Neaera 59.37 [4.8]

. . . Stephanus came to stay in Megara and was lodging in her [Neaera's] house as with a courtesan (*hetaira*), and had sex (*plesiazō*) with her, and she described everything that had happened including Phrynion's outrageous behaviour (*hybris*). She gave him everything she had taken from him [Phrynion] when she had left, because she wanted to live here [i.e. in Athens], but was afraid of Phrynion because of the wrong she had done him, because he was angry with her, and because she knew that he had a violent and reckless temper. So she made Stephanus here her protector.

S Prostitution and blackmail undertaken by 'citizen' Neaera

[Demosthenes], Against Neaera 59.41 [3.7; 3.8; 4.3; 5.9]
Now that she had security through Stephanus and was living with him, she was doing the same work she used to, no less than before, yet was exacting higher fees from those wishing to have sex with her (*plesiazō*), pretending now to be someone's wife living with (*synoikeō*) her husband (*anēr*). And he would also help her, if she took some rich, naïve foreigner (*xenos*) as her lover (*erastēs*), in blackmailing him as an adulterer (*moichos*) caught with (*epi*) her: he would lock him up inside and, naturally, exact a large sum of money from him.

T Laws on divorce and passing off non-citizen women as Athenian

[Demosthenes], Against Neaera 59.52 [1.1; 1.7; 1.14]
Stephanus gained permission to bring a suit (*dikē*) for alimony against him [Phrastor] in the Odeion according to the law that commands, 'If someone divorces (*apopempō*) his wife (*gynē*), he must return the dowry (*proix*); and if he does not, he must pay interest of 9 obols [i.e. monthly per 100 drachmas], and her guardian (*kyrios*) may bring a suit (*dikazomai*) for alimony in the Odeion on behalf of his wife (*gynē*).' Phrastor brought an indictment (*graphē*) against this man Stephanus before the Thesmothetae, on the grounds that he [Stephanus] had betrothed (*engyaō*) to him, an Athenian, the daughter of a foreign woman (*xenē*) as though she were his own. This was in accordance with the following law. Read it to me.

Law
If anyone gives in marriage (*ekdidōmi*) to an Athenian man a foreign (*xenos*) woman as though she belonged to himself, he shall be deprived of civic rights (*atimos*), and his possessions shall become public property, and one third will belong to the man convicting him. Anyone who is permitted to do so may bring an indictment (*graphomai*) before the Thesmothetae, just as in cases of usurpation of civic rights by a foreigner (*xenia*).

U Laws on adultery and an alleged blackmail plot

[Demosthenes], Against Neaera 59.64–7 [4.2; 4.3]

[64] . . . Epaenetus of Andros, who had been a lover (*erastēs*) of Neaera long ago and had spent large sums of money on her, used to stay with these people [Stephanus and Neaera] whenever he came to Athens owing to his affection (*philia*) for Neaera. [65] Stephanus here laid a plot against him. Sending for him to come to the country as if to make a sacrifice, he caught him as an adulterer (*moichos*) with (*epi*) the daughter of this here Neaera and extorted 30 minas from him in his fear, accepting as guarantors for this sum Aristomachus, who had once been a Thesmothete, and Nausiphilus, son of Nausilus who had served as archon. And he let him go on the condition that he would pay the money. [66] But when Epaenetus got out and became his own master again (*kyrios*) he brought an indictment (*graphē*) before the Thesmothetae against Stephanus here, on the grounds that he had been imprisoned unlawfully by him. This was in accordance with the law that commands, 'If anyone unjustly imprisons a man as an adulterer (*moichos*), the latter may indict (*graphomai*) him before the Thesmothetae for unjust imprisonment, and if he convicts the man that imprisoned him and proves that he has been unjustly plotted against, he himself is innocent and his guarantors are released of their surety; but if he proves to be an adulterer (*moichos*), [the law] commands that his guarantors hand him over to the one who caught him in the act, who may treat him in the courtroom in any way he wishes, as long as it is without a knife (or 'dagger': *encheiridion*), since the man is as an adulterer (*moichos*).' [67] Epaenetus indicted him in accordance with this law (*nomos*), and while he admitted having intercourse (*chraomai*) with the woman, he denied that he was an adulterer (*moichos*). His argument was that she was not Stephanus' daughter but Neaera's, and that her mother knew that she was having sex (*plesiazō*) with him. He also said that he had spent a considerable sum of money on them, supporting the whole household whenever he came to Athens. He referred to the law on these matters, which states that a man cannot be taken as an adulterer (*moichos*) with (*epi*) such women as are employed in a brothel (*ergasterion*) or who sell themselves openly. And he claimed that Stephanus' house was just this, a brothel (*ergasterion*), and that they were doing very nicely from this business.

V The law concerning the adulteress and her husband

[Demosthenes], Against Neaera 59.87 *[1.7; 4.4]*

Law on Adultery

If the adulterer (*moichos*) is caught (or 'convicted': *haireō/haliskomai*), the one who has caught him shall not be permitted to stay married (*synoikeō*) to his wife (*gynē*); and if he does stay married to her, he shall be deprived of his civic rights (*atimos*). Nor shall the woman (*gynē*) with (*epi*) whom the adulterer (*moichos*) was taken be allowed to attend the public rites; and if she does attend, let her suffer whatever punishment she may suffer with impunity, except for death.

W *Hetairai* should not be allowed to encroach on citizen women

[Demosthenes], Against Neaera 59.112–13 *[1.4; 3.10]*

[112] It would, therefore, be much better that this trial had not take place than if, now that it has taken place, you vote for an acquital. For in that case prostitutes (*pornē*) will immediately have freedom to live as wives (*synoikeō*) with whomever they want, and to say that their children are fathered by whomever they want; and your laws will become invalid, and those who are courtesans (*hetaira*) by nature would be able to do anything they pleased. Consider also, therefore, the citizen women (*politis*), so that the daughters of poor men are not deprived of marriage (*anekdotos*). [113] As it is now, even if a girl is poor, the law provides an adequate dowry (*proix*) for her, if nature has given her even a moderately attractive appearance. But if you treat the law with disrespect and render it invalid by acquitting her, the trade of the prostitute (*pornē*) will most certainly reach the daughters of citizens (*politēs*), who through poverty will not be able to get married (*ekdidomai*), and the honour of free women will pass to the courtesans (*hetaira*), should permission be granted to them to bear children (*paidopoieomai*) however they please and to participate in ceremonies, sacrifices and honours in the city.

X *Hetairai*, concubines and wives

[Demosthenes], Against Neaera 59.122 *[1.5; 1.11; 1.15; 1.17]*

For this is what being married to a woman (*synoikeō*) means [for a man]: to have children (*paidopoieomai*), to introduce his sons to his phratry-members and his demesmen, and to give his daughters to men in marriage (*ekdidōmi*). We have courtesans (*hetaira*) for pleasure (*hēdonē*), concubines (*pallakē*) for the everyday care of our bodies, but wives (*gynē*) to have legitimate (*gnēsios*) children (*paidopoieomai*) and to have as a faithful keeper of our household affairs.

Y Advice to a beloved on good and shameful conduct

[Demosthenes], Erotic Essay 3–6 *[2.2; 2.6]*

[3] When I observe that several of those who are admired (*erōmenos*) and in possession of good looks (*kallos*) use neither of these pieces of fortune in the correct manner, but rather put on airs because of the comeliness of their appearance, scorn association with their admirers (*erastēs*), and fail to judge what is best to such an extent that, because of those men who act outrageously in these matters, they also act peevishly towards those looking to associate with them with decency (*sōphrosynē*), I came to the conclusion that [youngsters] of this kind not only act in a way that is injurious to themselves but also engender [4] bad habits in others. Likewise those who are wise should not copy their foolhardiness and should, in particular, bear in mind that, since actions are neither noble (*kalos*) nor disgraceful in themselves, but rather differ for the most part depending on the person performing them, it is illogical to adopt the same attitude towards both types of men. Furthermore, it is the most absurd thing of all to envy those who have a vast number of firm friends (*philos*) while simultaneously rejecting admirers (*erastēs*), who are a breed apart and who are drawn by nature to form relationships, not with all and sundry, but only with the beautiful (*kalos*) and modest (*sōphrōn*). [5] Besides, for those who have never seen a friendship (*philia*) of this kind turn out well, or who have vigorously condemned themselves in the belief that they would be incapable of associating modestly (*sōphronōs*) with their acquaintances, perhaps it would not be illogical to hold this opinion. But for those of a disposition like yours, who are in no way closed to hearing how many benefits accrue through love (*erōs*) without shame (*aischynē*) and who have lived the rest of their lives with the utmost circumspection, it is unreasonable to suspect that they would do anything shameful (*aischros*). [6] In consequence, I was all the more impelled to write this speech, thinking that I would gain two particularly fine (*kalos*) prizes. By listing the virtues you possess, I hope to demonstrate both that you are a worthy object of admiration and that I am not foolish to love (*agapaō*) you, given your qualities; and by offering advice for which there is a particularly pressing need, I believe I will be

offering an example of my goodwill and starting point for our mutual affection (*philia*).

Dinarchus

An Attic orator, Dinarchus was born in Corinth in c. 360 BC, but moved to Athens as a child. *Against Demosthenes* was composed for a trial which took place in 323 BC.

A The harshness of Athenian juries

Dinarchus, Against Demosthenes *1.23 [4.8]*
You are the ones who have imposed great and irrevocable punishments on people for crimes far smaller than those committed by Demosthenes. It was you who killed Menon the miller, because he kept a free boy (*pais*) from Pellene in his mill. You punished Themistius of Aphidna with death, because he assaulted the Rhodian cithara-player (*kitharistria*) at the Eleusinian festival, and Euthymachus, because he set up the Olynthian girl (*paidiskē*) in a brothel (or 'cubicle': *oikēma*; i.e. as a prostitute).

Diogenes Laertius

Author of a work on the lives and teachings of ancient philosophers; active in the first half of the third century AD.

A A report of the 'bigamy concession' in Athens

Diogenes Laertius 2.26 (= Aristotle, *On Good Birth*, fr. 93 Rose) *[1.13]*
It is said that the Athenians, wanting to increase their population because of a shortage of men, passed a law that men could marry (*gameō*) one citizen woman but also have children (*paidopoieomai*) by another.

Drinking songs

The poems included in this section are anonymous drinking songs (*skolia*). *PMG* stands for *Poetae Melici Graeci* (Greek Lyric Poets).

A A song in honour of Harmodius and Aristogeiton

PMG 895 [2.6]

I shall carry my sword in a branch of myrtle just like Harmodius and Aristogeiton when, during sacrifices in Athens, they killed the tyrant Hipparchus.

B Another song in honour of Harmodius and Aristogeiton

PMG 896 [2.6]

You will always have fame on earth, beloved Harmodius and Aristogeiton, because you killed the tyrant and made Athens democratic.

Epicrates

Playwright of Middle Comedy, active in the fourth century BC.

A The decline of Laïs, an ageing courtesan

Epicrates, fr. 3.11–21 KA Antilaïs [3.7]

For when she was a young chick, and she had been driven wild by staters [i.e. gold coins worth 4 drachmas], you could have seen Pharnabazus [i.e. the satrap of Phrygia] more quickly than her. But now she is running the last lap of her years and the frame of her body is slack, it is easier to see her than to spit. She goes out everywhere already drunk, she accepts even a stater or a half-drachma coin, and she admits old and young men alike. And she has become so tame, my dear, that she even takes the money out of your hand.

Eubulus

Playwright of Middle Comedy, c. 380–335 BC, active in the mid-fourth century BC.

A The stealthiness of adultery compared to the openness of the brothel

Eubulus, fr. 67. 1–9 KA Nannion [3.4; 3.7; 5.4]

The man that beds a woman secretly in a shady marriage-bed, isn't he the most wretched man of all? After all, it is possible for him to look in broad daylight at naked women stationed in a line, standing in webs of fine fabric – such girls (*korē*) as Eridanus [a river which flowed through the agora and Kerameikos] rears in a garden with pure waters. And from them you can buy pleasure (*hēdonē*) with a small coin, rather than pursue stealthy Cypris, the ugliest of all diseases, to give insult (*hybris*) not satisfy desire (*pothos*).

B Scantily dressed prostitutes for hire in a brothel

Eubulus, fr. 82 KA Night Festival (Pannychis) [5.4]
. . . the young girls (lit. 'foal': *pōlos*) of Aphrodite, decked out, naked and drawn up in a row, standing in webs of fine fabric – such girls (*korē*) as Eridanus rears in a garden with pure waters. And from them you can buy pleasure (*hēdonē*) with a small coin in safety and security.

C The make-up of an older woman runs on a hot day [5.3]

Eubulus, fr. 97. 3–6 KA The Garland-Sellers (Stephanopōlides)
If you go outside during summer, from your eyes there flow two rivulets of black water, and from your cheeks the sweat traces a red furrow to your throat . . .

Euripides

Athenian tragic poet, active from the mid-450s until his death in 406 BC. Amongst those Euripidean plays that can be dated securely are *Medea* (431 BC), *Hippolytus* (428 BC) and *Trojan Women* (415 BC). The approximate dates of other plays cited here, in order of composition, are as follows: *Andromache*, 426 BC, *Hecabe*, 424 BC, *Electra*, 416 BC, and *Auge*, 414–406 BC. *Iphigenia at Aulis* was written towards the end of Euripides' life (408–406 BC).

A The advantage of virtue over beauty for a wife

Euripides, Andromache *205–8 [5.1]*
Andromache (*to Hermione*): Your husband does not despise you because of any drugs of mine, but rather because you are not fit to live with. For this, too, acts as a love potion (*philtron*). It is not beauty, my dear, but virtuous qualities (*aretē*) that please husbands.

B A wife's secure status compared to that of a concubine

Euripides, Andromache 869–75 [1.4; 1.7; 1.10]

Nurse (*to Hermione*): Your husband will not be persuaded to break off his marriage (*kēdos*) to you, because of some foreign woman's (*gynē*) mean words. [For he did not receive you as a captive from Troy,] but took you as the daughter (*pais*) of a noble man with many wedding gifts from a city of considerable good fortune. And your father will not betray you and let you be thrown out of this house in this way, as you fear, child.

C An apology for rape

Euripides, Auge, *fr. 272b [4.6; 4.7]*

[Heracles] (*to Auge*): Now, it was the wine that drove me out of my senses. I admit that I wronged (*adikeō*) you, but the wrong (*adikēma*) was not intentional.

D A warning to the adulterer who marries an adulteress

Euripides, Electra 921–4 [4.4]

Electra: [When a man has ruined (*diollymi*) someone else's wife (*damar*) in secret beds (*eunē*) and is then compelled to take her as his own wife, let him know that he is a wretched fool if he thinks that the self-control (*sōphrosynē*) she did not show there [i.e. with her previous husband], she will show for him.]

E Eye-contact between men and women

Euripides, Hecabe 974–5 [5.4]

Hecabe: [. . . custom forbids women (*gynē*) from meeting the gaze of men (*anēr*).]

F The wisdom of turning a blind eye to sexual misdemeanours

Euripides, Hippolytus 462–6 [4.5]

Nurse (*to Phaedra*): How many men do you think – men who have great soundness of mind, in fact – see their marriage-beds (*lektron*) suffering but pretend not to see? How many fathers give their wayward sons (*pais*) a hand with the deeds of Aphrodite? For it is one of the wisdoms possessed by mortals to turn a blind eye to acts that are unpretty (*mē kalos*).

G Theseus' condemnation of Hippolytus to death

Euripides, Hippolytus *885–90 [4.6]*

Theseus: Hippolytus dared to touch my marriage-bed (*eunē*) with violence (*bia*), dishonouring (*atimazō*) the august eye of Zeus. But, o father Poseidon, those three curses you promised me once, kill my son (*pais*) with one of them, let him not survive this day, if you really have granted me true curses!

H Punishing the son who has abused his father's marriage-bed

Euripides, Hippolytus *1038–44 [4.6]*

Theseus: Has this man not been born an enchanter and a cheat, who believes that with his gentleness of temper he will conquer my soul, despite dishonouring (*atimazō*) his father?

Hippolytus: I am likewise truly amazed at you, father; for if you were my son (*pais*), and I your father, I would have killed you instead of punishing you with banishment, if I really thought you had touched my wife (*gynē*).

I Preparations for a wedding

Euripides, Iphigenia at Aulis *425–39 [1.5]*

Messenger (*to Agamemnon*): Yes, the army has found out – for the rumour quickly spread – that your daughter (*pais*) has arrived. And the whole crowd comes running to the sight to catch a glimpse of your daughter. For those who are fortunate are famous the world over and attract men's attention. And they say: 'Is it some marriage (*hymenaios*) or what is happening? Was Lord Agamemnon missing (*pothos*) his daughter and brought the girl here?' You would have heard others saying: 'They are offering the girl (*neanis*) to Artemis, the Mistress of Aulis, in preparation for marriage. Who is it who is going to marry her?' But come now, get the sacrificial baskets ready for this and put wreaths on your heads. You, too, Lord Menelaus, prepare the wedding song (*hymenaios*), let the flute sound out under the roofs and let the feet begin their dance. For this has dawned a happy day for the girl (*parthenos*).

J The trials of marriage for a woman

Euripides, Medea *230–51 [1.7; 1.10]*

Medea: Of all creatures that have life and understanding, we women (*gynē*) are the most wretched. First we have to buy a husband (*posis*) at an extravagant price and take him as a master of our bodies, and, worse still, we take a huge gamble on whether we get a bad one or a good one. For there is no blame-free divorce (*apallagē*) for women (*gynē*), nor are they able to turn a husband (*posis*) down. And when she comes upon new customs and laws [i.e. in the marital house], she has to be a seer to predict how best to provide for her husband (*xyneunetēs*), since she has not learnt this at home. And if we get it right and our husband (*posis*) lives with us, bearing the yoke without violence (*bia*), our life is to be envied. But if not, it is better to die. The husband (*anēr*), when he's annoyed with the company of those inside, can go and ease his heart's vexation, [by turning to a friend or comrade]. But *we* have to look to one person alone. And they say that we live a life free from danger at home, while they go to war. Fools! I would rather stand three times in battle rank than give birth once.

K The modest behaviour of a dutiful wife

Euripides, Trojan Women *654–5 [5.4]*

Andromache: I offered a quiet tongue and a gentle eye to my husband (*posis*).

Greek Anthology

A huge collection of poems dating from the seventh century BC to the Byzantine era, arranged in its present form in the twelfth or thirteenth century AD.

A The unattractiveness of a woman now she is old

Rufinus, Greek Anthology *5.76 [5.2]*

She used to have the sexiest complexion, with youthful breasts and beautiful ankles. She was a good height and had lovely eyebrows and hair. But she was changed by time and old age and grey hair. And now she has not even a dream of her former looks, but has hair that is not hers and a wrinkled-looking face the like of which not even an old ape possesses.

B The appropriate age for a beloved boy

Straton, Greek Anthology *12.4 [3.8; 5.5]*

I take pleasure in the prime (*akmē*) of a twelve-year-old boy: but a thirteen-year-old is much more desirable (*potheinos*) than him. And the boy who's reached twice seven years is a sweeter flower of Eros, but the one who's just fifteen is more pleasant. The sixteenth year is divine. But to seek out a seventeen-year-old is not for me, but for Zeus. And if anyone has a longing (*pothos*) for older boys, he's no longer playing, but is now looking for someone to answer him back.

Herodotus

A native of Halicarnassus in Asia Minor, Herodotus wrote his *Histories* in the latter half of the fifth century BC.

A Mycerinus rapes his own daughter

Herodotus 2.131–2 [4.6; 5.8]

[131] . . . Some say . . . that Mycerinus passionately desired (*eraomai*) his own daughter and then he had intercourse (*mignymi*) with her against her will (*aekōn*). [132] Then, they say, the girl hanged herself in her distress . . . .

B Cleisthenes betroths his daughter to Megacles

Herodotus 6.130 [1.3]

'. . . to Megacles, the son of Alcmeon, I betroth (*engyaō*) my daughter (*pais*), Agariste, by the laws of the Athenians'. On Megacles' acceptance of the betrothal, Cleisthenes confirmed the marriage (*gamos*).

Hesiod

Boeotian poet, active sometime between 750 and 650 BC.

A A warning about deceitful women

Hesiod, Works and Days *373–5 [5.1]*

Do not let any sweet-talking, fancy-arsed woman beguile your good sense while she pokes around in your barn. Whoever trusts a woman, trusts thieves.

B Advice to men on choosing a wife

Hesiod, Works and Days *695–705 [1.6]*
Take a wife (*gynē*) to your house when you are ripe for it (*hōraios*), not much younger than thirty years of age nor much older; this is a timely marriage (*gamos*) for you. And the woman (*gynē*) should have attained puberty (*hebaō*) four years earlier, and in the fifth she should marry (*gameomai*). And you should marry (*gameō*) a young woman (*parthenikē*), so that you will be able to teach her the proper customs. Above all you should marry (*gameō*) a woman who lives close to you, after you have looked at everything around, so that your marriage does not provoke mockery from your neighbours. For a man acquires nothing better for himself than a good wife, yet again nothing more miserable than a bad one, a parasite, a woman who both singes her husband (*anēr*) without a torch, even if he is powerful, and gives him to premature old age.

Homer

The two epic poems ascribed to Homer, the *Iliad* and *Odyssey*, were probably composed c. 720–700 BC (maybe slightly later).

A Wedding celebrations in a city as depicted on Achilles' shield

Homer, Iliad *18.491–6 [1.5]*
In one city, there were weddings (*gamos*) and feasts, and they were leading the brides from the women's quarters (*thalamos*) under shining torches throughout the city and a great wedding song (*hymenaios*) rose up. And young men (*kouros*) were dancing and whirling, and among them flutes and lyres raised their cries. And the women (*gynē*) looked on in wonder, each standing on her doorstep.

Hyperides

An Attic orator, Hyperides was born in 390 BC and was executed in 322 BC. *Against Athenogenes* was composed at some point between 330 and 324 BC.

A A former courtesan arranges the sale of a beloved slave and his family

Hyperides, Against Athenogenes 3.3–4 [3.4; 3.6; 3.9]

[3] ... And so, jurors, there is probably nothing so very strange in my being taken in like this by Antigone, a woman who is said to be the most skilful courtesan (*hetaira*) of her generation, and who has continued to keep a brothel (*pornoboskeō*). [...] [4] And so, to cut a long story short, she finally sent for me again later and said that, having talked to Athenogenes for a long time, she had only just managed to convince him to release Midas and both his sons to me for 40 minas [i.e. 4,000 drachmas]. And she told me to provide the money as soon as possible, before Athenogenes could change his mind in any way.

B Appropriate adornment for a woman inside and outside the house

Hyperides, fr. 206 [5.3]

A woman should adorn herself however she wants for her husband; but if she adorns herself when she goes out, one should fear that it is no longer for her husband that she's doing it but for other men.

Ibycus

Lyric poet from Rhegium in South Italy, active at some point in the mid-sixth century BC.

A The effects of Eros on a seasoned campaigner

Ibycus, fr. 287 PMG [2.2; 2.5; 5.1]

Again Eros, looking at me tenderly from under his dark eyelids, throws me into the inescapable nets of Aphrodite with his manifold charms. Truly I tremble as he comes upon me, just as a victorious horse still bearing the yoke in old age goes unwillingly into the fray with his swift chariots.

Inscription

The following inscription forms part of a fourth- or third-century BC epitaph from the Peiraeus.

A A husband commemorates his wife [1.10]

Epigrammata Graeca *44.2–3 (Kaibel 1878)*

. . . Chaerestrate lies in this tomb. When she was alive
Her husband loved her. When she died he lamented. . . .

Isaeus

Attic orator, c. 420–340s BC, probably a native of Calchis in Euboea
(and therefore a metic in Athens). *On the Estate of Menecles* was probably delivered in the mid-350s BC and *On the Estate of Pyrrhus* likewise
seems to belong to the 350s or 340s BC.

A Male relatives' obligations towards unmarried women

Isaeus, On the Estate of Cleonymus *1.39 [1.4; 1.12]*
If Polyarchus, the father of Cleonymus and our grandfather, were alive
and could not afford living expenses, or if Cleonymus had died leaving
daughters unprovided for, because of our close family ties (*anchisteia*)
we would have been obliged to support our grandfather, and either
ourselves take Cleonymus' daughters as wives (*gynē*) or else provide
dowries (*proix*) and find other husbands for them (*ekdidōmi*). The ties
of kinship, the laws, and fear of dishonour in your eyes would have
forced us to do this or else become liable to heavy punishment and
extreme disgrace.

B Two brothers find husbands for two sisters

Isaeus, On the Estate of Menecles *2.3–4 [1.2; 1.3; 1.4; 1.11]*
[3] Our father, Eponymus of Acharnae, gentlemen, was a close
and intimate friend of Menecles. He had the four of us children,
two sons and two daughters. After my father's death we married
off (*ekdidōmi*) our elder sister, when she reached a suitable age, to
Leucolophus with a dowry of 20 minas. [4] And four or five years
later, when our younger sister was almost old enough to marry
(*synoikeō*) a man (*anēr*), Menecles' first wife (*gynē*) died. So once he
had carried out the customary rites over her, he asked us for our sister
in marriage, reminding us of the friendship (*philia*) which had existed
between our father and himself and of his friendly disposition towards
ourselves.

C A man finds a new husband for his childless wife

Isaeus, On the Estate of Menecles *2.6–9 [1.7; 1.10; 1.11]*

[6]. . . We proved our worth there [in Thrace as soldiers] and after saving a little money, we sailed back here. We found that our elder sister had two children (*pais*), but that the younger, the wife of Menecles, was childless. [7] Two or three months later, Menecles spoke to us, and after lavishing praise on our sister said that he was concerned about his increasing age and his childlessness. He said that our sister would not benefit from her goodness if she grew old with him without having children. He said it was enough that he himself was unfortunate. [8] So he begged us to grant him this favour of giving her in marriage (*ekdidōmi*) to someone else, with his own consent. And we told him that it was for him to persuade her about this; and we said we would do whatever she was persuaded to do. [9] And at first she could not bear to hear him talking like this, but as time went on she was persuaded, albeit with difficulty. So we gave her in marriage (*ekdidōmi*) to Elius of Sphettus and Menecles gave over the dowry (*proix*) to him . . . and gave her the clothes which she had brought with her when she came to his house and whatever gold jewellery there was.

D An ageing man takes action in regard to his childlessness

Isaeus, On the Estate of Menecles *2.10–12 [1.11; 1.12]*

[10] Some time after this Menecles began to consider how to resolve his childlessness so that he would have someone to look after him in old age, bury him when he died and then carry out the customary rites over him. He could see that this man, my opponent, had only one son, so he thought it inappropriate to ask him to let him adopt his son and thus leave him childless without male offspring. [11] Therefore, he could not find any relative closer than us. So he spoke to us and said that he thought it was right, since his fate was not to have children (*pais*) by our sister, that he should adopt (*poieomai*) a son out of the family from which he would have wished to have children (*pais*) naturally. 'So', he said, 'I would like to adopt whichever of you is willing.' [12] When my brother heard this, he approved of Menecles' proposal and agreed that his age and isolation required someone to look after him and live at his home; 'I,' he said, 'as you know, travel abroad; but my brother here' (meaning me) 'will look after your affairs as well as mine, if you want to adopt him.' Menecles said it was a good suggestion and in this way adopted me.

E Menecles' adoptive son and his wife care for him in old age

Isaeus, On the Estate of Menecles *2.18 [1.2; 1.6]*

After [the adoption] had been accomplished, Menecles began to look
for a wife for me, and said I ought to marry. So I married the daughter
of Philonides. And he showed the forethought that a father would naturally show for his son. In the same way, I tended him and respected
him as though he were my father by birth – both my wife (*gynē*) and I
did – so much so that he praised us to all his fellow demesmen.

F Inappropriate behaviour for a wife

Isaeus, On the Estate of Pyrrhus *3.13–14 [1.10; 3.6]*

[13] That the woman whom the defendant has sworn he betrothed
(*engyaō*) to him [our uncle] was a courtesan (*hetaira*) to anyone who
wanted her, and not our uncle's wife (*gynē*), has been testified to you
by all Phyrrhus' friends and neighbours. They have testified that, whenever the defendant's sister was with him, brawls, revelry and much
debauchery arose around her. [14] Yet no one, I presume, would dare
to carry on in this way with married women (*gametē gynē*). Nor do
married women (*gametē gynē*) accompany their husbands to dinners
or think of dining with them in the company of strangers, especially
not unexpected guests. However, they did not see fit to denounce the
evidence of any of those who testified to these things. And to prove that
what I say is true, read the deposition to them again.

G Concubinage with benefits

Isaeus, On the Estate of Pyrrhus *3.39 [1.15]*

Yes, by Zeus: in my view even those who give their female family
members away for concubinage (*pallakia*) all make an arrangement in
advance about what they are prepared to give their concubines (*pallakē*).

H The law of the heiress depriving men of their wives

Isaeus, On the Estate of Pyrrhus *3.63–5 [1.12]*

[63] . . . if Pyrrhus' uncles had known that their nephew had left a legitimate daughter and that none of us was willing to marry (*lambanō*)
her, they would never have allowed Xenocles, who was not related to
Pyrrhus by blood, to marry a woman who belonged to them by right of
kinship. That would have been very strange. [64] In respect of women

that have been given in marriage (*ekdidōmi*) by their fathers (for who could provide better counsel in such matters than a father?) and are living (*synoikeō*) as wives (*gynē*) with their husbands (*anēr*), although they have been given in marriage in this way, if their father dies without leaving any legitimate (*gnēsios*) brothers, the law commands that they pass to the jurisdiction (*epidikos*) of their closest relatives. And many husbands (*synoikōn*) before now have lost their wives in this way. [65] The necessary consequence of this law is that women who have been given in marriage by their fathers may be legally claimed. However, if she, Phile, were a legitimate (*gnēsios*) daughter left by him, would any of Pyrrhus' uncles have allowed Xenocles to marry a woman who belonged to them by right of kinship and thus make him heir to so large a fortune instead of themselves? Do not believe it, gentlemen.

I A family's likely reaction to a woman becoming an heiress

Isaeus, On the Estate of Pyrrhus *3.74 [1.12]*

For it is clear that, if he had left her as the heiress (*epiklēros*), he would have been well aware that one of two things was likely to happen to her: either one of us, the nearest relatives, would gain a ruling (*epidikazō*) and take her as wife (*gynē*); or, if none of us wanted to marry her, one of these uncles who were giving evidence just now would do so; or, failing that, one of the other relatives would in the same way gain a ruling (*epidikazō*) over the whole estate and take her as his wife.

J Euctemon chooses a concubine over his family

Isaeus, Philoctemon *6.19–21 [1.15; 3.6]*

[19] [Euctemon] had a freed-woman, gentlemen, who managed a tenement-house of his in the Peiraeus and kept girls (*paidiskē*). One of the girls she acquired went by the name of Alce, whom I think many of you know. After her purchase, this Alce spent a number of years in a brothel (or 'cubicle': *oikēma*) but left the brothel when she got too old. [20] . . . Euctemon then installed this woman, Alce, as the keeper of his tenement-house in the Kerameikos, near the postern gate, where wine is sold. [21] Her establishment there marked the beginning of many ills, gentlemen. For going there all the time to collect the rent, Euctemon spent most of his time in the tenement-house, and sometimes took his meals with the woman, abandoning his wife (*gynē*) and children (*pais*) and the house in which he lived. Although his wife and sons took this badly, not only did he not stop going there, but he ended up living

there entirely. He was reduced to such a state by drugs or disease or some other reason that he was persuaded by her to introduce the elder of her two boys (*pais*) to his phratry-members under his name.

K Public and private interest in preserving family households

Isaeus, Apollodorus 7.30 [1.11; 1.12]

All men, when they are about to die, take precautions for their own sake to prevent their families (*oikos*) from dying out and to ensure that there shall be someone to perform funerary sacrifices and carry out all the customary rites over them. For this reason, even if they die childless, they do at least adopt (*poieomai*) children to leave behind. And it is not just personal interests that prompt this, but the state has also taken public measures to ensure these things, since by law it entrusts the archon with the duty of preventing families (*oikos*) from dying out.

L Multiple marriages and the loss of a dowry

Isaeus, On the Estate of Ciron 8.7–8 [1.4; 1.8; 1.11]

[7] My grandfather, Ciron, gentlemen, married (*gameō*) my grandmother, who was his first cousin – the daughter of his own mother's sister. She was not married (*gameō*) to him for long; she gave birth to my mother, and died four years later. My grandfather, left with one only daughter, married the sister of Diocles, who bore him two sons. He brought up his daughter in the house with his wife (*gynē*) along with the children (*pais*) he had by her. [8] When the sons were still alive and his daughter had reached the proper age, he gave her in marriage (*ekdidōmi*) to Nausimenes of Cholargus, providing [as a dowry] 25 minas along with clothing and jewellery. Three or four years later Nausimenes fell ill and died without our mother having given him any children. My grandfather took her back again – without, however, recovering the dowry (*proix*) which he had given owing to the poverty of Nausimenes' estate – and gave her in marriage (*ekdidōmi*) a second time to my father with a dowry of 1,000 drachmas.

M Limits on financial transactions carried out by women and children

Isaeus, Against Aristarchus 10.10 [1.4]

. . .the law expressly forbids a child (*pais*) – or woman (*gynē*) – to make a contract for the disposal of more than a bushel [36 litres] of barley.

N A husband is loath to part with his heiress wife

Isaeus, Against Aristarchus *10.19 [1.12]*

After my mother was betrothed (*engyaō*) to him with a dowry (*proix*) my father married her (*synoikeō*), but since these men were enjoying their own use of the estate [i.e. of his wife's family], he did not have access to it. When he asked about it at my mother's insistence, they threatened to gain a ruling (*epidikazō*) and take her away if he was not content to have her with the dowry (*proix*) alone. And my father would have allowed them the use of twice as much property if it meant that he would not be deprived of my mother.

O Xenaenetus is accused of buggering away his inheritance

Isaeus, On the Estate of Aristarchus *10.25 [2.8; 3.9]*

But it is evidently not enough, gentlemen, for Xenaenetus to have buggered away (*katapaiderasteō*) his inheritance – he now thinks he should also dispose of this [i.e. the estate being contested] in the same manner.

P A view on the inheritance entitlement of an heiress and her sons

Isaeus, fr. 26 [1.12]

For we think that she should be married (*synoikeō*) to her closest relative, and for a time the property should belong to the heiress (*epiklēros*), but that, when the boys (*pais*) are two years past their puberty (*heboō*), they should get possession of it.

Lysias

A metic orator, born in Athens to a Syracusan father, active c. 403– c. 380 BC, to whom thirty-four surviving speeches are attributed. The composition date of *On the Murder of Eratosthenes* is probably c. 400 BC. *Against Simon* was delivered sometime after 394 BC.

A The speaker outlines his reasons for killing an alleged adulterer

Lysias, On the Murder of Eratosthenes *1.4 [4.8]*

But I need to show this, gentlemen, that Eratosthenes was committing adultery (*moicheuō*) with my wife (*gynē*), he corrupted (*diaphtheirō*) her, he dishonoured (*aischynō*) my children (*pais*) and he insulted (*hybrizō*) me myself by coming into my house (*oikia*). Furthermore, that he and I had no argument except for this, and that I didn't do this for the money to get rich instead of being poor, nor did I do it for any other benefit except retribution according to the laws.

B The early stages of a marriage

Lysias, On the Murder of Eratosthenes *1.6 [4.4]*
For, Athenians, when I decided to marry (*gameō*) and I took a wife (*gynē*) home, for some time I was disposed to treat her in such a way as not to annoy her, but I also didn't allow her to do whatever she wanted. I kept an eye on her as much as possible, and paid as much attention to her as was reasonable. But when my child (*paidion*) was born, I then started to trust her and put all my affairs in her hands, believing that there was the greatest intimacy (*oikeiotēs*) between us.

C The circumstances surrounding the beginning of the affair

Lysias, On the Murder of Eratosthenes *1.7–9 [1.10; 4.5]*
[7] And in the first instance, Athenians, she was the best of all wives (*gynē*), since she was a clever, frugal housekeeper (*oikonomos*), and kept everything in good order. But when my mother died, her death became the cause of all my troubles. [8] And so it was that while she was following her in the funeral procession, my wife (*gynē*) was seen by this man (*anthrōpos*), and was in time corrupted (*diaphtheirō*) by him. For he began watching out for the slave-girl on her way to market, and by sending messages [to her mistress], brought about her ruin (*apollymi*). [9] First I must tell you, sirs (for I have to explain these details), that my house is on two floors, the upper being equal in space to the lower, with the women's quarters (*gynaikōnitis*) above and the men's (*andrōnitis*) below. When our child was born, its mother breastfed it; and in order that, each time that it had to be washed, she might avoid the risk of descending by the stairs, I began to live above, and the women below.

D Advances towards a slave-girl

Lysias, On the Murder of Eratosthenes *1.12 [1.16; 5.7]*
But when I got angry and told her [my wife] to go away, she said, 'Yes, so that you can try it on here with your little slave-girl (*paidiskē*). You made a grab for her before, too, when you were drunk!'

E The affair is discovered

Lysias, On the Murder of Eratosthenes *1.15–17 [4.5]*

[15] After this, Athenians, some time had elapsed when I was still completely in ignorance of my own misfortunes; an old woman then approached me, sent in secret by a woman (*gynē*) with whom he had been committing adultery (*moicheuō*), as I later learnt. Because she was angry and felt mistreated, since he was no longer visiting her in the same way, she kept watch until she found out the reason. And so the woman approached me while she was keeping watch on my house, and said, 'Euphiletus, don't think that I am a busybody in coming to you. [16] But the man who brings insult (*hybrizō*) upon you and your wife (*gynē*) happens to be our enemy. If you take the slave-girl who goes to the marketplace (*agora*) and serves you and you torture her, you will learn everything.' She said, 'It is Eratosthenes of Oe [a deme in Attica] who does these things and has corrupted (*diaphtheirō*) not only your wife, but many others as well. [17] For this is a skill he has.'

F The adulterer is captured and killed

Lysias, On the Murder of Eratosthenes *1.23–9 [4.3]*

[23] . . . I went to sleep. But Eratosthenes, gentlemen, came in, and the slave-girl woke me immediately and said that he was inside the house. I told her to keep an eye on the door and, coming downstairs, I went out in silence. I called on one [neighbour] then another, and while I found some at home, others (who were out of town) I did not. [24] I collected as many as possible of those who were around and started walking. And taking torches from the nearest tavern we went into the house. The door had been opened by the woman in readiness. Pushing open the door of the bedroom, those of us who entered first saw him still lying beside my wife (*gynē*), while those who followed saw him standing naked on the bed. [25] And I, gentlemen, struck him, threw him down and, twisting his hands behind his back, tied him up. I asked him why he was committing this outrage (*hybris*) in entering my house. And he confessed to wrongdoing, but he kept begging and beseeching me not to kill him but to come to a financial agreement. [26] And I said that 'It is not *I* that will not kill you, but the law of the city. You have transgressed it and held it in less regard than your pleasures, and you chose to commit such a sinful action (*hamartēma*) against my wife and children rather than obey the laws and be decent (*kosmios*).' [27] Thus, gentlemen, what happened to him is what the laws command for

those committing such crimes. He was not seized and carried in from the street nor did he flee for protection to my hearth, as these men say. How could that be true since he was struck down in the bedroom and fell immediately, and I tied his hands behind him? And there were so many people in the house that he could not escape them, because he didn't have a knife, a club or anything else with which to defend himself against those coming in. [28] But, gentlemen, I think that you, too, know that those who act unjustly do not acknowledge that their enemies speak the truth. Rather, they lie themselves and devise such tricks as to rouse anger in the minds of the listeners against those acting justly. And so first read the law.

Law [the text of the law is missing]

[29] He did not dispute it, gentlemen, but agreed that he was doing wrong, and he kept on begging and beseeching not to be killed, and he was prepared to make financial recompense. But I didn't agree to his payment, and I considered the law of the city to have a higher authority. I took this revenge, which you deemed to be most just when you imposed it as punishment on those adopting such practices.

G An account of the laws on rape and adultery

Lysias, On the Murder of Eratosthenes *1.30–4 [1.15; 4.3; 4.6; 4.8; 4.9]*

[30] Read this law from the stele in the Areopagus.

Law [the text of the law is missing]

You hear, gentlemen, that it is explicitly stated by the Court of the Areopagus itself, to which it is assigned by our fathers and by us to try cases of murder, that you should not convict of murder a man who inflicts this retribution on an adulterer (*moichos*) that he has caught with (*epi*) his wife (*damar*). [31] And so strongly did the law-giver consider this to be just in respect of married women (*gametē gynē*), that he also assigned the same punishment in the case of concubines (*pallakē*), who are of inferior worth. Moreover, it is clear that, if he had any greater punishment in respect to married women, he would have imposed it. But as it is, he was unable to find a stronger punishment in relation to them, and so considered it right to impose the same punishment in respect of concubines (*pallakē*) as well. Read for me this law, too.

Law [the text of the law is missing]

[32] You hear, gentlemen, that [the law] commands, if anyone shames (*aischynō*) by force (*bia*) a free man or a free boy, he has to pay double damages; if he does this to a woman (*gynē*), in those cases where it is allowed to kill him, he is liable to the same penalty. Thus, gentlemen, he [the law-giver] thought that those using violence (*biazomai*) were worthy of a lesser penalty than those who use persuasion; for he condemned the latter to death, whilst for the former he doubled the damages. [33] He reasoned that men who use force (*bia*) are hated by those who have been assaulted (*biazomai*), but that men employing persuasion corrupt (*diaphtheirō*) their victims' souls in such a way as to make other men's wives (*gynē*) more closely attached to them than their husbands (*anēr*); the whole household is in their hands, and as for the children (*pais*) it is unclear whose they are – the husbands' (*anēr*) or the adulterers' (*moichos*). For these reasons the law-giver set death as the penalty. [34] Therefore where I am concerned, gentlemen, the laws not only acquit me of wrongdoing, but they also ordered me to take this retribution; it is for you to decide whether they [the laws] are valid or worth nothing.

H Affection for a boy and intrusion on a household's womenfolk

Lysias, Against Simon *3.3–7 [1.10; 2.2; 2.6; 2.11]*

[3] I am particularly upset, gentlemen (*boulē*), that I shall be compelled to tell you things about which I am ashamed (*aischynomai*). But since Simon has placed this necessity upon me, I shall recount to you every single event, leaving nothing undisclosed. [4] And I expect no mercy, gentlemen, if I am in the wrong. But, if I demonstrate to you that I am innocent of the things which Simon names in his affidavit, while in other respects you may think it very foolish of me to have an attachment to the youth (*meirakion*) at my age, I ask you not to think any the worse of me for that, since you know that all men have the capacity to feel desire (*epithymeō*) – and that the most noble and sensible man may be the one who is able to bear his misfortunes in the most orderly (*kosmios*) way. The plaintiff, Simon, has hindered all my efforts in this vein, as I shall now demonstrate.

[5] For we [both] felt desire for Theodotus, gentlemen, a youth (*meirakion*) from Plataea, and whilst *I* tried to win his affection by kind actions, the plaintiff thought that he would compel him to do what he wanted by acting aggressively (*hybrizō*) and contrary to the law. To tell

you about all the ills that boy suffered at his hands would be a lengthy affair. But as for the wrongs he inflicted on *me*, I think it is fitting for you to hear these. [6] For when he learnt that the boy was at mine, he came to my house at night, drunk, broke down the doors and entered the women's chambers, where inside were my sister and nieces who have lived such modest (*kosmios*) lives that they feel shame (*aischynomai*) at being seen even by their own family-members. [7] What is more, such was the outrageousness (*hybris*) of this man that he refused to go away until people who had arrived on the scene and those who had accompanied him, thinking that he was doing something shocking by intruding on young girls and orphans, drove him out by force (*bia*).

I The price of a boy

Lysias, Against Simon *3.22 [2.8; 3.6; 3.8; 3.9]*

For he dared to say that he had given 300 drachmas to Theodotus, after making an agreement with him, but that I plotted against him and took away his young man (*meirakion*).

J The penalty for adultery

Lysias, Against Agoratus *13.68 [4.3]*

Well then, because he [Agoratus] was that sort of man, he tried to commit adultery (*moicheuō*) with the wives of citizens and corrupt (*diaphtheirō*) free women, and he was captured (*lambanō*) as an adulterer (*moichos*). And the penalty for this is death.

Machon

Comic playwright, born in Corinth or Sicyon and active in the third century BC. Machon also wrote a book of anecdotes about notorious individuals, especially courtesans.

A A *hetaira* quips that her prices are flexible

Machon 450–5 [3.7; 3.9]

Morichus was trying it on with Phryne from Thespiae. And when she asked him for one mina [100 drachmas], Morichus said, 'That's a lot! Didn't you lately take two gold pieces [probably Persian darics, worth 20 drachmas each] to attend to a certain foreigner?' 'Well, wait until I'm horny, then,' she said, 'and I'll accept the same again!'

Menander

Playwright of New Comedy, c. 344–292 BC. Aside from *Bad-Tempered Man* (produced 316 BC; the sole New Comic play to survive [almost] intact), his works are difficult to date. *Woman from Samos* was probably written sometime between 417 and 407 BC.

A A stepbrother's reaction to a young man's interest in his stepsister

Menander, Bad-Tempered Man *(Dyskolos) 289–98 [4.6]*

Sostratus:	Do I seem to you to be doing something strange?
Gorgias:	I think that you're out to achieve a bad deed. You think you'll persuade a free-born girl (*parthenos*) to do wrong, or you're looking out for an opportunity to achieve a deed worthy of many death sentences.
Sostratus:	Apollo!
Gorgias:	Well, it's not right for a layabout like you to make yourself a nuisance for busy people like us. You should know that a poor man who has been wronged is the most troublesome (*dyskolos*) of them all. In the first place, he attracts sympathy; and secondly, he perceives what he has suffered not as wrongdoing (*adikia*) but as a personal insult (*hybris*).

B Eros contributes to a stable marriage

Menander, Bad-Tempered Man *(Dyskolos) 788–90 [1.10]*
(*Sostratus and Callippides emerge from the shrine, mid-conversation*)

Sostratus:	Your reaction to all this isn't what I wanted, father, nor is it what I was expecting from you.
Callippides:	What? Haven't I given my consent? I want you to marry the girl you love (*eraō*) – indeed, I say that you *should*.
Sostratus:	That's not what you seem to me to be saying.
Callippides:	By the gods, I am! For I know that for a young man a marriage (*gamos*) is all the more secure if he is induced to enter it out of love (*erōs*).

C A betrothal

Menander, The Girl with her Hair Cut Short *(Perikeiromene)*
1013–15 [1.3; 1.4; 1.11]

Pataecus:	I give this girl to you for the procreation (lit. 'plough- ing': *aroton*) of legitimate (*gnēsios*) children.
Polemon	I take her.
Pataecus:	And a dowry of three talents.
Polemon:	You're generous.

D A soldier laments his rejection by a concubine

Menander, The Hated Man *(Misoumenos) 37–40 [3.6]*
Thrasonides: I bought her, set her free, made her mistress of my house, gave her slaves, gold and clothes, and thought of her as my wife (*gynē*).

E Pay for a pimp

Menander, Men at Arbitration *(Epitrepontes) 136–7 [3.9]*
Smicrines (in a list of complaints about the young man, Charisius): He gives the pimp (*pornoboskos*) 12 drachmas a day.

F Evidence of a rape during the Tauropolia

Menander, Men at Arbitration *(Epitrepontes) 443–57 [4.6]*

Syrus:	Hey you! [Give me back] the ring – or show me the man you are going to give it to. We must settle this: I've got to go.
Onesimus:	The thing is like this, friend: I know perfectly well that it belongs to my master, Charisius, but I shrink from showing it to him. For by doing this I'm as good as making him the father of the baby (*paidion*) it was exposed with.
Syrus:	How on earth?
Onesimus:	You dim-wit! He lost it sometime during the Tauropolia – you know, the women's night-time festival. It must be the case that there was an assault (*biasmos*) on a young girl (*parthenos*). Clearly, she gave birth to the baby and exposed it. And so if anyone found the girl and presented her with the ring, he would be showing a clear piece of evidence. But for now all we have is suspicion and confusion.

G An unclaimed foundling and a description of a rape

Menander, Men at Arbitration (Epitrepontes) *464–90 [4.7]*

Habrotonon:	Onesimus, the baby boy the woman is now nursing inside, did the charcoal-maker find it?
Onesimus:	So he says.
Habrotonon:	(*thinking of the baby*) How sweet, poor dear!
Onesimus:	She found this ring of my master's besides.
Habrotonon:	Oh, the poor thing! But if the baby is really your young master's, will you see it brought up as a slave? Wouldn't that make you worthy of death?
Onesimus:	But as I say, no one knows who the mother is.
Habrotonon:	(*now examining the ring*) Do you say that he lost this at the Tauropolia?
Onesimus:	Yes, when he was drunk, just as the boy with him told me.
Habrotonon:	He clearly chanced upon the women celebrating when he was alone; for I was there when something similar happened.
Onesimus:	*You* were there?
Habrotonon:	Yes, last year at the Tauropolia; for I was playing for some young girls (*korē*), and I shared their games with them (*sympaizō*) myself. At that time I didn't yet know what men were like.
Onesimus:	Right!
Habrotonon:	I *didn't*, by Aphrodite!
Onesimus:	Do you know who the girl (*pais*) was?
Habrotonon:	I could always find out; for she was a friend (*philē*) of those women (*gynē*) I was with.
Onesimus:	Did you hear who her father was?
Habrotonon:	I know nothing; except that I would know her if I saw her. She is good-looking (*euprepēs*), by the gods, and they said she was wealthy.
Onesimus:	It could be her!
Habrotonon:	I don't know. She wandered off while she was there with us, then all of a sudden she runs towards us, alone and crying, pulling her hair out, her beautiful thin cloak utterly ruined – gods! – for it had been totally ripped to shreds.

H A husband's remorse at his double standards concerning rape

Menander, Men at Arbitration (Epitrepontes) 891–900 [4.7]
Onesimus (*relating the actions of his master*): When he [Charisius] had finally heard the whole story, he fled inside. Cue: wailing within, the tearing of hair, utter consternation. For he kept repeating again and again, 'I'm a scoundrel. I have committed a crime like this myself and am now the father of a bastard (*nothos*) child (*paidion*). I didn't feel nor did I show a single scrap of mercy to that unfortunate woman who was in the same wretched condition. I'm a brutal, merciless man.' He rebukes himself fiercely and he looks around with blood-shot eyes, quite overwrought.

I A woman learns that her husband is her rapist

Menander, Men at Arbitration (Epitrepontes) 920–2 [4.7]
Charisius (*reporting Pamphile's considered reaction following the revelation her husband is the same man who raped her before their marriage*): . . . she said, 'I am here as his partner (*koinōnos*) in life and I should not flee because of some mistake (*atychēma*) that has occurred.'

J Difficulties caused by marrying a rich heiress

Menander, The Necklace (Plokion), fr. 403 Koerte [1.12]
A: I have the heiress (*epiklēros*), Lamia, as a wife. Didn't I tell you?
B: Not that, you didn't.
A: Right away we have a mistress of our house, the fields – everything.
B: Apollo, how awkward.
A: Most awkward. And she's horrible to everyone, not just to me, mostly my son and daughter.
B: You're talking about a hopeless situation.
A: Don't I know it.

K One brother tells another that he is too old to marry a young girl

Menander, The Shield (Aspis) 256–69 [1.2; 1.6]
Chaerestratus: Have you lost all sense of decency, Smicrines?
Smicrenes: What do you mean, my boy?
Chaerestratus: A man of your age, proposing to marry a young girl (*pais*).

Smicrenes:	*My* age?
Chaerestratus:	I think you're too old.
Smicrenes:	Am I the only man to marry later in life?
Chaerestratus:	For heaven's sake, Smicrines, show some human feeling. Chaereas has grown up with her and intends to marry her. What can I say? You won't lose out at all. As far as the property is concerned that Cleostratus left, take it, every last bit of it! Be its owner (*kyrios*) – our gift! But let the girl (*paidiskē*) have a bridegroom (*nymphios*) her own age. I'll provide a dowry (*proix*) of two talents myself out of my own money.

L A young man relates how he got a girl pregnant

Menander, Woman from Samos (Samia*) 35–54 [1.2; 4.7]*

Moschion: The girl's (*korē*) mother was well disposed towards my father's Samian woman, and she was at their house most of the time, and sometimes in turn they came to our house. Indeed, coming back from the field, as it happened, I found them there gathered together at our house for the Adonia [i.e. an all-female religious festival], with a few other women. The festival provided a lot of fun, as you'd expect, and since I was there with them I became a sort of spectator; for the noise they were making was keeping me awake. You see, they were carrying their gardens onto the roof [i.e. as part of the festival], they were dancing, they were celebrating all night long, scattered all over the place. I shrink from saying the rest: perhaps there is no point in my being ashamed (*aischynomai*), but I am ashamed. The girl (*pais*) got pregnant. By saying this, I am also telling you what happened before that. I didn't deny that the blame was mine, but early on I spoke to the girl's (*korē*) mother, I promised to marry (*gameō*) her whenever my father came back. I swore an oath! After the baby (*paidion*) was born I took it in, not long ago.

M A man's dismissal of his courtesan-concubine

Menander, Woman from Samos (Samia*) 376–82; 390–7 [1.15; 3.6; 3.9]*

(*Demeas dismisses Chrysis, the Samian woman, since he is under the impression that she has had a child by another man.*)

Demeas:	You see, you did not understand how to live in luxury.
Chrysis:	Not understand? What do you mean?
Demeas:	And yet you came here in linen dress, Chrysis – do you see – a very plain one.

Chrysis:	What of it?
Demeas:	I was everything to you then, when you were poorly off.
Chrysis:	And who's everything to me now?
Demeas:	Don't whitter at me! You have all your possessions: I give you your servant girls as well, Chrysis. Leave my house! . . .
Demeas:	Such a big shot! In the city you'll now discover exactly what you are. Courtesans (*hetaira*) no better than you, Chrysis, earn just 10 drachmas by running off to dinner parties and drinking neat wine until they die – or go hungry if they don't readily do this and smartish. *You*'ll learn this faster than any of them, I daresay, and you'll realise who you really are and what a mistake you made.

Metagenes

Comic playwright active in the last part of the fifth century BC.

A An array of prostitutes

Metagenes, fr. 4 KA The Breezes *or* The Blockhead *(Aurai/ Mammakythos) [3.2; 3.4]*

I told you before about the young (*hōraios*) dancing-girl (*orchēstris*) courtesans (*hetaira*), now I am telling you about the flute-girls (*aulētris*) just getting their downy hair (*chnoazō*), who for a fee spread their legs as quick as you like under merchants.

Pausanias

Author of the extensive *Description of Greece*; active in the mid-second century AD.

A The rape of two girls near Leuctra

Pausanias, Description of Greece *9.13.5 [4.6]*

For Scedasus, who lived near Leuctra, had two daughters, Molpia and Hippo. When the girls had just reached their prime, they were raped (*biazomai*) against the law by two men from Sparta, Phrurarchidas and Parthenius. And because the assault (*hybris*) seemed unbearable to the girls (*parthenos*), they immediately hanged themselves. And when Scedasus went to Sparta but got no satisfaction, he returned to Leuctra and killed himself.

B The raid by the Gauls on the Callians in 279 BC results in mass rape

Pausanias, Description of Greece *10.22.4 [4.6]*
Not just the women but also those girls (*parthenos*) who had come of age and who had the resolve to do so killed themselves when the city was seized. Those still remaining suffered every kind of assault (*hybris*) under violent constraint at the hands of men equally lacking in pity and love (*erōs*). And any of the women finding the daggers of the Gauls killed themselves. For the others, death was soon to come through want of food and sleep, while the unbridled barbarians assaulted (*hybrizō*) every one in turn, having sex (*syngignomai*) even with those dying and already dead.

Philemon

Playwright of New Comedy, active in the late fourth and early third centuries BC.

A Democratic brothels offering men easy sex

Philemon, fr. 3 KA The Brothers (Adelphoi) *[3.4; 3.9; 3.10; 5.4]*
You contrived [laws] for everyone, Solon. For they say that you were the first to discover this practice – it's only democratic and a life-saver at that, by Zeus! (I can certainly vouch for that, Solon.) When you saw the city full of young men compelled by nature to do wrong in ways they should not, you bought women (*gynē*) and set them up in places where they were available to everyone, kitted out appropriately. They stand there naked, so you won't be fooled. Look at it all! You don't quite feel yourself? [Something's up . . .?] The door's open. One obol: jump on board! There's nothing to be prudish about, no nonsense, and she doesn't flinch. No, it's straight off to the woman you want, however you want it. You're done? Tell her to go to hell: she's a stranger to you!

Pindar

Lyric poet from Boeotia, active in the early fifth century BC.

A The compelling nature of boys' beauty

Pindar, fr. 123.10–12 [2.2; 2.5; 5.1; 5.5]
But I, because of her [i.e. Aphrodite], like the wax of holy bees bitten by the sun, am melting whenever I look upon the young-limbed youth (*hēbē*) of boys (*pais*).

Plato

Athenian philosopher, c. 429–347 BC. A number of Plato's works feature the historical figure of Socrates (469–399 BC) and fictional-ised versions of other real-life Athenians are likewise to be found in his dialogues, such as the orator Lysias and the comic playwright Aristophanes. The dramatic date of *Symposium* (which was written c. 385–380 BC) is 416 BC. *Phaedrus* was composed c. 370 BC.

A The beauty of Charmides stuns his admirers

Plato, Charmides *154c–154d [5.5]*
[154c] The young man [Charmides] appeared to me then to be a marvel of stature and beauty (*kallos*). And I could see all the rest were in love with (*eraō*) him, they were so surprised and confused when he came in; and he had a string of other admirers (*erastēs*) following behind him. It wasn't surprising that men (*anēr*) like us reacted in this way, but I could see that none of the boys (*pais*), not even the young-est, was looking at anything else, but they were all gazing at him as if he were a statue. Then [154d] Chaerephon called me and said, 'What do you think of this young man (*neaniskos*), Socrates? Hasn't he got a pretty face (*euprosōpos*)?'

'Absolutely,' I replied.

'But if he would just agree to strip,' he said, 'you would forget about his face; his body (*eidos*) is so perfect.'

B The effects of Charmides' beauty on Socrates

Plato, Charmides *155d–155e [5.5]*
[155d] [Charmides] gave me such an irresistible look with his eyes, and was just about to ask a question, and everyone in the wrestling school (*palaistra*) was milling around us on every side, and *then*, my dear friend, I saw inside his cloak, caught fire and was lost to myself. And I thought that Cydias was very wise about love (*ta erōtika*) when, talking

about a beautiful (*kalos*) boy (*pais*), he warns someone 'to be careful not to come as a fawn to a lion to be snatched as his share of meat'. [155e] For I felt I had been seized by such a creature.

C Adultery for cash

[Plato], Eryxias 396e [4.5]

Critias:	Do you think that a man who bribes the wives of his neighbours and commits adultery (*moicheuō*) acts justly or unjustly, when both the state and the laws forbid this?
Eryxias:	Unjustly.

D The life of the *kinaidoi*

Plato, Gorgias 494c–495a [2.9; 5.8]

Socrates:	. . . Keep going as you've started and don't be shy. And I mustn't be shy, either, it seems. First of all, tell me whether a man who has an itch and wants to scratch, and is allowed to scratch to his heart's content, can have a happy life scratching all the time. [494d]
Callicles:	What an odd person you are, Socrates, and your way of arguing is pretty odd, too!
Socrates:	Well yes, Callicles, I shocked and embarassed Polus and Gorgias, but you won't be shocked or embarrassed: you are such a brave fellow. But at least answer the question.
Callicles:	Then I agree that the man scratching himself could live pleasantly.
Socrates:	And if it's a pleasant life, it's a happy life, too?
Callicles:	Certainly.
Socrates:	[494e] Is it only if he wants to scratch his head? Or what else should I ask you? Look, Callicles, what would you answer if someone asked you everything in turn that follows from there? And the culmination of such things, the life of the *kinaidoi*, isn't that awful, shameful, and miserable? Or will you dare to say that these people are happy if they get enough of what they want?
Callicles:	Aren't you ashamed, Socrates, to bring the discussion round to such things?

Socrates: Is it me bringing the discussion to such things, or the person who freely claims that those who enjoy themselves, in whatever way, [495a] are happy, and who doesn't make a distinction between good and bad sorts of pleasure? But tell me whether you still say that pleasant and good are the same thing, or whether there are some forms of pleasure which are not good.

E The prescribed age for marriage in an ideal state

Plato, Laws *book 6 785b [1.6]*

Athenian: The limit of the marriage-age shall be from sixteen to twenty years for a girl (*korē*) – this shall be the longest time allowed – and for a boy (*koros*) from thirty to thirty-five.

F Male same-sex relationships fail to promote virtue

Plato, Laws *book 8 836c–e [2.9]*

Athenian: If we followed nature and enacted that law from before the time of Laius, arguing that people ought not indulge in the same kind of intercourse with men (*arrēn*) and boys (*neos*) as with women (*thēleios*), presenting as evidence for this the nature of animals, and pointing out in this respect how male (*arrēn*) animals do not touch other males (*arrēn*) for this purpose, since it is unnatural; if we did this, then perhaps we would be using an argument that was neither convincing nor in any way in agreement with the practice in your city-states. In addition, the thing that we say the law-giver always has to pay heed to [836d] does not correspond with all this. For we are always examining which of the proposed laws promote virtue and which do not. Come, then, let us even concede that this practice is currently legal and that it is acceptable, or at least not unacceptable – what would it contribute to our virtue? Will it call forth a courageous spirit in the man seduced (*peithō*), or will it engender in the soul of the seducer the quality of self-control (*sōphrōn*)? Nobody would ever believe this. On the contrary, just as everyone will continue to [836e] reproach the weakness of the man who yields to pleasures and is unable to hold out against them, will the man not also be blamed who imitates the woman (*thēlys*) in an analogous way? Is there anyone, then, who will ordain such a law as that? Hardly anyone, if he has a notion of what true law is.

G The power of the taboo against incest

Plato, Laws *book 8 838a–b [5.8]*

Athenian: Even as things stand we know that most people, even
                 if they are lawless, effectively and strictly abstain from
                 sexual intercourse (*synousia*) with beautiful (*kalos*)
                 people; and that far from doing this against their will,
                 they are as willing as can be.

Megillus: When do you mean?

Athenian: When someone has a brother or sister who is beauti-
                 ful. And [838b] the same unwritten law is most effec-
                 tive in holding a man back from sleeping with his son
                 or daughter, whether openly or secretly, or wishing
                 to lay hands on them in any way. Indeed most people
                 never so much as feel desire (*epithymia*) for any such
                 relationship.

Megillus: That is true.

H Lysias' rhetorical speech: reasons to gratify a friend over a lover

Plato, Phaedrus *231c–233b [2.6]*

[231c] If lovers (*erastēs*) deserve to be highly regarded for their claims
to have the greatest affection (*phileō*) for the ones they love (*eraō*), and
for their preparedness through their actions and words to incur others'
hatred so as to please their beloved (*erōmenos*), it is easy to see that, if
they are telling the truth, whenever they next fall in love (*eraō*), they
will care for the new love more than for the old and will certainly cause
pain to the old love, if that pleases the new. How can it be reasonable
in a matter of such importance [231d] to entrust oneself to someone
with the kind of affliction [i.e. being in love] that not even someone
of experience would attempt to cure? For [lovers] themselves admit
that they are ill rather than of sound mind (*sōphroneo*) and that they
know they are being stupid, but cannot control themselves. So, when
they have come to their senses, why should they think that they acted
wisely when they did the things they resolved to do while under the
influence of this affliction? And if you had to choose the best of your
lovers (*erōn*), your choice would be from a few; but it would be from
many if you were choosing the person most expedient to you [i.e. from
the world at large]. For this reason [231e] you would have much better
hope, in choosing among many, of finding the one most worthy of
your affection (*philia*). Now if you are afraid of public opinion, in case

you will be disgraced if people find out about your love affair, it is likely that [232a] a lover, thinking that they are envied by others as much as others are envied by themselves, will be elated by their catch and keen to show everyone their pride in the fact that their efforts in courtship have not gone unrewarded. In contrast, it is likely that those who are not in love (*eraō*), since they are in control of themselves, will choose the best course of action, rather than relying on the opinion of other people. Moreover, many people are bound to notice and see lovers following their beloveds (*erōmenos*) about, making this their main concern in life. So, when the two are seen talking to [232b] each other, people think they are together having just come from intercourse or just on their way to it. But no one would try to find fault with those who are not in love when they meet, since everyone knows that people need to talk to each other, either because of friendship (*philia*) or because it is pleasant in some other way. And if you are concerned by the thought of affection (*philia*) not lasting and, in such an event, if you gave up what you value most you would feel you were the chief sufferer, whereas in other circumstances an argument would be an equal misfortune to both parties, then it would be reasonable for you to be more afraid of those who are in love with you. [232c] They are pained by many things and think that everything that happens is aimed at hurting them. So they prevent their beloveds (*erōmenos*) from meeting with others in the fear that wealthy men would have an advantage over them because of their money or that educated men might prove more powerful in their intellegence, and they guard against [232d] the influence of everyone that possesses any other advantage. Either they persuade you to let yourself be hated by these men and deprive you of friends (*philos*), or, if you look out for your own needs by thinking more sensibly than them, you will quarrel with them. But those who are not in love, but who have got what they want through their own merits, would not be jealous of people associating with you, but would dislike those who did not want to, considering you slighted by the latter and benefited by the former. In consequence [232e] it is much more likely that you will gain friendship (*philia*) rather than hatred from the liaison. And then, too, many of those in love feel lust (*epithymeō*) for a person's body before they know their character and become acquainted with other members of the family, so that it is uncertain whether they will still want to be your friend (*philos*) when their lust (*epithymia*) has subsided. [233a] But in the case of those not in love, who were your friends (*philos*) before any liaison, the favours they receive are not likely to diminish the friendship (*philia*), but rather will remain as reminders of joys to come. And, indeed, it will be better for you to give in to me than to a lover (*erastēs*). For they over-praise what you say and what you do, partly out of fear that they will cause annoyance and partly [233b] because they have poor judgement as a result of their lust (*epithymia*).

I Stages of courtship between a lover and his beloved

Plato, Phaedrus *255a–256a [2.2; 2.5; 2.6; 5.5]*

Socrates: . . . [255a] Since the beloved receives all this attention from his lover (*erōn*), as if he were being worshipped as a god; and since the lover is not pretending, but is really in love; and since the beloved himself is naturally friendly (*philos*) to his worshipper, even though he may earlier have been prejudiced by his schoolfellows or others who said that it was a disgrace to associate with a lover (*erōn*) and may for that reason have rejected his lover, yet, as time goes on, his youth and obligation cause him [255b] to introduce him to his friends. For it is no law of destiny that bad men should be each other's friends (*philos*), or that good men should not. And when the lover (*erōn*) has been granted this intimacy and shares his conversation, the goodwill that emerges in this close association astonishes the beloved (*erōmenos*), who discovers that the friendship (*philia*) of all his other friends (*philos*) and relatives is nothing compared with that of his divinely inspired friend (*philos*). And as the intimacy progresses and the lover continues to come near and touch the beloved in gymnasia, and in their general interactions, [255c] then the source of that stream which Zeus, when he was in love (*eraō*) with Ganymede, called 'desire' (*himeros*) flows abundantly towards the lover (*erastēs*). Some of it flows into him, and some overflows after he is filled; and just as the wind or an echo rebounds from smooth, hard surfaces and is carried back whence it came, so the stream of beauty (*kallos*) passes back into the beautiful (*kalos*) one, passing through the eyes, the natural access to the soul, where [255d] it reanimates the passages of the feathers, waters them and makes the feathers begin to grow, filling the soul of the beloved (*erōmenos*) with love (*erōs*). So he is now in love (*eraō*), but he does not know who with; he does not understand what is wrong with him and cannot explain it. He is like someone who has caught an eye disease from another without being able to account for it. He sees himself in his lover (*erōn*) as in a mirror, but is not conscious of the fact. And when his lover is there, like him he stops feeling his pain; but when he is absent, like him he is filled with yearning (*potheō*) such as he inspires. [255e] He is experiencing reciprocal love (*anterōs*), love's (*erōs*) reflection; but he calls it, and believes it to be, not love (*erōs*), but affection (*philia*). Like the lover, though less strongly, he desires (*epithymeō*) to see his friend, to touch him, kiss him, and lie down with him (*synkatakeimai*); and naturally these things are soon brought about. Now as they lie together, the lover's (*erastēs*) unruly horse has something to say to the charioteer, and demands a little enjoyment in return for his many troubles; [256a] and the beloved (*ta paidika*) says nothing, but teeming with passion and confused emotions he embraces and kisses his lover (*erastēs*), caressing him as his best friend; and when they lie together, he would not refuse to grant any favour (*charizomai*) that his lover (*erōn*) might ask; but the other horse and the charioteer oppose all this with modesty and reason.

J Sophocles' view of sex in old age

Plato, Republic *book 1 329b–c [5.8]*

Cephalus: ... I was once present when someone asked the poet Sophocles, 'How are you with sex (*aphrodisia*), Sophocles? Are you still able to make love (*syngignomai*) to a woman (*gynē*)?' And *he* said, 'Least said the better! I'm over the moon to have left it behind me, like escaping a fierce and frenzied master.'

K Phaedrus' speech: the power of Eros and the army of lovers

Plato, Symposium *178d–179c [2.7; 1.10]*

Let me then say that a man in love (*eraō*), caught out in some shameful act or putting up with shameful treatment at another's hands, would not feel half as much distress at being observed, whether by his father or friends or anyone in the world, as by his beloved (*paidika*); [178e] and in the same way we see how the beloved (*erōmenos*) is especially ashamed before his lovers (*erastēs*) when he is observed to be engaged in some shameful business. So that if we could somehow arrange to have a city or an army composed of lovers (*erastēs*) and their beloveds (*paidika*), there could be no better way to organize a community than this since they would abstain from everything shameful [179a] in a mutual rivalry for honour. Fighting side by side, one might almost consider such men – even a few of them – capable of defeating many others. For a man in love (*eraō*) would surely find it less acceptable for his beloved (*paidika*) to see him desert his station or fling away his arms than all others; sooner than this, he would prefer to die many deaths. And, as for leaving one's beloved (*ta paidika*) or not going to his aid when he is in danger, no man is so cowardly that Eros cannot inspire him to such courage that he is equal to the best in nature. [179b] And without doubt what Homer calls a 'fury inspired' by a god in certain heroes is the effect produced on those in love (*eraō*) by Eros' power.

Furthermore, only those who are in love (*eraō*) will agree to die for others; not merely men (*anēr*), but women (*gynē*), too. Sufficient evidence of this statement is provided for the Greeks by Alcestis, daughter of Pelias, who was the only one willing to die in place of her husband, although both his father [179c] and mother were still alive . . . .

L Phaedrus' speech: Achilles and Patroclus

Plato, Symposium *179e–180b [2.2; 2.7 1.10]*
They [the gods] honoured Achilles, the son of Thetis, and sent him to the Isles of the Blest. He had learnt from his mother that he would die if he killed Hector, but that if he didn't kill him, he would return home and live to be an old man. Despite this, he dared to choose to go to the rescue of his lover (*erastēs*) Patroclus, [180a] to avenge him, and to die not only *for* his dead friend but *after* him, too. For this reason, the gods admired him exceedingly and honoured him greatly, because he had valued his lover (*erastēs*) so highly. And Aeschylus is talking nonsense when he says that it was Achilles who was in love (*eraō*) with Patroclus, for he was more beautiful (*kalos*) not only than Patroclus but than all the other heroes and he was still beardless and much younger according to Homer. For the gods really do [180b] hold this sort of courage in particular honour, the kind that relates to love (*erōs*). And they are even more full of wonder and delight and act favourably when the beloved (*erōmenos*) loves (*agapaō*) his lover (*erastēs*) than when the lover (*erastēs*) loves (*agapaō*) his beloved (*ta paidika*), because the lover (*erastēs*) is something more divine than his beloved (*ta paidika*), for he is filled with divine spirit. It is for this reason that they honoured Achilles rather than Alcestis, and sent him to the Isles of the Blest.

M Pausanias' speech: Common and Heavenly Aphrodite

Plato, Symposium *181a–3e; 185b–c [2.6; 2.7; 2.11]*
Not all loving (*eraō*) and Love (*erōs*) is good and worth celebrating, but only the Love (*erōs*) that compels us to love (*eraō*) in a good way.

The love that belongs to Common Aphrodite (*Pandēmos Aphroditē*) is truly popular [181b] and does whatever work comes his way. This is the sort of love that lesser men have, men who, first, love (*eraō*) women (*gynē*) no less than boys (*pais*), and, secondly, love (*eraō*) the body more than the soul, and thirdly, choose the most ignorant people they can find, since they are only thinking of achieving their goal and don't care if it is a good thing or not. For this reason it transpires that they do whatever chance brings their way, whether it is good or the opposite. [181c] This is because this love comes from the goddess who is by far the younger of the two who, owing to her birth, shares in both the female (*thēlys*) and the male (*arrēn*). But the love that derives from Heavenly Aphrodite (*Ourania [Aphroditē]*) first contains nothing of the female (*thēlys*) but only of the male (*arrēn*) – and this is the love (*erōs*) of boys (*pais*); secondly, she is older and knows no outrageousness (*hybris*). For this reason, those who are inspired by this love (*erōs*) turn to the male (*arrēn*), loving (*eraō*) those with a vigorous body and a stronger mind. You can see in the love of boys (*paiderastia*) how those who are spurred on by this love (*erōs*) [181d] don't love boys until they begin to acquire the rational maturity that comes with the growth of down on their chins. For I believe that those who begin to love (*eraō*) them then are prepared to stay with them and share the rest of their lives with them, rather than taking advantage of a young boy's (*neos*) inexperience to deceive him and make a mockery of him by running off to someone else. A law should be enacted against this love [181e] of boys (*pais*) to prevent a great deal of effort being wasted on a doubtful outcome. For who can tell how a boy will end up, vicious or virtuous in body and soul? Good men, however, voluntarily make this law for themselves, and lovers of the 'common' sort (*pandēmos erastēs*) ought to be forced to obey such a rule, just as [182a] we force them, as much as we can, to refrain from loving (*eraō*) our free-born women (*gynē*). For these are the people who have brought down the reproach that leads some people to dare to say it is shameful to gratify (*charizomai*) one's lover (*erastēs*). They say this, thinking about their lack of judgement and lawlessness, since surely whatever is done in an orderly and lawful manner can never justly bring reproach.

Moreover, it is easy to consider the customs concerning love (*erōs*) in other cities, where it is laid down in simple terms, while ours [182b] here and in Lacedaemonia are complicated (*poikilos*). For in Elis and Boeotia and places where people are not skilled at speaking they have a simple ruling that it is a good thing to gratify (*charizomai*) lovers (*erastēs*). Neither young nor old would call it shameful, I reckon, so they don't have to try to persuade the young (*neos*) by speech, since they are incapable of speaking. But in Ionia and many other regions where they live under the rule of barbarians, it is counted as shameful. Because of tyranny [i.e. the fact that they are governed by a monarch], barbarians consider this shameful, [182c] as well as all training in philosophy and sports. For I imagine it doesn't suit the rulers that there should be clever ideas engendered in their subjects – or any strong friendships (*philia*) and common interest groups (*koinōnia*) – all of which the other things, but love (*erōs*) in particular, tend to bring about. It is a lesson that the tyrants here learnt by experience; for Aristogeiton's love (*erōs*) and Harmodius' friendship (*philia*) grew to be so strong that it destroyed their power . . . .

[183c] . . . So, you might think that here in our city both loving (*eraō*) someone and being a friend (*philos*) to lovers (*erastēs*) are considered completely acceptable. But when fathers put tutors (*paidagōgos*) in charge of their boys when they are beloved (*erōmenos*) by someone to prevent them from conversing with their lovers (*erastēs*), with the tutor given strict instructions on the matter, and when his contemporaries and companions reproach him if they see anything of that sort going on, [183d] while his reproachers are not in their turn stopped or scolded by their elders as speaking amiss, from this you might think that such behaviour is held to be a great disgrace. But I think it is like this: the matter is not simple. As I said at the beginning, by itself it is neither good (*kalos*) nor shameful (*aischros*), but it is good if conducted in a good manner, and shameful if done in a shameful manner. Doing the thing shamefully is to grant favours (*charizomai*) to a wicked man in a wicked way; doing it in a good way means granting favours to an honest man in a good way. By 'wicked' we mean that common lover (*erastēs ho pandēmos*), who lusts for the body rather than the soul. [183e] Since he is not in love (*eraō*) with what is constant, he himself is not constant. As soon as the bloom of the body he used to love (*eraō*) begins to fade he 'flies away' leaving many words and promises unhonoured. But the lover (*erastēs*) of a worthy nature lasts throughout life, as though joined as one with something lasting. . . .

This is the love (*erōs*) that belongs to the Heavenly Goddess, which is heavenly and valuable to both the city and private individuals, since it compels both the lover (*erastēs*) and the beloved (*erōmenos*) [185c] to take great care in their own virtue. But all the other forms of love belong to the other Goddess, the Common one.

N Aristophanes' speech: love is the pursuit of our other half

Plato, Symposium *191d–193a [2.7; 2.10; 2.11; 4.4]*

Each of us, then, is only half a person, cut just like a flat-fish into two pieces, and is always searching for our other half. So all the men (*anēr*) who are cut from the whole that was originally called 'androgynous' (*androgynos*) are lovers of women (*philogynē*). Many of the adulterers (*moichos*) are from that sex (*genos*), [191e] as are the women (*gynē*) that love men (*philandros*) and the 'adulteresses' (*moicheutria* [N.B. this is the only attested use of this word from the classical era]). All the women who are cut from the 'woman' original (*gynē*) don't really pay attention to men, but turn to women, and this is the sex (*genos*) that *hetairistriai* [lesbians?] come from. And those cut from the 'male' (*arrēn*) original seek out men (*arrēn*). While they are still young (*pais*) they show themselves to be slices of the male by sowing affection (*phileō*) for men and enjoying [192a] lying with them and being joined with them; these are the finest boys (*pais*) and youths (*meirakion*), because they are the most masculine (*andreios*). Some say they are shameless, but that's not true. They do it not through shamelessness but through courage, manliness and virility since they are welcoming their like. Strong evidence for this is that, on reaching maturity, it is only men like this that enter politics. When they grow to be men [192b] they love boys (*paiderasteō*), and they are not naturally inclined towards marriage (*gamos*) and having children, but do these things through force of custom. They are quite happy to live together unmarried for the rest of their lives. At all events, such a man is born to be a lover of boys (*paiderastēs*) and someone who is well disposed to lovers (*philerastēs*), always welcoming his own kind. So, when one of them finds his or her own half, whether he is a lover of boys (*paiderastēs*) or a lover of any other sort, [192c] then the two of them are struck in an amazing way by affection (*philia*), intimacy (*oikeiotēs*) and desire (*erōs*), and don't want to leave each other's side for a single moment. These are the ones who stay together throughout life, even if they couldn't say what they want from each other. No one could imagine this to be sexual intercourse (*aphrodisiōn synousia*) – that this alone could be why each is so ecstatic in the other's company. Obviously the soul of each is wishing for something else that it cannot express, [192d] only surmising and hinting at what it wishes. And if, as they lay together, Hephaestus stood over them, holding the tools of his trade, and asked, 'What is it, mortals, that you want of each other?' And if they weren't sure, he asked them again: 'Do you want to be joined as closely as possible, so that you cannot be divided, [192e] night or day? If that is your wish, I am ready to weld and fashion you together in a single piece, so that instead of being two you can be made one. As long as you live, the pair of you would share a single life as a unit, and when you die you would also be a unit there in Hades, instead of two, having shared a single death. Think about whether this is what you desire (*eraō*), and whether you will be quite happy with this outcome.' On hearing this, we know that no one would reject it or would want anything else, but everyone would simply consider that he had heard just what he was longing for (*epithymeō*) all the time, namely, to be joined and fused with his beloved (*erōmenos*) so that the two might be made one.

The cause of all this is that our original form was like that, and we used to be one whole. And the desire (*epithymia*) and pursuit [193a] of that whole is called love (*erōs*).

Plato Comicus

A comic playwright of the late fifth and early fourth centuries BC, with a career spanning from approximately the mid-420s to the 380s BC, making him roughly contemporary with Aristophanes. He is called Plato Comicus ('the comic Plato') to differentiate him from the philosopher.

A Payments for different sexual positions

Plato Comicus, 188.17–18 KA Phaon *[3.9]*

. . . to Miss Bend-Over-Backwards (*Lordō*) a drachma, to Miss Bent-Forwards (*Kybdasos*) three obols, to the hero, Racehorse (*Kelēs*), a skin and incense (*thylēma*: alternatively 'barley cakes').

Plutarch

A prolific writer from Chaeronia, active in the late first and early second centuries AD, Plutarch wrote a series of parallel lives of famous Greeks and Romans.

A Hipparete's dowry and her attempt at divorcing Alcibiades

Plutarch, Life of Alcibiades *8.2–5 [1.4; 1.7]*

[2] But others say that it wasn't Hipponicus, but Callias, his son, who gave Hipparete to Alcibiades, with a dowry of 10 talents, and they say that afterwards, when she had borne a child, Alcibiades demanded

another 10 talents, claiming that this had been agreed if children were born. And Callias was so afraid of a plot that he offered his property and house (*oikos*) to the people in case he died without his own natural heirs.

Hipparete was an orderly and affectionate (*philandros*) wife, [3] but in her distress about her marriage (*gamos*) because of her husband's affairs with courtesans (*hetaira*), both citizen (*astos*) and foreign (*xenos*), she left his house and went to her brother's. Alcibiades didn't care about this, but kept up his decadent lifestyle, and so she lodged an application for divorce (*apoleipsis*) with the archon. And rather than someone doing it for her, [4] she went in person. And when she turned up to do this according to the law, Alcibiades came and seized her, carrying her off home with him through the marketplace (*agora*), and no one dared to stand up to him or take her from him. So, she lived with him until her death; and she died soon after, while Alcibiades was sailing to Ephesus.

[5] This violence (*bia*) was not considered against the law or inhumane at all. Indeed, the law seems to encourage this by requiring the wife seeking a divorce (*apoleipō*) to appear in public in person, so that her husband (*anēr*) can go up to her and seize her.

B Pericles' love life and Aspasia's infamy

Plutarch, Life of Pericles 24.5–7 [1.7; 1.15; 5.4]

[5] Nevertheless, the affection (*agapēsis*) of Pericles for Aspasia appears to have been of the erotic sort (*erotikos*). For his wife (*gynē*) was a relation of his, and had been previously been married to Hippolicus, to whom she had borne Callias the Rich. She also gave birth to Xanthippus and Paralus while she was with Pericles. But when wedded life (*symbiōsis*) stopped being pleasing to them, he gave her in marriage (*synekdidōmi*), with his wife's consent, to someone else. And he took up with Aspasia and felt particular affection for her (*stergō*). [6] For, they say, both on going out and coming in from the marketplace (*agora*) each day, he greeted her with a kiss.

In comedies she is called a new Omphale, Deianeira and Hera. And Cratinus openly called her a concubine (*pallakē*) in these lines: 'Buggery (*katapygosynē*) gave birth to Aspasia – his Hera – a shameless concubine (*pallakē*).' And it seems that she bore him an illegitimate (*nothos*) son, about whom Eupolis in his *Demes* made him ask, 'Is my bastard (*nothos*) alive?' And Myronides replied 'He would have become a man a while ago, if he wasn't shrinking in fear of the prostitute's (*pornē*) wickedness.' [7] They say that Aspasia was so famous and renowned that even Cyrus, the one who fought the king for the sovereignty of Persia, named the concubine (*pallakē*) he was most fond of (*agapaō*) 'Aspasia', although she was previously called 'Milto'.

C Pericles' 'citizenship' law

Plutarch, Life of Pericles *37.3 [1.1]*

Pericles . . . framed a law that only those born from two Athenians could be Athenian citizens.

D Solon's laws concerning the heiress

Plutarch, Life of Solon *20.2–3 [1.11; 1.12]*

The law seems absurd and ridiculous in the case of an heiress (*epiklēros*) where the man who has authority over her and has become her guardian (*kyrios*) by law is not able himself to have sex (*plesiazō*) with her, in which case the law allows her to be married (*hypyō*) to one of his next of kin. But some say that this was a wise provision directed at those men unable to have sex (*syneimi*), but who take heiresses (*epiklēros*) for their money, and thereby violate nature under cover of law. For seeing that the heiress can live with (or 'have intercourse with'? *syneimi*) whomever she wishes, they will either opt against the marriage (*gamos*), or they will cling to it shamefully and be punished for their money-grubbing, insolent behaviour (*hybris*). [3] It is good that the heiress (*epiklēros*) cannot choose just anyone, but only from amongst her husband's (*anēr*) relations: in this way, the child will still belong to his household line (*oikeios*) and be part of his family (*genos*). In this regard, the requirement for the bride (*nymphē*) to be shut up with the groom (*nymphios*) and eat a quince is also appropriate, as is requiring the man who has married the heiress (*epiklēros*) to have intercourse (*entynchanō*) with her at least three times a month. For even if no children (*pais*) are born, this is nevertheless a way for a husband to honour a dutiful (*sōphrōn*) wife and a kindness which removes many of the vexations that build up over time and which prevents them being completely estranged by their differences.

E Solon's laws on rape and adultery

Plutarch, Life of Solon *23.1–2 [4.3; 4.4; 4.8]*

[1] In general, the strangest of Solon's laws seem to be those concerning women (*gynē*). For he allowed a man capturing an adulterer (*moichos*)

to kill him. But if someone seized a free woman and raped her (*biazo-mai*), he set a fine at 100 drachmas. And for someone acting as a pimp (*proagōgeuō*), [the fine was] 20 drachmas, except in the case of those women who sell themselves openly, meaning courtesans (*hetaira*), of course. Because they openly go with (*phoitaō*) whoever pays them. [2] Moreover, no one is allowed to sell their daughters or their sisters, unless he finds out that she has had sexual intercourse (*syngignomai*) with a man (*anēr*) while still a girl (or 'virgin': *parthenos*). Yet it is absurd to punish the same deed severely and irrevocably at one time, but at another to punish it lightly as if were mere play, making the penalty an arbitrary fine. Unless money was scarce in the city at that time, and difficulty in obtaining it made these fines large.

F Wedding feasts

Plutarch, Moralia *666f–667a [1.5]*
... a wedding feast gives itself away with the shouting aloud of the marriage song (*hymnaios*), the torches, and the flutes (*aulos*) – things Homer says that even the women stand at their doors to watch and wonder at. Since no one is unaware that we have invited and are receiving guests, we are ashamed to leave anyone out and invite all our relatives, acquaintances and anyone with whom we have with the least connection.

Sappho

Lyric poet from Lesbos, born in the second half of the seventh century BC.

A The physical effects of watching a loved one converse with a man

Sappho, fr. 31 [5.5; 2.11]
That man seems to me equal to the gods, who sits opposite you and listens attentively to you speaking sweetly and laughing your lovely laugh. This has truly roused my heart in my chest, for whenever I look at you briefly, it seems that I can no longer speak, but even my tongue is frozen and at once a thin cloak of fire runs under my skin. With my eyes I see nothing, my ears are ringing. Cold sweat pours down upon me and shivering seizes me all over. I am greener than fresh grass, and am on the verge of dying. But even that can be endured ... [a poor man] ...

B A tender farewell between two women and recollection of sweeter times

Sappho, fr. 94.1–23 [2.11]

I really want to die. She was leaving me in tears and kept saying, 'Oh, how dreadfully we suffer, Sappho! Truly I don't want to leave you.' And I replied to her, 'Go and take care and remember me, for you know how we cherished you; I can remind you, if you have forgotten, that we also had good times; [. . .] with many wreaths of violets and roses [. . .] together [. . .] by my side, and you placed many woven garlands upon your tender neck made [. . .] of flowers. And [. . .] with royal perfume [. . .]. And on a soft couch, tender [. . .] you would satisfy your longing (*pothos*) . . . There was neither [. . .] a shrine [. . .] from which we were absent, no grove [. . .] dance . . . sound . . .'

Semonides

Iambic poet from the island of Amorgos, active in the mid-seventh century BC. The longest fragment of his poetry, the Catalogue of Women, details seven kinds of women supposedly created from different animals. All have their considerable faults save for the one good type: the bee woman.

A The qualities of the good 'bee' wife

Semonides 7.83–95 [1.10]

Another [type of woman] comes from a bee. Whoever marries her is fortunate; for to her alone reproach does not cling, but life thrives and increases because of her. Loving and loved, she grows old with her husband (*posis*), having borne him beautiful and famous-named offspring. And she is pre-eminent amongst all women, and divine grace surrounds her. Nor does she enjoy sitting among women when their conversation turns to sex (*aphrodisioi logoi*). Zeus bestows his favour on men with women such as these, who are the best and most wise. Through Zeus' scheme, these other types of women [i.e. the other six kinds of 'animal' women] both are and remain a misery for mankind.

Solon

Athenian statesman and poet, active in the early sixth century BC. Solon served as archon in 594 BC, which is perhaps the time when his legal and political reforms were made.

A The longed-for attractions of a boy

Solon, fr. 25 West [2.3; 5.1; 5.5]
[. . .] one may love boys (*paidophileō*) for the lovely flowers of youth (*hēbē*), longing for their thighs and their sweet mouths.

Sophocles

Athenian tragic playwright, active from the early 460s to his death in 406 BC.

A Antigone's address to her tomb

Sophocles, Antigone *891 [1.14]*
Antigone: O tomb! O bridal chamber!

B Antigone's lament before death

Sophocles, Antigone *917–18 [1.14]*
Antigone: I have enjoyed no marriage bed or bridal song and have not received any portion of marriage or the nurture of children.

C Dreams of incest

Sophocles, Oedipus the King *981–2 [5.8]*
Jocasta: . . . many mortals before now have slept with their mothers in their dreams.

D The blind Oedipus laments his fate

Sophocles, Oedipus the King *1360–8 [5.8]*

Oedipus:	Now I am godless, the son of unholy parents, and I shared the bed of those from whom I was born, damn me. And if there is any worse evil than this, it has fallen on me: Oedipus.
Chorus:	I cannot say that you have chosen well. You would be better off dead than alive and blind.

E The sweetness of a girl's childhood compared to marriage

Sophocles, Tereus, *fr. 583.3–10 (524) [1.5; 1.10]*

[Procne]: When we are young we live the sweetest life of all, I think, in our father's home; for ignorance always raises happy children. But when we reach maturity (*hēbē*) and intelligence, we are thrust out and sold away from our ancestral gods and our parents. Some go to foreign (*xenos*) husbands (*anēr*), some to barbarians, some to joyless homes, and others to reproachful ones.

Theognis

The elegiac poetry attributed to Theognis is generally thought to be a collation of two or three poets' work (indeed, these poems are often referred to as the *Theognidea*). The poems date from the late seventh and sixth centuries BC.

A The fickleness of boys and horses

Theognis 1267–70 [2.2; 2.5]

A boy (*pais*) and a horse are of the same mind; for the horse doesn't cry for its charioteer lying in the dust, but gives the next man a ride once it has had its fill of barley. Likewise a boy loves (*phileō*) whoever is at hand.

B A plea to a boy for mercy

Theognis 1305–10 [2.2; 5.5]

Since you know in your heart that the flower of much-loved youth (*paideia*) passes more swiftly than the course of a race, understanding this let loose my bonds, lest you also be constrained one day, mightiest of boys (*pais*), and you experience the harsh workings of Aphrodite just as I now experience with you. You should be on your guard lest the bad behaviour [of a boy] should defeat you.

C Praise of a smooth-cheeked boy

Theognis 1327–8 [2.5; 5.1; 5.5]

Boy (*pais*), as long as you have a smooth cheek, I will never stop praising you, not even if I am destined to die.

D The hard yoke of pederasty

Theognis 1357–60 [2.10]
A hard yoke always lies on the neck of those who love boys (*paidophilēs*)
as a painful memory of affectionate hospitality (*philoxenia*). For you
have to work hard indeed to gain the affection (*philotēs*) of a boy (*pais*)
– just like putting your hand into a fire of vine-twigs.

Theopompus

Comic playwright active from c. 410 to c. 370 BC and whose career thus
spanned the transition from Old to Middle Comedy.

A Sex between youthful age-mates

Theopompus, fr. 30 KA The Mede *(Medos) [2.11]*
Lycabettus: My place is where the all too youthful lads (*meirakion*)
grant favours (*charizomai*) to their age-mates.

Timocles

Playwright of Middle Comedy, active from c. 330 BC onwards.

A The advantages of innocence over experience in a girl

Timocles, fr. 24 KA The Marathonians *(Marathonioi) [5.2]*
What a big difference there is between spending the night with a young
girl (*koriskē*) and with a whore (*chamaitypē*; lit. 'ground-beater').
Wow! Her firmness, her complexion, her breath – ye gods! The fact
that everything isn't there on a plate – you have to struggle a bit and
get slapped in the face and beaten by soft hands: it's sweet by almighty
Zeus . . . !

Xenarchus

Playwright of Middle Comedy, active in the fourth century BC.

A Adultery compared unfavourably to the delights of a brothel

Xenarchus, fr. 4 KA The Pentathlete *(Pentathlos) [3.4; 4.3; 5.2; 5.4; 5.9]*
Awful, awful and not to be endured are the things the younger men

do in the city. For there are very good-loking (*euprepēs*) young girls (*meirax*) here in the brothels (*porneion*) whom you can see sunbathing with their breasts uncovered, naked and drawn up in rank and file. From among these a man can choose whomever he fancies – thin, fat, curvy, tall, shrivelled, young, old, middle-aged, fully ripe – without setting up a ladder to go inside secretly, or crawling under the roof through the chimney-hole, or artfully getting himself carried inside in a heap of chaff. For these women [i.e. prostitutes] force themselves (*biazomai*) on people and drag them inside, calling the old men (*gerōn*) 'little daddies', while others, the younger ones, they call 'kid brothers'. And each of them can be had without fear, cheaply, during the day, towards evening, in any way you like. But as for those women [i.e. respectable women] that men either can't see or can't see clearly, since they are perpetually trembling in a state of fear and dread, with their life on the line [. . .] how, Lady Mistress Aphrodite, can they ever fuck (*bineō*) them if – mid-screw – they recall the laws of Draco [i.e. on adultery]?

Xenophon

Athenian soldier and prose author, c. 428–354 BC. Xenophon's works are extremely varied in nature, ranging from history to technical treatises to Socratic dialogues (in which the real-life Socrates features as a character). The dramatic date of *Oeconomicus* ('The Estate Manager') is around 400 BC, shortly before Socrates' death: it was probably written in the early 360s.

A Adulterers as destroyers of marital affection

Xenophon, Hiero 3.3 [1.10; 4.4]

Nor does it escape the notice of city-states (*polis*) that friendship is the greatest and most pleasant good for people. At any rate, many states think it right to kill only adulterers (*moichos*) with impunity, because they clearly think of them as destroyers of the wives' (*gynē*) affection (*philia*) for their husbands (*anēr*).

B The perils of adultery

Xenophon, Memorabilia 2.1.5–6 [4.3]

[Socrates is speaking to Aristippus] '. . . Surely, then, you think that it is shameful (*aischros*) for a man to be in the same plight as the most senseless of wild animals? Just in this way do adulterers (*moichos*) enter the women's apartments, in the knowledge that a man who commits adultery (*moicheuō*) is in danger of incurring the penalties that the law threatens, namely being trapped, caught, and abused (*hybrizō*). And although such miserable and shameful penalties hang over the adulterer's head, and although there are many ways in which he might relieve his need for sex (*ta aphrodisia*) safely, to put oneself in danger all the same, isn't this absolutely a trait of a man possessed?' 'I agree', he said.

C Heracles' vision of Virtue and Vice

Xenophon, Memorabilia *2.1.22 [5.2; 5.3; 5.9]*
There appeared two women of great stature walking towards him. The first woman [Virtue] had a pleasant appearance (*euprepēs*) and a noble bearing. Her body was clothed with purity, her eyes with modesty (*aidōs*), and her figure with good sense (*sōphrosynē*). She was dressed in white. The other [Vice] had been reared to be plump and soft and was made-up in such a way that her skin appeared too white and too red to be real, and her comportment served to exaggerate her height. Her eyes were wide open and she was dressed the better to show off all her charms. And she regularly looked at herself and checked, too, whether anyone was watching her, and often even looked admiringly at her own shadow.

D Marital sex and parents' commitment to their offspring

Xenophon, Memorabilia *2.2.4–5 [1.10; 1.11; 3.1]*
[4] Socrates: You don't suppose that people have children (*paidopoieo-mai*) just for the sake of sex (*ta aphrodisia*), when the streets and the brothels (or 'cubicles': *oikēma*) are full of ways to satisfy that need. It is plain to see that we consider which woman (*gynē*) we would father the best children (*teknon*) from. Then we have intercourse (*synerchomai*) with them, and have children (*teknopoieomai*). [5] And the man (*anēr*) supports the woman who will bear his offspring, prepares in advance for his future children (*pais*) everything he thinks will be an asset in life, as well as he can. The woman conceives the child (*phortion*) and bears its burden, putting her life in danger and sharing with it part of the food she eats. After bearing it to term and giving birth with great pain, she nurses and takes care of it. She does not derive any benefit beforehand, nor is the infant (*brephos*) aware of who is caring for it.

Nor is it able to communicate what it wants: the mother guesses and tries to give it what is good for it and what it likes. And she brings it up for a long time, enduring her labour both day and night, not knowing if she will receive any gratitude (*charis*) in return.

E The qualities of a good matchmaker

Xenophon, Memorabilia *2.6.36 [1.2]*

[Aspasia] said that good matchmakers (*promnēstris*) were skilled at bringing people together in marriage by presenting their good qualities truthfully, and resisting the urge to over-praise them, since anyone who had been deceived like that would hate both each other and the matchmaker.

F A courtesan's household and her means of income

Xenophon, Memorabilia *3.11.4 [3.7; 5.4; 5.9]*

At this point Socrates, noticing that she [Theodote] was adorned in sumptuous fashion and that her mother, who was there with her, was well dressed and got up in no casual manner, and that she was accompanied by many beautiful servants who were well cared for, too, and that their house was unstintingly provided for in all other respects, said, 'Tell me, Theodote, do you have a farm?' 'No, I don't', she said. 'Do you have a house that brings you income?' 'Nor a house', she said. 'Maybe some craftsmen?' 'No, no craftsmen', she said. 'How, then,' he said, 'do you meet your daily needs?' 'If a friend I have made', she said, 'wishes to benefit me, this is my livelihood.'

G Socrates rebukes a young man in poor physical shape

Xenophon, Memorabilia *3.12.1 [5.5; 5.9]*

Seeing that Epigenes, one of the men present, was a young man in poor physical condition, he said, 'You haven't been in training, Epigenes.'

'I'm just an ordinary citizen, Socrates', he replied.

'But [you ought to train] no less than someone planning to compete at the Olympian games. Or do you think so little of the struggle to the death that the Athenians will have against her enemies sooner or later?'

H Communication between husband and wife

Xenophon, Oeconomicus 3.12–13 [1.10]

[12] . . . [Socrates said,] 'Is there anyone you talk to less than your wife (*gynē*)?'

[13] He [Critobulus] answered, 'If there is anyone, there can't be many.'

'And you married (*gameō*) her as a very young girl (*pais*) and pains had been taken so that she had seen and heard nothing?'

'Certainly.'

I The upbringing of Ischomachus' young wife

Xenophon, Oeconomicus 7.5 [1.6]

'She [my wife] came to me when she wasn't yet fifteen years old, and before that much care had been taken that she should see, hear and discover as little as possible.'

J A bolted door and sexual relations between slaves

Xenophon, Oeconomicus 9.5 [1.16]

'I also showed [my new wife] the women's apartments (*gynaikōnitis*), which are divided from the men's (*andrōnitis*) by a bolted door, to prevent items being removed from the house that shouldn't be and to stop the slaves having children (*teknopoieomai*) without our consent. When good slaves have children (*paidopoieomai*), their loyalty is usually increased; but when bad ones join together (*synzeugnymi*), they are more inclined to crime.'

K A husband praises natural looks over make-up

Xenophon, Oeconomicus 10.2–8 [5.3]

[2] Then Ischomachus said, 'I saw her once, Socrates, wearing a lot of white lead (*psimythion*), so that she would seem whiter than she was, and rouge (*enchousa*), so as to appear redder than reality, and wearing high shoes, so that she would seem taller than she naturally was. [3] 'Tell me, woman (*gynē*),' I said, 'would you, as a partner in our assets, judge me to be more worthy of affection (*axiophilētos*) if I showed you how our finances stand in reality, without boasting that I have more than I have or hiding anything that I do have, or if I tried to deceive you by saying that I have more than I do, showing you counterfeit silver

and fake necklaces and claiming that the purple garments which are fading won't lose their colour?' [4] And answering straight away, she said, 'Don't talk like that. I couldn't hold you dear in my heart, if you were that sort of man.' And I said, 'Surely, we were joined together, woman (*gynē*), to share our bodies with each other, too?' 'This is what people say, at any rate', she said. [5] 'And so,' I said, 'as a partner of your body, would you think me more worthy of affection if I strove to present you with a body that I had looked after, ensuring that it is fit and powerful and that I have a genuine healthy colour, or if I rubbed myself with red lead (*miltos*) and smeared pigment (*andreikelos*) beneath my eyes, presenting myself to you and living with (*syneimi*) you deceitfully, and providing for your sight and touch red lead instead of my own skin?' [6] And she said, 'I would rather touch you than red lead or pigment, and I would rather see your own colouring than pigment, and I would rather see your eyes looking healthy than smeared with pigment.' [7] 'So believe me, woman (*gynē*),' Ischomachus said . . . , 'that I, too, prefer your own colouring to that of white lead and rouge. But just as the gods made horses to be pleasing to horses, cattle to be pleasing to cattle, and sheep to be pleasing to sheep, in the same way men also think that an unadorned (*katharos*) human body is the most pleasing. [8] Perhaps these tricks can deceive outsiders who don't know any better, but people living together (*syneimi*) are always bound to be found out if they try to deceive each other. For either they are caught getting out of bed before getting ready, or they are shown up by sweat or tears, or they are seen for what they are while bathing.'

L A wife compared to a slave-girl

Xenophon, Oeconomicus *10.12 [1.16; 5.3]*
'As for her [my wife's] appearance, when you compare her to a slave-girl, because she's less made-up (*katharos*) and more tastefully dressed, she is desirable, especially since she grants her favours (*charizomai*) willingly, unlike the slave who has no choice but to submit.'

M Socrates praises the smell of olive oil in the gymnasium

Xenophon, Symposium *2.3–4 [5.5]*
'The odour of olive oil in the gymnasium, when a man has it on him, is sweeter than myrrh on women (*gynē*), and when it is absent it is more longed for.'

N Socrates claims that boys take no pleasure in sex

Xenophon, Symposium *8.21 [2.3]*

'For a boy (*pais*) does not share with a man the joys of sex (*ta aphro-disia*) as a woman (*gynē*) does; rather he looks on, sober, at the man who is drunk with desire (*aphroditē*).'

Illustrations

Figure 1 [1.5; 5.4]
Attic red-figure lebes gamikos by the Washing Painter, c. 430–420 BC. The bride binds her hair as an Eros figure and female companions look on. National Archaeological Museum, Athens 14790. Image courtesy of DAI Athen, neg. no. NM 4712. © Hellenic Ministry of Education and Religious Affairs, Culture and Sports / Archaeological Receipts Fund

Figure 2 [1.5; 5.2; 5.4]
Red-figure pyxis attributed to the Eretria Painter, c. 430–420 BC. Adornment scene showing a seated woman (Thaleia) being presented with a box, whilst a companion (Glauce) stands behind her, holding a necklace. © Trustees of the British Museum, London E774 (1874,0512.1)

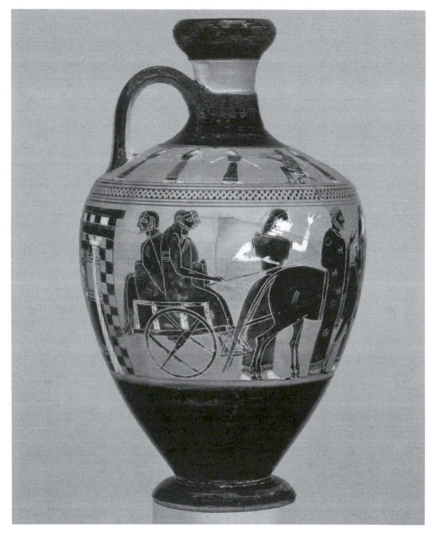

Figure 3 [1.5]
Attic black-figure lekythos attributed to the Amasis Painter, c. 550–530 BC. Mules
draw the cart in which the bride and groom ride to the bridegroom's house.
© The Metropolitan Museum of Art, New York, Purchase, Walter C. Baker Gift,
1956 (56.11.1)

Figure 4 [1.5]
As before (Figure 3). © The Metropolitan Museum of Art, New York, Purchase,
Walter C. Baker Gift, 1956 (56.11.1)

Figure 5 [1.5; 1.6; 1.10; 5.4]
Attic red-figure cup by the Amphitrite Painter, c. 460–450 BC. The groom takes the
bride's hand as she is escorted towards the bridegroom's house, with torches and
musical accompaniment. Photograph © bpk, Berlin; Antikensammlung, Staatliche
Museen zu Berlin F2530

Figure 6 [1.5; 1.6; 1.10; 5.4]
Red-figure loutrophoros by the Washing Painter, c. 430–420 BC. The groom clutches
the wrist of the bride, whose veil is being adjusted by her *nympheutria* (bridesmaid),
while a winged Eros plays the *aulos*. National Archaeological Museum, Athens 1174.
Image courtesy of DAI Athen, neg. no. NM 16279. © Hellenic Ministry of Education
and Religious Affairs, Culture and Sports /Archaeological Receipts Fund

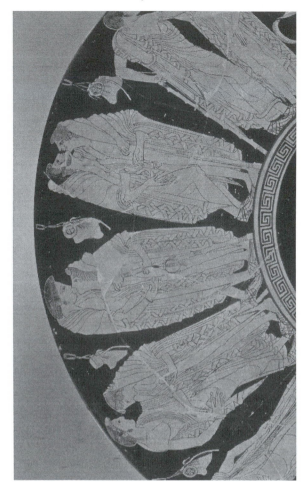

Figure 7 [2.2; 2.4; 2.5; 5.5]
Athenian red-figure kylix signed by Peithinos, c. 500 BC. Youths and boys at various stages of courtship. Photograph © bpk, Berlin; Antikensammlung, Staatliche Museen zu Berlin F2279

Figure 8 [2.3; 2.4; 5.5]
Black-figure amphora by the Phrynos Painter, c. 550–540 BC. An adult man courts a youth. © Martin von Wagner Museum der Universität Würzburg L 241. Photograph: P. Neckermann

Figure 9 [2.3; 5.5]
Black-figure amphora by the Painter of Berlin 1686, c. 540 BC. Men courting youths.
© Trustees of the British Museum, London W39 (1865,1118.39)

Figure 10 [2.3; 2.10; 5.5; 5.6]
Black-figure hydria, c. 550 BC. On the left a man and a youth engage in intercrural intercourse, while on the right a larger youth penetrates a more slender youth anally. A youth in the centre holds aloft a hare. Private collection. Line drawing courtesy of Lloyd Llewellyn-Jones

Figure 11 [2.3; 5.5]
Red-figure pelike by the Triptolemos Painter, c. 490–480 BC. Intercrural copulation between a man and a youth, who looks away at a hare. Mykonos Museum (21st Ephorate of Antiquities). © Hellenic Ministry of Education and Religious Affairs, Culture and Sports/Archaeological Receipts Fund

Figure 12 [2.3; 2.10; 5.5]
Red-figure kylix in the style of the Epeleios Painter, c. 520–500 BC. Orgy scene with youths. Museo di Antichità, Turin, inv. no. 4117. ©Archivio della Soprintendenza per i Beni Archeologici del Piemonte e del Museo Antichità Egizie

Figure 13 [2.3; 2.10; 2.11; 5.5; 5.6]
As before (Figure 12). ©Archivio della Soprintendenza per i Beni Archeologici del Piemonte e del Museo Antichità Egizie

Figure 14 [2.4; 2.6]
Red-figure cup by the Painter of Munich 2660, c. 480–470 BC. A man offers a boy a
cockerel. The wording reads *ho pais kalos*, 'the boy is beautiful'. Ashmolean Museum,
University of Oxford AN1896–1908 G.279

Figure 15 [2.5; 5.5]
Red-figure stamnos, c. 430 BC. A lyre-playing youth admires a naked serving boy, while a man playing kottabos reclines with a youth on another couch. A flute-girl plays in the centre of the scene. Staatliche Antikensammlungen und Glyptothek, Munich 2410. Photograph: Renate Kühling

Figure 16 [2.11; 5.5]
Red-figure kylix attributed to the Carpenter Painter, c. 510–500 BC. A youth draws
the head of an adult man towards him. The J. Paul Getty Museum, Villa Collection,
Malibu, California, Malibu 85.AE.25

Figure 17 [2.11; 5.6]
Red-figure kylix attributed to Apollodoros, c. 470–460 BC. One woman touches
the genitals of another. Immagini della Soprintendenza per i Beni Archeologici
dell'Etruria Meridionale. Museo Nazionale Archeologico, Tarquinia RC87778

Figure 18 [3.4; 5.2; 5.4]
Red-figure pelike attributed to the Nikoxenos Painter, c. 490 BC. Side A: An ithyphallic man lifts a woman's skirt and looks at her genitalia. Immagini della Soprintendenza per i Beni Archeologici dell'Etruria Meridionale. Museo Nazionale Archeologico, Tarquinia RC2989

Figure 19 [3.9; 5.2]
As before (Figure 18). Side B: A man and woman engage in standing rear-entry sex.
Immagini della Soprintendenza per i Beni Archeologici dell'Etruria Meridionale.
Museo Nazionale Archeologico, Tarquinia RC2989

Figure 20 [3.5; 5.2; 5.4]
Red-figure kylix by the Gales Painter, c. 520–510 BC. An ithyphallic youth fondles
a woman's breast as they both recline on couch. Yale University Art Gallery, Gift of
Rebecca Darlington Stoddard, New Haven 1913.163

Figure 21 [3.5; 5.2]
Red-figure kylix attributed to the Brygos Painter, c. 490–480 BC. Side A: Symposium scene. Two male diners recline in the company of a seated woman and musicians. © Trustees of the British Museum, London E68 (1848,0619.7)

Figure 22 [3.5; 5.2]
As before (Figure 21). Side B: Symposium scene. A bearded diner looks on as a youth reclines with a female companion. A naked youth clutching a wine dipper and strainer stands beside a seated flute-player. © Trustees of the British Museum, London E68 (1848,0619.7)

Figure 23 [3.5]
Red-figure kylix attributed to the Brygos Painter, c. 490–480 BC. A flute-girl and another woman in the company of male revellers. © Martin von Wagner Museum der Universität Würzburg L 479. Photograph: P. Neckermann

Figure 24 [3.7; 3.10; 5.2; 5.4; 5.6]
Red-figure kylix by the Pedieus Painter, c. 510–500 BC. Side A: Orgy scene, including three-way sex, (forced?) fellatio and slipper beating. © Photo RMN – les frères Chuzeville; Musée du Louvre, Paris G13

Figure 25 [3.7; 3.10; 5.4; 5.6]
As before (Figure 24). Side B: Orgy scene with women and youths.
© Photo RMN – les frères Chuzeville; Musée du Louvre, Paris G13

Figure 26 [4.7; 5.6]
Red-figure hydria attributed to the Coghill Painter, c. 450–440 BC. Apollo pursues a woman (Creusa?). © Trustees of the British Museum, London E170 (1873,0820.355)

Figure 27 [5.2; 5.4]
Red-figure cup attributed to Makron, c. 490–480 BC. A seated female musician plays
for a dancing-girl wearing a see-through chiton and holding krotala (castanets).
© Trustees of the British Museum, London E61 (1867,0508.1063)

Figure 28 [5.2; 5.6]
Red-figure kylix attributed to the Nikosthenes Painter, c. 520–500 BC. A naked
woman holds one olisbos (dildo) to her mouth, another to her vulva. © Trustees of
the British Museum, London E815 (1867,0508.1064)

Figure 29 [5.4]
Red-figure alabastron, c. 480–470 BC. A young woman in a long-sleeved chiton holds a fold of material in her teeth as she ties her belt while a young man (not pictured) looks on. © Trustees of the British Museum, London E719 (1892,0718.10)

Figure 30 [5.4; 5.6]
Red-figure kylix, attributed to the Triptolemos Painter, c. 490–480 BC. A balding man and a woman have sex on a *klinē* (couch). Immagini della Soprintendenza per i Beni Archeologici dell'Etruria Meridionale. Museo Nazionale Archeologico, Tarquinia RC2983

Figure 31 [5.5; 5.6]
Attic red-figure cup (school of the Nikosthenes Painter), c. 500 BC. Four satyrs engage in oral and anal intercourse, while another attempts intercourse with one of the vase's decorative sphinxes. Photograph © bpk, Berlin; Antikensammlung, Staatliche Museen zu Berlin 1964.4

Figure 32 [5.6]
Red-figure kylix by Douris, c. 480 BC. A man and woman engage in rear-entry, plausibly anal, sex. The wording reads *heche hēsychos*, 'hold still'. Photograph © 2013 Museum of Fine Arts, Boston 1970.233. Gift of Landon T. Clay

Further Reading

There is certainly no shortage of modern publications on ancient Greek sex and sexuality: indeed, in the face of such an overwhelming choice, the problem for the reader new to this area is where to start. The following is a list of some of the more accessible works on ancient Greek sex and sexuality and some suggested ways into the ancient evidence. Also provided is a chapter-by-chapter summary of key works to consult in order to gain a better overview of relevant academic debates.

General

Perhaps the best starting point for an overview of Greek sex is to be found in chapters 3 and 4 of M. Skinner, *Sexuality in Greek and Roman Culture* (Oxford: Blackwell, 2005). Also hugely accessible is J. N. Davidson, *Courtesans and Fishcakes: The Consuming Passions of Classical Athens* (London: HarperCollins, 1997), which provides an entertaining and provocative account of aspects of Athenian sex life such as homosexuality and prostitution (see esp. chapters 3, 4 and 5).

Useful sourcebooks include:

Hubbard, T. K. 2003. *Homosexuality in Greece and Rome: A Sourcebook of Basic Documents*, Berkeley/Los Angeles/London: University of California Press

Johnson, M. and T. Ryan. 2005. *Sexuality in Greek and Roman Literature and Society: A Sourcebook*, London/New York: Routledge

Larson, J. 2012. *Greek and Roman Sexualities: A Sourcebook*, London: Bloomsbury

Ancient sources

Texts

Taken together, the translated extracts in Part II provide a valuable collection of the types of sources upon which scholars of sex and sexuality in classical Athens routinely draw. Context is so often key, however, and there is no substitute for reading an ancient work in its entirety. The following texts, available in a variety of translations, are all worth reading in full (a brief description and areas of interest are given in parentheses).

Aeschines 1, *Against Timarchus* (Aeschines' prosecution speech of 346–345 BC: homosexuality and male prostitution)

Aristophanes, *Lysistrata* and *Thesmophoriazusae* (comic plays produced in 411 BC: female stereotypes and women's sexuality)

[Demosthenes] 59, *Against Neaera* (the prosecution of Neaera by Apollodorus in the late 340s BC: marriage, rape and adultery; female prostitution)

Lysias 1, *On the Murder of Eratosthenes* (a prosecution speech, written c. 400 BC, defending the killing of an adulterer as justifiable homicide: marriage, rape and adultery)

Menander, *The Women from Samos* (*Samia*) (comic play produced c. 320 BC: domestic life; marriage; the *hetaira*/concubine)

Plato, *Symposium* and *Phaedrus* (philosophical dialogues written c. 385–380 and c. 370 BC respectively: the reality and ideology of pederasty)

Xenophon, *Oeconomicus* (philosophical dialogue written c. 360 BC on the subject of the management of the household and the training of a new bride: marriage and domestic life; attitudes towards women)

Xenophon, *Symposium* (philosophical dialogue, probably written after Plato's work of the same name: homosexuality; beauty and attractiveness)

Images

Between them, the following richly illustrated volumes contain a broad range of material relating to the sex lives of classical Athenians.

Dierichs, A. 1993. *Erotik in der Kunst Griechenlands*, Mainz: von Zabern

Dover, K. J. 1978. *Greek Homosexuality*, London: Duckworth

Johns, C. 1982. *Sex or Symbol: Erotic Images of Greece and Rome*, London: British Museum Press

Kilmer, M. F. 1993. *Greek Erotica on Attic Red-Figure Vases*, London: Duckworth

Lear, A. and E. Cantarella. 2008. *Images of Ancient Greek Pederasty: Boys Were Their Gods*, London/New York: Routledge

Lewis, S. 2002. *The Athenian Woman: An Iconographic Handbook*, London/New York: Routledge

Oakley, J. H. and R. H. Sinos. 1993. *The Wedding in Ancient Athens*, Madison/London: University of Wisconsin Press

An online repository of vase images is available as part of the Perseus Project (Tufts University); images can be found by searching under 'keyword': http://www.perseus.tufts.edu/hopper/artifactBrowser?object=Vase

Chapter 1 Sexual Unions: Marriage and Domestic Life

Blundell, S. 1995. *Women in Ancient Greece*, London: British Museum Press [esp. chapters 10, 11 and 12]

Cantarella, E. 2005. 'Gender, Sexuality and Law', in M. Gagarin and D. Cohen (eds), *The Cambridge Companion to Ancient Greek Law*, Cambridge: Cambridge University Press: 236–53

Cohn-Haft, L. 1995. 'Divorce in Classical Athens', *Journal of Hellenic Studies* 115: 1–14

Hunter, V. 1989. 'The Athenian Widow and her Kin', *Journal of Family History* 14: 291–311

Just, R. 1989. *Women in Athenian Law and Life*, New York/London: Routledge [esp. chapters 4, 5 and 7]

Lacey, W. K. 1968. *The Family in Classical Greece*, London: Thames & Hudson [chapters 4–7 cover classical (and pre-classical) Athenian material on the *oikos*, marriage, property and women respectively]

Oakley, J. H. and R. H. Sinos. 1993. *The Wedding in Ancient Athens*, Madison/London: University of Wisconsin Press

Ogden, D. 1996. *Greek Bastardy in the Classical and Hellenistic Periods*, Oxford: Clarendon Press [chapters 1–6: some complex detail at times but hugely informative, both on bastardy and on broader issues of marriage and marriage laws; particularly useful for its coverage of non-citizens]

Oldenziel, R. 1987. 'The Historiography of Infanticide in Antiquity: A Literature Stillborn', in J. Blok and P. Mason (eds), *Sexual Asymmetry: Studies in Ancient Society*, Amsterdam: J. C. Gieben: 87–107

Patterson, C. 1998. *The Family in Greek History*, Cambridge, MA/London: Harvard University Press [a dense book, but a mine of important information on marriage and the family]

Chapter 2 Same-Sex Relationships

Cohen, D. 1991. *Law, Sexuality, and Society: The Enforcement of Morals in Classical Athens*, Cambridge: Cambridge University Press [chapter 7]

Dover, K. J. 1978. *Greek Homosexuality*, London: Duckworth

Fisher, N. R. E. 2001. *Aeschines: Against Timarchos*, Oxford: Oxford University Press [pp. 25–53 on Athenian law and attitudes towards homosexuality, and modern scholarship]

Golden, M. 1984. 'Slavery and Homosexuality at Athens', *Phoenix* 38.4: 308–24

Halperin, D. M. 1990. *One Hundred Years of Homosexuality: And Other Essays on Greek Love*, New York/London: Routledge [esp. chapters 1 and 2]

Hubbard, T. K. 1998. 'Popular Perceptions of Elite Homosexuality in Classical Athens', *Arion* 6: 48–78

—2003. *Homosexuality in Greece and Rome: A Sourcebook of Basic Documents*, Berkeley/Los Angeles/London: University of California Press [introduction]

Kilmer, M. 1997. 'Painters and Pederasts: Ancient Art, Sexuality, and Social History', in M. Golden and P. Toohey (eds), *Inventing Ancient Culture: Historicism, Periodization, and the Ancient World*, London/New York: Routledge: 36–49

Lear, A. and E. Cantarella. 2008. *Images of Ancient Greek Pederasty: Boys Were Their Gods*, London/New York: Routledge

Parker, H. 2001. 'The Myth of the Heterosexual: Anthropology and Sexuality for Classicists', *Arethusa* 34: 313–62

Rabinowitz, N. S. 2002. 'Excavating Women's Homoeroticism in Ancient Greece: The Evidence from Attic Vase Painting', in N. S. Rabinowitz and L. Auanger (eds), *Among Women: From the Homosocial to the Homoerotic in the Ancient World*, Austin: University of Texas Press: 106–66

Chapter 3 Prostitution

Cohen, E. 2006. 'Free and Unfree Sexual Work: An Economic Analysis of Athenian Prostitution', in C. A. Faraone and L. K. McClure (eds), *Prostitutes and Courtesans in the Ancient* World, Madison /London: University of Wisconsin Press: 95–124

Glazebrook, A. 2006. 'The Bad Girls of Athens: The Image and Function of *Hetairai* in Judicial Oratory', in C. A. Faraone and L. K. McClure (eds), *Prostitutes and Courtesans in the Ancient* World, Madison / London: University of Wisconsin Press: 125–38

—2011. '*Porneion*: Prostitution in Athenian Civic Space', in A. Glazebrook and M. Henry (eds), *Greek Prostitutes in the Ancient Mediterranean 800 BCE–200 CE*, Madison /London: University of Wisconsin Press: 34–59

Halperin, D. M. 1990. *One Hundred Years of Homosexuality: And Other Essays on Greek Love*, New York/London: Routledge [chapter 5 on male prostitution and citizenship]

Hamel, D. 2003. *Trying Neaira: The True Story of a Courtesan's Scandalous Life in Ancient Greece*, New Haven, CT/London: Yale University Press

Henry, M. 1988. *Menander's Courtesans and the Greek Comic Tradition*, *Studien zur klassischen Philologie* 20, Frankfurt /Bern/New York/ Paris: Peter Lang

Loomis, W. 1998. *Wages, Welfare Costs and Inflation in Classical Athens*, Ann Arbor: University of Michigan Press [chapter 9 on the wages of prostitutes and pimps]

Miner, J. 2003. 'Courtesan, Concubine, Whore: Apollodorus' Deliberative Use of Terms for Prostitutes', *American Journal of Philology* 124: 19–37

Chapter 4 Sex and the Law: Adultery and Rape

Carey, C. 1995. 'Rape and Adultery in Athenian Law', *Classical Quarterly* n.s. 45: 407–17

Cohen, D. 1991. *Law, Sexuality, and Society: The Enforcement of Morals in Classical Athens*, Cambridge: Cambridge University Press [chapters 5 and 6 on adultery]

Cole, S. 1984. 'Greek Sanctions against Sexual Assault', *Classical Philology* 79: 97–113

Deacy, S. and K. Pierce (eds). 1997. *Rape in Antiquity: Sexual Violence in the Greek and Roman Worlds*, London: Duckworth [a valuable collection of essays on various aspects of rape]

Harris, E. 1990. 'Did the Athenians Regard Seduction as a Worse Crime than Rape?', *Classical Quarterly* 40: 370–7

—2004. 'Did Rape Exist in Classical Athens? Further Reflections on the Laws about Sexual Violence', *Dike* 7: 41–83

Kapparis, K. 1996. 'Humiliating the Adulterer: The Law and the Practice in Classical Athens', *Revue Internationale des Droits de l'Antiquité* 43: 63–77

Keuls, E. 1985. *The Reign of the Phallus: Sexual Politics in Ancient Athens*, Berkeley/Los Angeles/London: University of California Press [chapters 6, 7 and 8: the discussion in this book also touches on a range of other issues relevant to the study of Greek sexuality]

Lefkowitz, M. 1993. 'Seduction and Rape in Greek Myth', in A. E. Laiou (ed.), *Consent and Coercion to Sex and Marriage in Ancient and Medieval Societies*, Washington, DC: Dumbarton Oaks Research Library and Collection: 17–37

Porter, J. R. 1997.'Adultery by the Book: Lysias I (*On the Murder of Eratosthenes*) and Comic Diegesis', *Echos du Monde Classique/ Classical Views* 40 (n.s. 16): 421–53

Stewart, A. 1995. 'Rape?', in E. D. Reeder (ed.), *Pandora: Women in Classical Greece*, Princeton: Princeton University Press: 74–90

Chapter 5 Beauty, Attractiveness, Fantasy and Taboo

Cairns, D. 2002. 'Bullish Looks and Sidelong Glances: Social Interaction and the Eyes in Ancient Greek Culture', in D. Cairns (ed.), *Body Language in the Greek and Roman Worlds*, Swansea: Classical Press of Wales: 123–55

Gerber, D. E. 1978. 'The Female Breast in Greek Erotic Literature', *Arethusa* 11: 203–12

Glazebrook, A. 2008/9. 'Cosmetics and *Sophrosyne*: Ischomachus' Wife in Xenophon's *Oikonomikos*', *Classical World* 102.3: 233–48 [good on ancient cosmetics, their use and ideology]

Hawley, R. 1998. 'The Dynamics of Beauty in Classical Greece', in D. Montserrat (ed.), *Changing Bodies, Changing Meanings: Studies on the Human Body in Antiquity*, London/New York: Routledge: 37–54

Henderson, J. 1991. *The Maculate Muse: Obscene Language in Attic Comedy* (2nd edn), New York/Oxford: Oxford University Press

Holt, P. 1998. 'Sex, Tyranny, and Hippias' Incest Dream (Herodotos 6.107)', *Greek, Roman and Byzantine Studies* 39: 221–41 [on the sexual excesses and taboo-breaking acts associated with tyrants]

Kilmer, M. 1993. *Greek Erotica on Attic Red-Figure Vases*, London: Duckworth

Llewellyn-Jones, L. (ed.). 2002. *Women's Dress in the Ancient Greek World*, London: Duckworth/Classical Press of Wales [a useful collection of essays, esp. contributions by Thomas, Dalby, Blundell and Llewellyn-Jones]

Osborne, R. 2011. *The History Written on the Classical Greek Body*, Cambridge: Cambridge University Press

Richlin, A. (ed.). 1992. *Pornography and Representation in Greece and Rome*, New York/Oxford: Oxford University Press [essay collection, including thought-provoking pieces by Sutton and Zweig]

Stafford, E. 2011.'Clutching the Chickpea: Private Pleasures of the Bad Boyfriend', in S. D. Lambert (ed.), *Sociable Man: Essays on Ancient Greek Social Behaviour in Honour of Nick Fisher*, Swansea: Classical Press of Wales: 337–63 [on masturbation and the penis]

Glossary

Terms in **bold** within definitions have their own entries in the glossary.

alabastron	A type of ceramic vessel traditionally used as an oil or perfume container, usually small in size with a long neck.
amphora	A type of ceramic vessel with two handles, typically used for the storage and transportation of goods.
archon	The archon was the civilian head of state in Athens in any given year. He belonged to a board of nine (later, ten) archons, elected by lot from a shortlist, other members including the archon basileus (head of religious matters) and the polemarch ('war ruler') in addition to the six **Thesmothetae** (to which a secretary to the Thesmothetae was added at some point in the classical era).
Areopagus	The 'Hill of Ares' in central Athens, giving its name to the ancient council which sat there. Exercising huge authority in early Athens, the Areopagus saw many of its powers curtailed in the mid-fifth century, although it retained its right to try certain homicide and religious cases, amongst others.
aulētris (pl. *aulētrides*)	'Flute-girl': a female prostitute trained in playing the *aulos*.
aulos (pl. *auloi*)	A musical instrument resembling a modern flute, but whose two reeded pipes,

	when played simultaneously, would probably have sounded more like an oboe; see also *aulētris*.
black-figure vase	A vase with figures painted in black on a red terracotta background (cf. **red-figure vase**). Black-figure vases were principally produced in Athens in the sixth century BC.
chiton	A loose-fitting tunic, worn by both men and women.
deme	One of the 139 'districts' or 'communes' into which Attica was divided: these could be rural, urban or coastal areas. In the classical era, a man's deme membership also determined to which of Athens' ten tribes he belonged.
dikē (pl. *dikai*)	A civil 'suit' in Athenian law (cf. *graphē*).
drachma	The basic unit of currency in Athens, comprising six **obol**s. A drachma represented two days' pay for a juror and perhaps a single day's pay for a skilled workman or hoplite (armed citizen soldier) during the late fifth century BC (see Loomis 1998, esp. 232–4, on wage variation).
the Eleven	Athenian officials, appointed by lot, who were in charge of prisons and prisoners. These men were also empowered to execute certain categories of self-confessed criminal, such as those committing serious theft and kindnapping, if caught red-handed.
endogamy	Marriage within the family group (cf. **exogamy**).
engyē (pl. *engyai*)	Betrothal, i.e. the a pledging in marriage of a woman by her current legal guardian to her future husband (also called *engyēsis*; see Chapter 1.3).
epidikasia (pl. *epidikasiai*)	A judicial procedure which ultimately determined which man an *epiklēros* (heiress) would marry and/or who would act as her legal guardian (see Chapter 1.12).

epiklēros (pl. *epiklēroi*)	Usually translated 'heiress' (lit.'on the estate' or 'with the property'): a woman on whom the family's property was settled in the absence of a male heir of the same or closer proximity to the deceased (see Chapter 1.12).
erastēs (pl. *erastai*)	A 'lover' or 'admirer', usually of a 'beloved' boy or youth (**erōmenos**; Chapter 2.2), but alternatively of a girl, a woman or even an adult man.
erōmenos (pl. *erōmenoi*)	The 'beloved' of a same-sex **erastēs**, i.e. 'lover' or 'admirer' (see Chapter 2.2). The *erōmenos* (also referred to as *ta paidika*) was typically a boy or youth.
erōs	'Love', 'desire', 'sexual desire'.
exogamy	Marriage outside the family group (cf. **endogamy**).
graphē (pl. *graphai*)	An 'indictment' in the Athenian legal system, signifying a case in which injury to the public was alleged (cf. *dikē*).
hetaira (pl. *hetairai*)	'Courtesan' or 'prostitute' (lit. 'companion') (cf. **pornē**; see Chapter 3.3).
hydria	A vessel used for carrying water, equipped with two horizontal handles for carrying and a third vertical handle for pouring. Ceramic hydriae were often painted with mythological scenes.
hybris	Outrageous and insolent behaviour (see Chapter 4.6).
intercrural sex	A homosexual sex act, whereby one partner inserted his penis between the other's thighs (Chapter 2.3).
kottabos	A game played at the **symposium** in which drinkers would flick the dregs of wine from their cups at a target set up in the middle of the room.
kylix (pl. kylikes)	A ceramic wine cup comprising a broad shallow dish, a low foot, and two handles. Scenes could be painted on the outside of the cup as well as on the inside. This round inner scene, the 'tondo', would only have

	been revealed to the drinker in stages as he drank.
kyrios (pl. *kyrioi*)	The head of a household, i.e. the adult male owner and custodian of the family's estate (**oikos**) who also acted as the legal protector of the household's children and womenfolk (see Chapter 1.1).
lebes gamikos	A ceramic vessel used in the wedding ceremony and taking a variety of (ornate) shapes. Their nuptial context often led to the painting of lebetes gamikoi with wedding imagery, such as a procession or mythological marriage.
lekythos	A ceramic vessel used for storing (olive) oil. Lekythoi traditionally found use in funerary contexts.
loutrophoros	A ceramic vessel used for transporting (ritual) bathwater, traditionally for a wedding or funeral bath. Loutrophoroi characteristically had elongated necks with two handles.
metic	A resident foreigner in Athens and/or his or her descendants (Gk: *metoikos*; pl. *metoikoi*).
mina	A sum of money worth 100 **drachma**s.
moicheia	A sexual crime usually translated as 'adultery', committed when a woman had sex with a man without the permission of her **kyrios** (see Chapter 4.2).
moichos (pl. *moichoi*)	Usually translated as 'adulterer': a man who committed **moicheia**.
nothos (pl. *nothoi*)	The male 'bastard' offspring of, say, a citizen man and metic woman (see Chapter 1.15; a female 'bastard' was a *nothē*, pl. *nothai*).
obol	One sixth of a **drachma**.
oikos (pl. *oikoi*)	The ancient Greek 'household', a concept which encompassed the family's 'house', its 'property' and the 'family' itself (see Chapter 1.1).
palaistra (pl. *palaistrai*)	'Wrestling ground', sometimes attached to a public gymnasium.

pallakē (pl. *pallakai*)	A woman who co-habited with a man on a less formal basis than a wife; usually translated 'concubine' (see Chapter 1.15).
pederasty	The institution of 'boy-love' (Gk: *paiderastia*). The two same-sex partners in a pederastic relationship were known as the **erastēs**, 'lover', and the **erōmenos** or *ta paidika*, 'beloved'.
pelike	A ceramic vessel similar to an **amphora**, with a rounded body and flat base.
phratry	One of the kinship groups to which all native-born male Athenian citizens belonged and which evidently played an important role in regulating matters of legitimacy and descent.
pornē (pl. *pornai*)	'Whore' or 'prostitute' (cf. **hetaira**; see Chapter 3.3).
pyxis	A box, ceramic or otherwise, usually comprising a round vessel with a separate lid. Pyxides were often used as containers for cosmetics and jewellery.
red-figure vase	A terracotta painted vase where black was used to fill in the background of the image, leaving the figures to stand out in red. These vases began to be produced in Athens at around 530–525 BC (cf. **black-figure vase**).
stele (pl. stelai)	A stone slab, especially one carved with decoration or engraved with text.
symposium (pl. symposia)	An all-male 'drinking party' which provided a focus for both homo- and hetero-erotic activity (see Chapters 2.5 and 3.5).
talent	A sum of money worth 60 **mina**s, i.e. 6,000 **drachma**s.
Thesmothetae (sing. Thesmothete)	The six junior **archon**s in Athens, appointed annually by lot, whose main role was to oversee the trials of various categories of offender whose alleged crimes had a bearing on public life in the city (e.g. treason and a number of types of **graphē**).

Bibliography

Amundsen, D. W. and C. J. Diers. 1969. 'The Age of Menarche in Classical Greece and Rome', *Human Biology* 41: 124–32

Angel, J. L. 1972. 'Ecology and Population in Eastern Mediterranean', *World Archaeology* 4: 88–105

Bakewell, G. W. 2008/9. 'Forbidding Marriage: "Neaira" 16 and Metic Spouses at Athens', *Classical Journal* 104.2: 97–109

Bakewell, G. W. and J. P. Sickinger (eds). 2003. *Gestures: Essays in Ancient History, Literature and Philosophy presented to Alan L. Boegehold*, Oxford: Oxbow

Beazley, J. D. 1947. 'Some Attic Vases in the Cypriot Museum', *Proceedings of the British Academy* 33: 3–31

—1950. 'Some Inscriptions on Greek Vases', *American Journal of Archaeology* 54: 310–22

Bérard, C. and C. Bron (eds). 1989. *A City of Images: Iconography and Society in Ancient Greece*, transl. D. Lyons, Princeton: Princeton University Press

Blazeby, C. K. 2011. 'Women + Wine = Prostitute in Classical Athens?', in Glazebrook and Henry 2011a: 86–105

Blok, J. and P. Mason (eds). 1987. *Sexual Asymmetry: Studies in Ancient Society*, Amsterdam: J. C. Gieben

Blundell, S. 1995. *Women in Ancient Greece*, London: British Museum Press

—1998. *Women in Classical Athens*, London: Bristol Classical Press/Duckworth

—2002. 'Clutching at Clothes', in Llewellyn-Jones 2002c: 143–69

Blundell, S. and N. S. Rabinowitz. 2008. 'Women's Bonds, Women's Pots: Adornment Scenes in Attic Vase-Painting', *Phoenix* 62: 115–44

Boegehold, A. and A. Scafuro (eds). 1994. *Athenian Identity and Civic Ideology*, Baltimore: Johns Hopkins University Press

Bonfante, L. 1989. 'Nudity as Costume in Classical Art', *American Journal of Archaeology* 93.4: 543–70

Boswell, J. 1990. 'Concepts, Experience, and Sexuality', *differences* 2: 67–87

Bremmer, J. 1990. 'Adolescents, *Symposion*, and Pederasty', in Murray 1990: 135–48

—1991. 'Walking, Standing and Sitting in Ancient Greek Culture' in Bremmer and Roodenburg 1991: 15–35

Bremmer, J. and H. Roodenburg (eds). 1991. *A Cultural History of Gesture*, Ithaca, NY: Cornell University Press

Brown, P. 1993. 'Love and Marriage in Greek New Comedy', *Classical Quarterly* n.s. 43: 189–205

Brownmiller, S. 1975. *Against Our Will: Men, Women and Rape*, New York: Ballantine Books

Burguière, A., C. Klapisch-Zuber, M. Segalen and F. Zonabend (eds). 1996. *A History of the Family, Volume 1: Distant Worlds, Ancient Worlds*, transl. S. Hanbury-Tenison, R. Morris and A. Wilson, Oxford: Polity

Byl, S. 1990. 'L'étiologie et la stérilité féminine dans le Corpus Hippocratique', in Potter et al. 1990: 303–22

Cairns, D. 2002a. 'Bullish Looks and Sidelong Glances: Social Interaction and the Eyes in Ancient Greek Culture', in Cairns 2002b: 123–55

—(ed.). 2002b. *Body Language in the Greek and Roman Worlds*, Swansea: Classical Press of Wales

Cantarella, E. 1987. *Pandora's Daughters: The Role and Status of Women in Greek and Roman Antiquity*, Baltimore and London: Johns Hopkins University Press

—2005a. 'Gender, Sexuality and Law', in Gagarin and Cohen 2005: 236–53

—2005b. 'La condizione femminile alla luce della Grande Iscrizione', in Greco and Lombardo 2005: 71–83

Carey, C. 1993. 'Return of the Radish or Just When You Thought It Was Safe to Go Back into the Kitchen', *Liverpool Classical Monthly* 18.4: 53–5

—1995. 'Rape and Adultery in Athenian Law', *Classical Quarterly* n.s. 45: 407–17

Carson, A. 1985. *Eros the Bittersweet: An Essay*, Princeton: Princeton University Press

—1990. 'Putting Her in her Place: Women, Dirt and Desire', in Halperin et al. 1990: 135–69

Cartledge, P., P. Millett and S. C. Todd (eds). 1990. *Nomos: Essays in Athenian Law, Politics and Society*, Cambridge/New York: Cambridge University Press

Cleland, L., M. Harlow and L. Llewellyn-Jones (eds). 2005. *The Clothed Body in the Ancient World*, Oxford: Oxbow

Cohen, B. 1997. 'Divesting the Female Breast of Clothes in Classical Sculpture', in Koloski-Ostrou and Lyons 1997: 66–92

Cohen, D. 1984. 'The Athenian Law of Adultery', *Revue Internationale des Droits de l'Antiquité* 31: 147–65

—1990. 'The Social Context of Adultery at Athens', in Cartledge et al. 1990: 147–65

—1991. *Law, Sexuality, and Society: The Enforcement of Morals in Classical Athens*, Cambridge: Cambridge University Press

—1993. 'Consent and Sexual Relations in Classical Athens', in Laiou 1993: 5–16

Cohen, E. 2000a. '"Whoring under Contract": The Legal Context of Prostitution in Fourth-Century Athens', in Hunter and Edmondson 2000: 113–47

—2000b. *The Athenian Nation*, Princeton: Princeton University Press

—2003. 'Athenian Prostitution as a Liberal Profession', in Bakewell and Sickinger 2003: 214–36

—2005. 'Laws Affecting Prostitution at Athens', *Symposion: Vorträge zur griechischen und hellenistischen Rechtsgeschichte* 19: 201–24

—2006. 'Free and Unfree Sexual Work: An Economic Analysis of Athenian Prostitution', in Faraone and McClure 2006: 95–124

Cohn-Haft, L. 1995. 'Divorce in Classical Athens', *Journal of Hellenic Studies* 115: 1–14

Cole, S. 1984. 'Greek Sanctions against Sexual Assault', *Classical Philology* 79: 97–113

Cox, C. A. 1998. *Household Interests: Property, Marriage Strategies, and Family Dynamics in Ancient Athens*, Princeton: Princeton University Press

Cudjoe, R. V. 2005. 'The Purpose of the "Epidikasia" for an "Epikleros" in Classical Athens', *Dike* 8: 55–88

Dalby, A. 2002. 'Levels of Concealment: The Dress of *Hetairai* and *Pornai* in Greek Texts', in Llewellyn-Jones 2002c: 111–24

Davidson, J. N. 1997. *Courtesans and Fishcakes: The Consuming Passions of Classical Athens*, London: HarperCollins

—2006. 'Revolutions in Human Time: Age-Class in Athens and the Greekness of Greek Revolutions', in Goldhill and Osborne 2006: 29–67

—2008. *The Greeks and Greek Love: A Radical Reappraisal of Homosexuality in Ancient Greece*, London: Weidenfeld & Nicolson

de Brauw, M. and J. Miner. 2004. 'Androtion's Alleged Prostitution Contract: Aes. 1.165 and Dem. 22.23 in the Light of P.Oxy VII 1012', *Zeitschrift der Savigny-Stiftung für Rechtsgeschichte* 121: 301–13

Deacy, S. and K. Pierce (eds). 1997. *Rape in Antiquity: Sexual Violence in the Greek and Roman Worlds*, London: Duckworth

DeForest, M. (ed.). 1993. *Woman's Power, Man's Game: Essays on Classical Antiquity in Honor of J. K. King*, Wauconda, IL: Bolchazy-Carducci

Devereux, G. 1968. 'Greek Pseudo-Homosexuality and the "Greek Miracle"', *Symbolae Osloenses* 42.1: 69–92

—1970. 'The Nature of Sappho's Seizure in Fr. 31 LP as Evidence of her Inversion', *Classical Quarterly* 20: 17–31

DeVries, K. 1997. '"The Frigid Eromenoi" and Their Wooers Revisited: A Closer Look at Greek Homosexuality in Vase Painting', in Duberman 1997: 14–24

Dover, K. J. 1973. 'Classical Greek Attitudes towards Sexual Behaviour', *Arethusa* 6: 59–73

—1974. *Greek Popular Morality in the Time of Plato and Aristotle*, Oxford: Blackwell

—1978. *Greek Homosexuality*, London: Duckworth

Duberman, M. B. (ed.). 1997. *Queer Representations: Reading Lives, Reading Cultures*, New York: New York University Press

Fantham, E., H. P. Foley, N. Kampen, S. Pomeroy and H. A. Shapiro (eds). 1994. *Women in the Classical World: Image and Text*, New York/Oxford: Oxford University Press

Faraone, C. A. and L. K. McClure (eds). 2006. *Prostitutes and Courtesans in the Ancient World*, Madison/London: University of Wisconsin Press

Fisher, N. R. E. 1992. *Hybris: A Study in the Values of Honour and Shame in Ancient Greece*, Warminster: Aris & Phillips

—1995. 'Hybris, Status and Slavery' in Powell 1995: 44–84

—1998. 'Violence, Masculinity and the Law in Classical Athens', in Foxhall and Salmon 1998b: 68–97

—2001. *Aeschines: Against Timarchos*, Oxford: Oxford University Press

Foucault, M. 1985. *The History of Sexuality 2: The Use of Pleasure*, transl. R. Hurley, New York: Random House

Foxhall, L. and J. Salmon (eds). 1998a. *Thinking Men: Masculinity and its Self-Representation in the Classical Tradition*, Leicester-Nottingham Studies in Ancient Society vol. 7, London: Routledge

—(eds). 1998b. *When We Were Men: Masculinity, Power and Identity in Classical Antiquity*, London: Routledge

French, A. 1994. 'Pericles' Citizenship Law', *Ancient History Bulletin* 8.3: 71–5

Frontisi-Ducroix, F. 1996. 'Eros, Desire, and the Gaze', transl. N. Kline, in Kampen 1996: 81–100

Gagarin, M. and D. Cohen (eds). 2005. *The Cambridge Companion to Ancient Greek Law*, Cambridge: Cambridge University Press

Garland, R. 1990. *The Greek Way of Life: From Conception to Old Age*, London: Duckworth

Gerber, D. E. 1978. 'The Female Breast in Greek Erotic Literature', *Arethusa* 11: 203–12

Gilhuly, K. 2009. *The Feminine Matrix of Sex and Gender in Classical Athens*, Cambridge: Cambridge University Press

Glazebrook, A. 2005. 'The Making of a Prostitute: Apollodoros' Portrait of Neaira', *Arethusa* 38.2: 161–87

—2006a. 'The Bad Girls of Athens: The Image and Function of *Hetairai* in Judicial Oratory', in Faraone and McClure 2006: 125–38

—2006b. 'Prostituting Female Kin (Plut. Sol. 23.1–2)', *Dike* 8: 33–53

—2008/9. 'Cosmetics and *Sophrosyne*: Ischomachus' Wife in Xenophon's *Oikonomikos*', *Classical World* 102.3: 233–48

—2011. '*Porneion*: Prostitution in Athenian Civic Space', in Glazebrook and Henry 2011a: 34–59

Glazebrook, A. and M. Henry (eds). 2011a. *Greek Prostitutes in the Ancient*

Mediterranean 800 bce–200 ce, Madison/London: University of Wisconsin Press

—2011b. 'Introduction: Why Prostitutes? Why Greek? Why Now?', in Glazebrook and Henry 2011a: 3–13

Golden, M. 1984. 'Slavery and Homosexuality at Athens', *Phoenix* 38.4: 308–24

—1990. *Children and Childhood in Classical Athens*, Baltimore: Johns Hopkins University Press

Golden, M. and P. Toohey (eds). 1997. *Inventing Ancient Culture: Historicism, Periodization, and the Ancient World*, London/New York: Routledge

Goldhill, S. and R. Osborne (eds). 2006. *Rethinking Revolutions through Ancient Greece*, Cambridge: Cambridge University Press

Gomme, A. W. and F. H. Sandbach. 1973. *Menander: A Commentary*, Oxford: Oxford University Press

Greco, E. and M. Lombardo (eds). 2005. *La Grande Iscrizione di Gortyna: centoventi anni dopo la scoperta, Atti del I Convegno Internazionale di Studi sulla Messarà*, Athens: Scuola Archeologica Italiana di Atene

Grillet, B. 1975. *Les femmes et les fards dans l'antiquité grecque*, Lyon: Centre national de la recherche scientifique

Halperin, D. M. 1990. *One Hundred Years of Homosexuality: And Other Essays on Greek Love*, New York/London: Routledge

Halperin, D. M., J. J. Winkler and F. I. Zeitlin (eds). 1990. *Before Sexuality: The Construction of Erotic Experience in the Ancient Greek World*, Princeton: Princeton University Press

Hamel, D. 2003. *Trying Neaira: The True Story of a Courtesan's Scandalous Life in Ancient Greece*, New Haven, CT/London: Yale University Press

Hannah, P. A. 1998. 'The Reality of Greek Male Nudity: Looking at African Parallels', *Scholia* 7: 17–40

Hansen, M. H. 1976. *Apagoge, Endeixis and Ephegesis against Kakourgoi, Atimoi and Pheugontes*, Odense: Odense University Press

Harris, E. 1990. 'Did the Athenians Regard Seduction as a Worse Crime than Rape?', *Classical Quarterly* 40: 370–7

—2004. 'Did Rape Exist in Classical Athens? Further Reflections on the Laws about Sexual Violence', *Dike* 7: 41–83

Harrison, A. R. W. 1968–71. *The Law of Athens: The Family and Property*, Oxford: Clarendon Press

Harrison, T. 1997. 'Herodotus and the Ancient Greek Idea of Rape', in Deacy and Pierce 1997: 185–208

Harvey, F. D. and J. Wilkins (eds). 2000. *The Rivals of Aristophanes: Studies in Athenian Old Comedy*, London: Duckworth/Classical Press of Wales

Hawley, R. 1998. 'The Dynamics of Beauty in Classical Greece', in Montserrat 1998: 37–54

Henderson, J. 1991. *The Maculate Muse: Obscene Language in Attic Comedy* (2nd edn), New York/Oxford: Oxford University Press

—2000. 'Pherekrates and the Women of Old Comedy', in Harvey and Wilkins 2000: 135–50

Henry, M. 1988. *Menander's Courtesans and the Greek Comic Tradition, Studien zur klassischen Philologie* 20, Frankfurt /Bern/New York/Paris: Peter Lang

Holt, P. 1998. 'Sex, Tyranny, and Hippias' Incest Dream (Herodotos 6.107)', *Greek, Roman and Byzantine Studies* 39: 221–41

Hubbard, T. K. 1998. 'Popular Perceptions of Elite Homosexuality in Classical Athens', *Arion* 6: 48–78

—(ed.). 2000. *Greek Love Reconsidered*, New York: W. Hamilton Press

—2002. 'Pindar, Theoxenus, and the Homoerotic Eye', *Arethusa* 35: 255–96

—2003. *Homosexuality in Greece and Rome: A Sourcebook of Basic Documents*, Berkeley/Los Angeles/London: University of California Press

Humphreys, S. 1983. *The Family, Women and Death: Comparative Studies*, London/Boston, MA/Melbourne/Henley: Routledge & Kegan Paul

—2002 'Solon on Adoption and Wills', *Zeitschrift der Savigny-Stiftung für Rechtsgeschichte* 119: 340–7

Hunter, V. 1989. 'The Athenian Widow and her Kin', *Journal of Family History* 14: 291–311

Hunter, V. and J. Edmondson (eds). 2000. *Law and Social Status in Classical Athens*, Oxford: Oxford University Press

Ingalls, W. 2002. 'Demography and Dowries; Perspectives on Female Infanticide in Classical Greece', *Phoenix* 56.3/4: 246–54

Johnston, A. 1991. 'Greek Vases in the Marketplace', in Rasmussen and Spivey 1991: 203–32

Just, R. 1989. *Women in Athenian Law and Life*, New York/London: Routledge

Kaibel, G. 1878. *Epigrammata Graeca ex Lapidus Conlecta*, Berlin: G. Reimer

Kampen, N. (ed.). 1996. *Sexuality in Art*, Cambridge: Cambridge University Press

Kapparis, K. 1996. 'Humiliating the Adulterer: The Law and the Practice in Classical Athens', *Revue Internationale des Droits de l'Antiquité* 43: 63–77

Katz, M. 1992. 'Patriarchy, Ideology and the Epikleros', *Studi italiani di filologia classica*: 692–708

Keuls, E. 1985. *The Reign of the Phallus: Sexual Politics in Ancient Athens*, Berkeley/Los Angeles/London: University of California Press

Kilmer, M. 1993. *Greek Erotica on Attic Red-Figure Vases*, London: Duckworth

—1997a. 'Painters and Pederasts: Ancient Art, Sexuality, and Social History', in Golden and Toohey 1997: 36–49

—1997b. '"Rape" in Early Red-Figure Pottery: Violence and Threat in Homo-Erotic and Hetero-Erotic Contexts', in Deacy and Pierce 1997: 123–41

Kinzl, K. (ed.). 2006. *A Companion to the Classical Greek World*, Malden, MA/Oxford/Chichester: Wiley-Blackwell

Koloski-Ostrou, A. O. and C. L. Lyons (eds). 1997. *Naked Truths: Women,*

Sexuality, and Gender in Classical Art and Archaeology, London/New York: Routledge

Konstan, D. 2000. 'οἰκία δ' ἐστί τις φιλία: Love and the Greek Family', *Syllecta Classica* 11: 106–26

Kurke, L. 1997. 'Inventing the *Hetaira*: Sex, Politics, and Discursive Conflict in Archaic Greece', *Classical Antiquity* 16.1: 106–50

Lacey, W. K. 1968. *The Family in Classical Greece*, London: Thames & Hudson

Laiou, A. E. (ed.). 1993. *Consent and Coercion to Sex and Marriage in Ancient and Medieval Societies*, Washington, DC: Dumbarton Oaks Research Library and Collection

Lambert, S. D. (ed.). 2011. *Sociable Man: Essays on Ancient Greek Social Behaviour in Honour of Nick Fisher*, Swansea: Classical Press of Wales

Lape, S. 2006. 'The Psychology of Prostitution in Aeschines' Speech against Timarchus', in Faraone and McClure 2006: 139–60

Lear, A. forthcoming, 'Was Pederasty Problematized? A Diachronic View', in Masterson et al., forthcoming

Lear, A. and E. Cantarella. 2008. *Images of Ancient Greek Pederasty: Boys Were Their Gods*, London/New York: Routledge

Leduc, C. 1992. 'Marriage in Ancient Greece', in Schmitt Pantel 1992: 235–94

Lefkowitz, M. 1993. 'Seduction and Rape in Greek Myth', in Laiou 1993: 17–37

Lewis, S. 2002. *The Athenian Woman: An Iconographic Handbook*, London/New York: Routledge

Lissarrague, F. 1990. 'The Sexual Life of Satyrs', in Halperin et al. 1990: 53–81

Llewellyn-Jones, L. 2002a. 'Body Language and the Female Role Player in Greek Tragedy and Japanese *Kabuki* Theatre', in Cairns 2002b: 73–105

—2002b. 'A Woman's View: Dress, Eroticism, and the Ideal Female Body in Athenian Art', in Llewellyn-Jones 2002c: 171–202

—(ed.). 2002c. *Women's Dress in the Ancient Greek World*, London: Duckworth/Classical Press of Wales

—2003. *Aphrodite's Tortoise: The Veiled Woman of Ancient Greece*, Swansea: Classical Press of Wales

—2011. 'Domestic Abuse and Violence Against Women in Ancient Greece', in Lambert 2011: 231–66

Loman, P. 2004. 'Women's Participation in Ancient Warfare', *Greece & Rome* n.s. 51.1: 34–54

Loomis, W. 1998. *Wages, Welfare Costs and Inflation in Classical Athens*, Ann Arbor: University of Michigan Press

MacCary, W. T. and M. M. Willcock. 1976. *Plautus: Casina*, Cambridge: Cambridge University Press

MacDowell, C. 1989. *Shoes: Fashion and Fantasy*, London: Thames & Hudson

MacDowell, D. M. 1989. 'The *oikos* in Athenian Law', *Classical Quarterly* 39: 10–21

—2000. 'Athenian Laws about Homosexuality', *Revue Internationale des Droits de l'Antiquité* 47: 13–27

Maffi, A. 2005. 'Family and Property Law', in Gagarin and Cohen 2005: 254–66

Masterson, M., N. S. Rabinowitz and J. E. Robson (eds). forthcoming. *Sex in Antiquity: New Essays on Gender and Sexuality in the Ancient World*, London: Routledge

Miner, J. 2003. 'Courtesan, Concubine, Whore: Apollodorus' Deliberative Use of Terms for Prostitutes', *American Journal of Philology* 124: 19–37

Montserrat, D. (ed.). 1998. *Changing Bodies, Changing Meanings: Studies on the Human Body in Antiquity*, London/New York: Routledge

Murray, O. (ed.). 1990. *Sympotica: A Symposium on the Symposion*, Oxford: Clarendon Press

Nowak, M. 2010. 'Defining Prostitution in Athenian Legal Rhetorics', *Legal History Review* 78.1–2: 183–97

Oakley, J. H. and R. H. Sinos. 1993. *The Wedding in Ancient Athens*, Madison/London: University of Wisconsin Press

Ogden, D. 1996. *Greek Bastardy in the Classical and Hellenistic Periods*, Oxford: Clarendon Press

—1997. 'Rape, Adultery and the Protection of Bloodlines in Classical Athens', in Deacy and Pierce 1997: 25–41

Oldenziel, R. 1987. 'The Historiography of Infanticide in Antiquity: A Literature Stillborn', in Blok and Mason 1987: 87–107

Omitowoju, R. 1997. 'Regulating Rape: Soap Operas and Self Interest in the Athenian Courts', in Deacy and Pierce 1997: 1–24

Osborne, R. 1996. 'Desiring Women on Athenian Pottery', in Kampen 1996: 65–80

—2011. *The History Written on the Classical Greek Body*, Cambridge: Cambridge University Press

Parker, H. 2001. 'The Myth of the Heterosexual: Anthropology and Sexuality for Classicists', *Arethusa* 34: 313–62

Passmann, C. 1993. 'Re(de)fining Women: Language and Power in the Homeric Hymn to Demeter', in DeForest 1993: 54–77

Patterson, C. 1981. *Pericles' Citizenship Law of 451–50 BC*, Salem, NH: Ayer

—1985. '"Not Worth the Rearing": The Causes of Infant Exposure in Ancient Greece', *Transactions of the American Philological Association* 115: 103–23

—1991. 'Marriage and the Married Woman in Athenian Law', in Pomeroy 1991: 48–72

—1998. *The Family in Greek History*, Cambridge, MA/London: Harvard University Press

—2005. 'Athenian Citizenship Law', in Gagarin and Cohen 2005: 267–89

Pierce, K. F. 1997. 'The Portrayal of Rape in New Comedy', in Deacy and Pierce 1997: 163–84

Pomeroy, S. 1975. *Goddesses, Whores, Wives and Slaves: Women in Classical Antiquity*, New York: Schocken

—(ed.). 1991. *Women's History and Ancient History*, Chapel Hill/London: University of North Carolina Press

—1994. *Xenophon, Oeconomicus: A Social and Historical Commentary*, Oxford: Clarendon Press

—2006. 'Women and Ethnicity in Classical Greece: Changing the Paradigms', in Kinzl 2006: 350–66

Porter, J. R. 1997. 'Adultery by the Book: Lysias I (*On the Murder of Eratosthenes*) and Comic Diegesis', *Echos du Monde Classique/Classical Views* 40 (n.s. 16): 421–53

Potter, P., G. Maloney and J. Desautels (eds). 1990. *La maladie et les maladies dans la Collection Hippocratique: Actes du VIe Colloque International Hippocratique*, Quebec: Éditions du Sphinx

Powell, A. (ed.). 1995. *The Greek World*, London/New York: Routledge

Rabinowitz, N. S. 2002. 'Excavating Women's Homoeroticism in Ancient Greece: The Evidence from Attic Vase Painting', in Rabinowitz and Auanger 2002: 106–66

—2011. 'Greek Tragedy: A Rape Culture?', *Eugesta (Journal on Gender Studies in Antiquity)* 1 (http://eugesta.recherche.univ-lille3.fr/revue/)

Rabinowitz, N. S. and L. Auanger (eds). 2002. *Among Women: From the Homosocial to the Homoerotic in the Ancient World*, Austin: University of Texas Press

Rasmussen, T. and N. Spivey (eds). 1991. *Looking at Greek Vases*, Cambridge: Cambridge University Press

Redmond, J. (ed.). 1989. *Women in Theatre: Themes in Drama*, Cambridge: Cambridge University Press

Reeder, E. D. (ed.). 1995. *Pandora: Women in Classical Greece*, Princeton: Princeton University Press

Rehm, R. 1994. *Marriage to Death: The Conflation of Wedding and Funeral Rituals in Greek Tragedy*, Princeton: Princeton University Press

Richlin, A. (ed.). 1992. *Pornography and Representation in Greece and Rome*, New York/Oxford: Oxford University Press

Riddle, J. M. 1992. *Contraception and Abortion from the Ancient World to the Renaissance*, Cambridge, MA: Harvard University Press

Robson, J. E. 1997. 'Bestiality and Bestial Rape in Greek Myth', in Deacy and Pierce 1997: 65–96

—2009. *Aristophanes: An Introduction*, London: Duckworth

—forthcoming, 'Fantastic Sex: Fantasies of Sexual Assault in Aristophanes', in Masterson et al., forthcoming

Rosivach, V. J. 1984. '*Aphairesis* and *apoleipsis*: A Study of the Sources', *Revue International des Droits de l'Antiquité* 31: 193–230

Roy, J. 1991. 'Traditional Jokes about the Punishment of Adulterers in Ancient Greek Literature', *Liverpool Classical Monthly* 16: 73–6

Rubenstein, L. 1993. *Adoption in IVth Century Athens*, Copenhagen: Museum Tusculanum Press

Sanders, E., C. Thumiger, C. Carey and N. Lowe (eds). 2013. *Erôs in Ancient Greece*, Oxford: Oxford University Press

Scafuro, A. 1990. 'Discourses of Sexual Violation in Mythic Accounts and Dramatic Versions of "The Girl's Tragedy"', *differences* 2: 126–59

—1994. 'Witnessing and False Witnessing: Proving Citizenship and Kin Identity in Fourth-Century Athens', in Boegehold and Scafuro 1994: 156–98

—1997. *The Forensic Stage: Settling Disputes in Greco-Roman Comedy*, Cambridge: Cambridge University Press

Schaps, D. M. 1979. *Economic Rights of Women in Ancient Greece*, Edinburgh: Edinburgh University Press

Schmitt Pantel, P. (ed.). 1992. *A History of Women in the West I: From Ancient Goddesses to Christian Saints*, transl. A. Goldhammer, Cambridge, MA/ London: Belknap Press of Harvard University Press

Schnapp, A. 1989. 'Eros en chasse', in Bérard and Bron 1989: 67–83

—1997. *Le Chasseur et la cité: chasse et érotique en Grèce ancienne*, Paris: Éditions Albin Michel

Seaford, R. 1987. 'The Tragic Wedding', *Journal of Hellenic Studies* 107: 106–30

Sealey, R. 1990. *Women and Law in Classical Greece*, Chapel Hill: University of North Carolina Press

Sebesta, J. L. 2002. 'Visions of Gleaming Textiles and a Clay Core: Textiles, Greek Women, and Pandora', in Llewellyn-Jones 2002c: 125–42

Shapiro, H. A. 1981. 'Courtship Scenes in Attic Vase Painting', *American Journal of Archaeology* 85: 133–43

—1992. 'Eros in Love: Pederasty and Pornography in Greece', in Richlin 1992: 53–72

—2000. 'Leagros and Euphronios', in Hubbard 2000: 12–32

Sissa, G. 1996. 'The Family in Ancient Athens (Fifth–Fourth Century BC)', in Burguière et al. 1996: 156–98

Skinner, M. 2005. *Sexuality in Greek and Roman Culture*, Oxford: Blackwell

Sommerstein, A. H. 1998. 'Rape and Young Manhood in Athenian Comedy', in Foxhall and Salmon 1998a: 100–14

Sourvinou-Inwood, C. 1988. *Studies in Girls' Transitions: Aspects of the Arkteia and Age Representation in Attic Iconography*, Athens: Kardamitsa

Stafford, E. J. 2000. *Worshipping Virtues: Personification and the Divine in Ancient Greece*, London: Duckworth/Classical Press of Wales

—2005. 'Viewing and Obscuring the Female Breast: Glimpses of the Ancient Bra', in Cleland et al. 2005: 96–110

—2011.'Clutching the Chickpea: Private Pleasures of the Bad Boyfriend', in Lambert 2011: 337–63

—2013. 'From the Gymnasium to the Wedding: Erôs in Athenian Art and Cult', in Sanders et al. 2013: 175–208

Stewart, A. 1995. 'Rape?', in Reeder 1995: 74–90

—1997. *Art, Desire, and the Body in Ancient Greece*, Cambridge: Cambridge University Press

Strauss, B. 1993. *Fathers and Sons in Athens: Ideology and Society in the Era of the Peloponnesian War*, London: Routledge

Sutton, R. F. Jr. 1981. *The Interaction Between Men and Women on Attic Red-Figure Pottery*, PhD diss., University of North Carolina at Chapel Hill

—1992. 'Pornography and Persuasion on Attic Poetry', in Richlin 1992: 3–35

—1997/8. 'Nuptial Eros: The Visual Discourse of Marriage in Classical Athens', *Journal of the Walters Art Gallery* 55/6: 27–8

Thomas, B. M. 2002. 'Constraints and Contradictions: Whiteness and Femininity in Ancient Greece', in Llewellyn-Jones 2002c: 1–16

Thornton, B. 1991. 'Constructionism and Ancient Greek Sex', *Helios* 18: 181–93

Thorp, J. 1992. 'The Social Construction of Homosexuality', *Phoenix* 46.1: 54–61

Todd, S. C. 1993. *The Shape of Athenian Law*, Oxford: Clarendon Press

Tomaselli, S. and R. Porter (eds). 1986. *Rape: An Historical and Cultural Enquiry*, Oxford: Blackwell

Walton, F. T. 1946. 'My Lady's Toilet', *Greece & Rome* 43: 68–73

Wiles, D. 1989. 'Marriage and Prostitution in Classical New Comedy', in Redmond 1989: 31–48

Wilson, P. 2000. *The Athenian Institution of the Khoregia: The Chorus, the City and the Stage*, Cambridge: Cambridge University Press

Winkler, J. J. 1990a. *The Constraints of Desire: The Anthropology of Sex and Gender in Ancient Greece*, London/New York: Routledge

—1990b. 'Laying Down the Law: The Oversight of Men's Sexual Behaviour in Classical Athens' in Halperin et al. 1990: 171–209

Yates, V. 2005. '*Anterastai*: Competition in Eros and Politics in Classical Athens', *Arethusa* 38: 33–47

Zeitlin, F. I. 1986. 'Configurations of Rape in Greek Myth', in Tomaselli and Porter 1986: 122–51

Zweig, B. 1992. 'The Mute, Nude Female Characters in Aristophanes' Plays', in Richlin 1992: 73–89

Index

Note: page numbers in *italics* denote illustrations